All the Shah's Men

An American Coup and the Roots of Middle East Terror

STEPHEN KINZER

John Wiley & Sons, Inc.

Published by John Wiley & Sons, Inc., Hoboken, New Jersey
Published simultaneously in Canada

Wiley Bicentennial Logo: Richard J. Pacifico

Design and production by Navta Associates, Inc.

For general information about our other products and services, please contact our Customer Care Department within the United States at (800) 762-2974, outside the United States at (317) 572-3993 or fax (317) 572-4002.

Wiley also publishes its books in a variety of electronic formats. Some content that appears in print may not be available in electronic books. For more information about Wiley products, visit our web site at www.wiley.com.

Library of Congress Cataloging-in-Publication Data

Kinzer, Stephen.
    All the Shah's men : an American coup and the roots of Middle East terror / Stephen Kinzer. — 2008 ed.
        p. cm.
    Includes bibliographical references and index.
    ISBN 978-0-470-18549-0 (pbk.)
    1. Iran—Politics and government—1941–1979. 2. Mosaddeq, Mohammad, 1880–1967.
    3. United States—Relations—Iran. 4. Iran—Relations—United States. I. Title.
    DS318.K49 2008
    955.05'3—dc22   2007041614

Printed in the United States of America

15

For the People of Iran

*There is nothing new in the world except
the history you do not know.*

—Harry Truman

CONTENTS

The Folly of Attacking Iran

More than half a century has passed since the United States deposed the only democratic government Iran ever had. This book describes that fateful operation and reviews its disastrous consequences. It tells a story that should serve as an object lesson. Violent intervention in Iran seemed like a good idea in 1953, and for a time it appeared to have succeeded. Now, however, it is clear that this intervention not only brought Iran decades of tragedy, but also set in motion forces that have gravely undermined American national security.

As militants in Washington urge a second American attack on Iran, the story of the first one becomes more urgently relevant than ever. It shows the folly of using violence to try to reshape Iran. In 1953, the United States sought to promote its strategic interest by attacking an Iranian regime of which it disapproved. The results were exactly the opposite of those for which American leaders had hoped.

If the United States had not sent agents to depose Prime Minister Mohammad Mossadegh in 1953, Iran would probably have continued along its path toward full democracy. Over the decades that followed, it might have become the first democratic state in the

Muslim Middle East, and perhaps even a model for other countries in the region and beyond. That would have profoundly changed the course of history—not simply Iranian or even Middle Eastern history, but the history of the United States and the world.

From the perspective of today—the perspective of those who have lived through the September 11 attacks, the Iraq war, and all the attendant threats that have emerged to destabilize the modern world—the 1953 intervention in Iran may be seen as a decisive turning point in twentieth-century history. By placing Mohammad Reza Shah back on his Peacock Throne, the United States brought Iran's long, slow progress toward democracy to a screeching halt. The Shah ruled with increasing repression for twenty-five years. His repression produced the explosion of the late 1970s, later known as the Islamic Revolution. That revolution brought to power a radical clique of fanatically anti-Western clerics who have worked relentlessly, and often violently, to undermine American interests around the world.

In 1953, the United States deposed a popular Iranian nationalist who embraced fundamental American principles and replaced him with a tyrant who despised much of what the United States stands for. Today the West finds itself facing a regime in Tehran that embodies threats far more profound than those that it sought to crush in 1953. In the White House, the impulse to attack Iran seems just as strong as it was then. It is not difficult to imagine the argument some of President Bush's advisers might make in seeking to persuade him. We suffered the September 11 attacks because President Clinton was not bold enough to crush a growing threat, they would say, so let's be real men and crush the threat that's emerging now, rather than leave it to the next administration.

Why attack Iran? Those who favor the idea offer a variety of answers: Iran must not be allowed to become a nuclear power; Iran poses an existential threat to Israel; Iran is the heart of an emerging "Shiite crescent" that destabilizes the Middle East; Iran supports radical groups in nearby countries; Iran is helping to kill American soldiers in Iraq; Iran has ordered terror attacks in foreign countries; Iran's people are oppressed and need Americans to liberate them.

There is also a geopolitical argument for attacking Iran. Since the beginning of the Cold War era, the United States has used one country in the Middle East as a platform from which to project power across the region. For a quarter-century it was the Shah's Iran. Now it is Saudi Arabia, but prospects for long-term stability there are uncertain. The fantasy that Iraq would become America's key regional ally after a U.S. invasion has dissipated. Some in Washington have a new one: that when the dust clears after an American attack on Iran, it will be stable and friendly to the United States.

The most obvious reason for attacking Iran would be to win access to its vast oil supply. When Winston Churchill helped to seize Iran's oil industry in the 1920s, he called it "a prize from fairyland beyond our wildest dreams." It still is. Regardless of what policymakers in Washington or anywhere else may say, no country ever acts in Iran without thinking about its oil reserves. That is especially true of the Bush administration, which is more closely allied with the oil industry than any other administration in American history.

President Bush and those around him may have other reasons to feel tempted by the idea of invading Iran. Some believe, against all evidence, that the key to victory in Iraq is crushing the regime in Iran. Bush himself has said several times that he expects history to absolve him, an argument that can be used to justify even the craziest presidential decisions. Beneath these arguments lies another, more diffuse impulse.

American leaders, emphatically including President Bush himself, believe that since the United States is a great power, it has the right and responsibility to act dramatically whenever trouble emerges anywhere in the world. This impulse dates at least to the age of Thucydides, who wrote that nations have "an innate compulsion to rule when empowered." More recently, in a study of the Spanish-American War that holds great relevance for today, the British historian Joseph Smith wrote that America's eagerness to attack foreign lands stems from "an aggressive national egoism and a romantic attachment to national power." Some in Washington believe that invading, overthrowing, and occupying are simply what great nations do. Otherwise, they argue, there is no point in having power.

"At this moment in history, if there's a problem, we're expected to deal with it," President Bush said before launching the invasion of

Iraq. By his standards, Iran has certainly become "a problem." That suggests he may decide to order an attack in order to "deal with it."

Before great powers take far-reaching decisions that can reshape the world, their leaders normally consider the lessons of history. Any serious discussion about modern Iran, and certainly any debate about whether the United States should intervene there, must include an assessment of what happened after the last intervention. In 1953, eager to achieve short-term goals, the United States launched an operation that brought calamity to both Iran and itself. Some in Washington, however, reject the idea that this history has any relevance to the present era. They believe that this time, the United States can attack Iran and emerge triumphant.

A variety of prominent Americans have described President George Bush's decision to invade Iraq in 2003 as the worst strategic blunder in their country's history. Attacking Iran now might prove even more disastrous. It would turn that country's oppressive leaders, who are now highly unpopular at home, into heroes of Islamic resistance; give them a strong incentive to launch a violent counter-campaign against American interests around the world; greatly strengthen Iranian nationalism, Shiite irredentism, and Muslim extremism, thereby attracting countless new recruits to the cause of terror; undermine the democratic movement in Iran and destroy the prospects for political change there for at least another generation; turn the people of Iran, who are now among the most pro-American in the Middle East, into enemies of the United States; require the United States to remain deeply involved in the Persian Gulf indefinitely, forcing it to take sides in all manner of regional conflicts and thereby make a host of new enemies; enrage the Shiite-dominated government in neighboring Iraq, on which the United States is relying to calm the violence there; and quite possibly disrupt the flow of Middle East petroleum in ways that could wreak havoc on Western economies.

Given these likely outcomes, why would the United States attack Iran? Those who like the idea say it will accomplish three things: stop Iran from developing weapons of mass destruction, depose an aggressively anti-American regime, and bring to power a new government that would be democratic and pro-American. That government would, they presume, allow American oil companies free access to Iranian petroleum and give the United States a chance to rebuild the influence it once had in Iran. These fantasies are as dangerous as they are delusional.

Iran is one of the world's oldest nations. Its history is full of glories, peopled by titanic leaders like Cyrus, Xerxes, and Darius, and also by poets and thinkers who have made immeasurable contributions to world culture. This rich tradition has given Iranians a powerful sense of communal pride, a passionate attachment to their heritage, and a national identity that transcends the flag-waving and sloganeering that characterize more superficial forms of patriotism. Many Iranians detest the regime under which they now live, but that does not weaken their attachment to the Iranian nation. All of them know that when the United States came into being, their state had already existed for more than two thousand years. Regardless of their political beliefs, most bristle with anger when they hear threats from Washington.

The idea that the United States might be able to bomb Iran into democracy sounds increasingly absurd in the wake of the debacle in Iraq. For Iranians, though, it has a special, tragic irony. All of them know, as many American do not, that democracy was taking root in Iran when the United States intervened to suppress it in 1953. Given this historical fact, Iranians may be pardoned for considering it passing strange that Americans now propose to be their liberators. They are painfully aware that the United States helped create the oppressive theocracy under which they now live.

Few Iranians believe that Americans who favor attacking their country wish to do so in order to bring them freedom. Many also doubt that the United States is focused mainly on destroying Iran's nuclear program—a program that the United States first proposed to Iran in the 1970s, when the Shah was in power, and that most Iranians believe is their country's natural right. Behind these stated motives, behind the threats that are intensifying as war drums beat ever more loudly in Washington, Iranians see a more cynical project. They believe the United States wants to turn Iran into something between an ally and a vassal, extracting its oil and building bases on its soil. That was the real reason the United States intervened in Iran in 1953, and there is no reason to believe that its goals have substantially changed.

Rhetorical attacks on Iran have been a staple of Washington rhetoric since the Bush administration came to power in 2001. President Bush famously portrayed Iran as part of a global "axis of evil." In his second inaugural address he called Iran "the world's primary state sponsor of terror," and later he warned that Iran's emergence as a nuclear power would be "unacceptable." Vice President Dick Cheney has placed Iran "at the top of the list" of world trouble spots. Secretary of State Condoleezza Rice called Iran's human rights record "a thing to be loathed." John Bolton, the former U.S. ambassador to the United Nations, insists that it is time "to massively increase the pressure" on Iran, and that if sanctions and other coercive measures do not force the Iranian regime to change course, "then I think we need to look at the use of force." Senator Joseph Lieberman, one of President Bush's most loyal supporters on foreign policy issues, told a television interviewer that if Iranians "don't play by the rules, we've got to use our force, and to me that would include military action to stop them from doing what they're doing."

Lieberman used a new argument to justify his call for attacking Iran. He charged that Iran is aiding insurgents in Iraq, and that its aid has resulted in the deaths of as many as two hundred American soldiers. This is a remarkable argument. During the Vietnam War, the Soviet Union supplied North Vietnam with weapons and ammunition that killed tens of thousands of American soldiers. China did the same for its North Korean allies in the 1950s. The United States did not attack the arms suppliers then. Nor did the Sandinista government in Nicaragua try to attack the United States during the 1980s, when American weapons and American-trained fighters were killing Nicaraguan soldiers and civilians. Helping friends during wartime is a tactic as old as proxy war itself. Now, with the Bush administration eager to find a scapegoat for its failures in Iraq, Lieberman is urging that the United States "take aggressive military action against the Iranians to stop them from killing Americans in Iraq."

This threatening rhetoric might intimidate countries that are small, poor, isolated, and insecure. When directed against a nation as proud as Iran, it has the opposite effect. It stiffens resistance and unites people who, like people everywhere, don't like being ordered around by those they consider bullies.

Britain, which has been Iran's enemy for considerably longer than the United States has, seems to have learned this lesson. In 1953, the British secret service worked with the CIA to depose Prime Minister Mossadegh, and over the course of the twentieth century, anti-British fervor has nearly always been more intense than anti-Americanism in Iran. Yet when an Iranian patrol captured nineteen British sailors and marines whom they said entered Iranian waters illegally in the spring of 2007, British leaders responded in a way that was startlingly different from the way American leaders would probably have responded if the captured soldiers had been from the U.S. Army. Prime Minister Tony Blair repeatedly insisted that he would pursue only diplomatic means to free the captives and categorically ruled out the use of force. The Iranian government, evidently impressed, soon released its captives. An incident that might have burgeoned into a long-running and highly destabilizing crisis was resolved through negotiation, without either side losing face.

American leaders not only seize every chance to snarl at Iran, but have launched a series of operations aimed at destabilizing the Islamic regime. These might be considered covert operations if the regime in Tehran were not so fully aware of them. Part of the American project is to send tens of millions of dollars, openly appropriated by Congress, to groups within Iran that it considers pro-democracy. This, not surprisingly, has led the ruling mullahs to consider every private organization in Iran a potential tool of American aggression or subversion. They have launched brutal crackdowns that have sent hundreds of idealistic Iranians into the netherworld of Evin prison in Tehran, where the abuse of inmates and the withholding of legal rights are at least as pervasive as they are at the American prison in Guantánamo. Iranian dissidents now report that when they are arrested, their interrogators focus almost exclusively on questions about where their money comes from and whether any of it is American. By publicly appropriating funds for a program aimed explicitly at destabilizing the Iranian regime, the United States has helped to set off a fierce crackdown on dissent, narrowed the space for democratic development in Iran, and set back the cause of freedom to which it claims to be committed.

Besides this clumsy attempt to reshape the political landscape inside Iran, the United States is also engaged in more direct forms of intervention. It has sent carrier groups to the Persian Gulf and moved heavy bombers to Qatar. In addition, according to news reports, the United States has begun covertly funding armed bands of Kurds, Baluchis, Azeris, and other ethnic minorities in Iran that have taken credit for assassinating Iranian officials and Revolutionary Guard fighters. These are forms of pressure intended to frighten or unnerve the regime in Tehran. Instead, they are leading the regime to repress its domestic critics ever more fiercely.

The theory behind U.S. policy toward Iran seems to be that the Iranian regime is weak and vulnerable to conventional forms of pressure. In fact, the regime is stronger than it has ever been. The collapse of the Soviet Union, which eased pressure on Iran's northern border and led to the emergence of half a dozen new nations with Muslim majorities, opened a host of new strategic opportunities for Iran. High oil prices gave it new economic power in the first years of the new century. Then, most unexpectedly, the United States, which clamors to lead an international anti-Iran coalition, did Iran the huge favor of destroying the two regimes it feared most: the Taliban government of Afghanistan, which was run by fanatically anti-Iranian Sunni extremists, and Saddam Hussein's government in Iraq, with which Iran fought a devastating war in the 1980s.

Iranian influence in the Middle East has grown steadily since the U.S. invasion of Iraq. The new Iraqi government is dominated by Shiites who admire and work closely with Iran. President Hamid Karzai of Afghanistan embraces Iran as "our very dear friend." In Lebanon, the Iranian regime won what many Muslims considered a great victory in 2006, when the Iran-backed Hezbollah militia resisted a withering Israeli assault and then took charge of postwar reconstruction efforts.

With Iraq in chaos, and Syria and Egypt consumed by domestic challenges, Iran has become the only Muslim power in the Middle East able to shape events beyond its own borders. Iran has increased its influence over Iraq, Lebanon, Syria, and the Palestinians, as well as over "nonstate actors," including Hezbollah, Hamas, and Islamic Jihad. Never in modern history has Iran been as strong as it is today. Most perversely, this is largely the work of the United States. Iran's surge in power and influence is not due to its own efforts; its leaders simply take advantage of American mistakes.

The United States violently interrupted Iran's progress toward freedom by overthrowing Prime Minister Mossadegh in 1953, and the long-term result was devastating for both countries. Half a century later, another group of American leaders ordered the invasion of Iraq, with comparably catastrophic effect. Despite these debacles, some in Washington still believe that military force can produce positive change in Iran. No one is more horrified by this than the brave corps of Iranian democrats who, at great risk, are campaigning for reform in their homeland.

"The Iranian state is certainly guilty of violating many of its citizens' basic rights," the Iranian dissident Akbar Ganji, who spent six grueling years in prison after writing a book that accused Iranian officials of ordering political assassinations, told an interviewer in 2007. "But a military attack is not a just or effective response. . . . An attack would be calamitous for the innocent people of Iran and the region. . . . It would foster the growth of fundamentalism in the region [and] reignite the conviction that the Judeo-Christian West, led by the United States, is assaulting the world of Islam, from Afghanistan and Palestine to Iraq and Iran. . . . The current U.S. military threat has given the Iranian government a freer hand in repressing Iran's budding civil society in the name of national security, and so eclipsed democratic discourse that some Iranian reformists see themselves caught between domestic despotism and foreign invasion. Political change in Iran is necessary, but it cannot be achieved by foreign intervention."

In the same interview, Ganji made a point that can never be made often enough. The United States, he said, has no credibility as a bearer of democracy to Iran because of its role in crushing democracy there half a century ago—and because of its failure since then to show any interest in developing Iran's civil society.

"Most Iranians, I believe, share a broad outlook on American foreign policy," Ganji reported. "They think that Iran is valued only for its vast energy resources and its role in regional politics, and that Iranian culture and economic development, and the peace, welfare and basic rights of Iranian citizens, are largely irrelevant to American policymakers. . . . Iranians will never forget the 1953 U.S.-supported coup that toppled the nationalist, moderate, democratic government of Dr. Mohammad Mossadegh and ushered in a closed, dictatorial

political system. Iranian society lost one of its most important historical opportunities for the establishment of a democracy."

The United States is still paying the price—and it is a terrible
one—for its violent intervention in Iran decades ago. If it attacks
Iran again now, Iranians will revile the United States for another
half-century. Wise Americans recognize this. Professor A. Richard
Norton of Boston University, an authority on Muslim political
movements who was an adviser to the bipartisan Iraq Study Group,
has warned that "a U.S. attack would undermine pragmatic voices
in Iran, provide incentives for Iran to make life extremely difficult
for the U.S. in Iraq and elsewhere, and probably impede the international trade in petroleum." Milt Bearden, the veteran CIA officer
who directed the American-sponsored war in Afghanistan during
the 1980s, has called the idea "insane" and asserted, "Going to war
with Iran would have no good outcome for anyone except Iran."
Even Robert Gates, before he became secretary of defense, was part
of a team that studied American options toward Iran and recommended "a revised strategic approach" based on engagement and
dialogue.

The first essential aspect of that revised approach would have to
be a commitment by the United States to talk directly and uncondi-
tionally with the Iranian government. Given America's willingness
to negotiate with all manner of odious regimes, its refusal to sit
down with Iran is not simply perplexing but self-defeating. On the
surface, it is based on the odd principle that one should not negotiate with enemies. Officials in the Bush administration have said
they oppose wide-ranging talks with Iran because they do not want
to reward "bad behavior." Countries that are enemies and engage in
"bad behavior," however, are precisely the ones with which any
nation should want to engage most urgently—especially when
those countries have great influence and, as is the case with Iran
today, pose growing threats to global security. Hectoring, denouncing, threatening, and making shrill demands cannot be the basis of
sound foreign policy.

There is, however, another, deeper reason why the United States
has found itself unable to negotiate with Iran for the last quarter-century. The American political class has never recovered from the shock
of losing the Shah and the humiliation of the hostage crisis that fol-

lowed. It blames the current Islamic regime for those offenses. Some in Washington seem more determined to take long-delayed revenge on Iran than they are to build a new relationship with its government and people. Until the United States is able to leap this psychological barrier and abandon its petulant refusal to talk seriously with Iran, there will be no real improvement in relations.

The intensifying crisis over Iran's nuclear program makes negotiations more urgent now than ever. In order to have a chance to succeed, these negotiations would have to be direct and bilateral, since only the United States has the power to give Iran the security guarantees it would require as part of any future agreement. They would also have to be unconditional, with both sides encouraged to raise every point of disagreement. Meetings between American and Iranian diplomats to discuss ways of stabilizing Iraq, the first such meetings since the Islamic Revolution, could serve as a stepping-stone to more wide-ranging talks. Both sides described these meetings as "positive," but they will only turn out to have been truly positive if they lead to comprehensive negotiations.

An ideal model for such negotiations would be the policy the United States and China followed as they rebuilt relations in the 1970s. The first document to emerge from that process, the Shanghai Communiqué, was deceptively simple. In it, neither side made any commitment or concession. The communiqué was simply a list of each side's concerns and a pledge that both would negotiate seriously to resolve them. A comparable document would be a fine beginning for a new relationship between the United States and Iran.

What might the two countries list as their concerns about each other? The United States would certainly place Iran's nuclear program at the top of the list, closely followed by Iranian support for international terror. Iran would wish to address American actions aimed at destabilizing its regime. Each side believes the other is perpetuating violence in the Middle East.

Beyond these and other areas of obvious disagreement, however, there are a remarkable number of areas in which the United States and Iran might find common ground. These two countries are not fated to be enemies forever. In fact, they share many strategic goals and may even be seen as potential allies. Both desperately want to stabilize Iraq and Afghanistan. Both detest radical Sunni movements like al-Qaeda and the Taliban. Both, for different reasons, seek to assure a steady supply of petroleum to Western markets. Iran's oil industry is in a parlous state and needs tens of billions of dollars in investment; the United States has huge reserves of capital and a voracious appetite for oil.

Americans have much to gain from a new relationship with Iran, especially if it could lead to some calming of the raging passions that are now tearing the Middle East apart. Iran would also benefit. The cleavage between the Iranian regime and its people, like the gap between rich and poor in Iran, is now wider than it has been in decades. Inflation is relentless. Unemployment is painfully high, especially among young people. Social ills such as drug addiction and prostitution are reaching epidemic proportions. The non-oil economy is all but nonexistent, largely because of stifling government controls and lack of foreign investment. Endless cycles of recrimination between Washington and Tehran prevent the two sides from testing a new approach that could benefit them both.

It is far from certain that comprehensive negotiations between the United States and Iran would ultimately succeed. Not to make the effort, however, would be a grand historical error. Simply making an offer of comprehensive talks might produce a mini-crisis within the Iranian regime, with hard-liners battling pragmatists over whether to accept it.

Once talks begin, the only way they could succeed would be by compromise, something neither side has been willing to accept so far. That, however, is the purpose of negotiations. Opening comprehensive talks with Iran would not be a reward for "bad behavior" but a search for solutions that could ease a volatile conflict and contribute to global security.

The only way Iran can reasonably be expected to curb its nuclear ambitions would be through some kind of "grand bargain" in which its own security concerns would be addressed. That would probably require a solution that goes beyond Iran's borders and creates a new security architecture for the Middle East. It is not reasonable to expect Iran to abandon its nuclear program as long as its main regional enemy, Israel, and its main world enemy, the United States, are nuclear-armed and issuing a stream of barely veiled threats to Iran.

One accord to which negotiators might look is the one signed in 2007 between the United States and North Korea. In exchange for a promise that North Korea will accept the "eventual abandonment" of its nuclear weapons program, the United States agreed to "move toward full diplomatic relations" with North Korea; ease economic sanctions on the North Korean regime; "begin the process" of removing North Korea from the list of state sponsors of terror and from the list of countries with which business contacts are restricted by the Trading with the Enemy Act; and establish working groups to negotiate the denuclearization of the region and a new "northeast Asia peace and security mechanism." If these principles can shape an accord between the United States and North Korea, they should also be applicable to Iran, which has greater potential than North Korea to contribute to—or undermine—global security.

In order to be successful over the long term, a new American approach to Iran would have to involve more than just talks with the regime. Before Iran or any country can become stable and democratic, it must have a strong middle class. It is in the urgent interest of the United States to promote all manner of social, political, and economic contacts with people at every level of Iranian society. In a new climate, U.S. businesses would no longer be forbidden to trade with Iran but encouraged to do so. Rather than tightly restricting the number of visas issued to Iranians, the United States would do the opposite: invite as many Iranians as possible to the United States and flood Iran with Americans, ranging from students and professors to farmers and entrepreneurs to writers and artists.

Iran is well prepared to take advantage of this kind of engagement. It has a thriving civil society that thirsts for contacts with the outside world, and also a democratic consciousness that is more than a century old. As the failures in Iraq have so painfully shown, democracy cannot be imposed on a country from outside. Democracy is not an election but a way of life and an approach to solving problems. In any society, awareness of democratic values grows slowly. Unlike other countries in its neighborhood, Iran has been advancing toward democracy since adopting its first constitution more than a century ago. Iranian constitutions have not always been observed, and Iranian elections have not always been fair. Over this long period, however, the Iranian people have developed a deep understanding of what democracy means. Many thirst for it. There is more fertile ground for democratic change in Iran than in almost any other Muslim country. Remarkably, many ordinary Iranians also feel a residual admiration for the United States. American leaders should take advantage of this potential.

The idea of attacking Iran and seeking to decapitate its regime carries within itself a highly dangerous assumption: that whatever comes afterward would be an improvement. Iranians have a painful experience that disproves this belief. In the late 1970s they banded together—communists, religious fundamentalists, liberal admirers of Mossadegh—to overthrow the Shah. They did so because they assumed that whatever regime came next would be better. Many now agree this was a terrible mistake.

Some in Washington argue that any new regime in Iran would be an improvement over the repressive and xenophobic mullahs. They are dangerously mistaken. An attack on Iran might well throw that country into chaos like that which has enveloped Iraq. In such an anarchic environment, there would be no central authority to control violent radicals. Most frighteningly, those radicals might include enraged nuclear technicians and scientists. The chance that these Iranians might use their technological know-how to pass weapons of mass destruction on to terrorist groups would be far greater after an attack than it is now. Bombing nuclear facilities in Iran—assuming they could all be found and destroyed—would be at best a temporary solution. It would almost certainly lead to the emergence of more terrifying threats than those Iran poses today. As the director of the International Atomic Energy Agency, Mohammad AlBare-dei, likes to point out, buildings can be attacked and destroyed, but "you cannot bomb knowledge."

By violently pushing Iran off the path to democracy in 1953, the United States created a whirlpool of instability from which undreamed-of threats emerged years later. A long American campaign of isolation, pressure, and warnings has produced no change in Iran's behavior. Continuing it will mean a steady increase in tension that some in Washington believe should culminate in a military attack. Such an attack would usher in another era of upheaval in Iran and the surrounding region, this time with the overlay of nuclear-tinged terror.

Operation Ajax, as the CIA plot to depose Prime Minister Mossadegh was code-named, brought immeasurable tragedy to Iran, contributed to the rise of anti-American terror, and, in the end, greatly weakened the security of the United States. Few episodes of twentieth-century history more perfectly epitomize the concept of "blowback." Today, as anti-Iran rhetoric in Washington becomes steadily more strident, it is urgent that Americans understand how disastrous the last U.S. attack on Iran turned out to be. They might also ponder the question of what moral responsibility the United States has to Iran in the wake of this painful history.

By abandoning a quarter-century of bitter American antagonism toward China, President Richard Nixon showed an ability to conceive a rearrangement of the global balance of power. His gamble reshaped the course of history. The world is crying out for an American leader with comparable audacity, one who can visualize a relationship between Iran and the United States different from the one that has existed since 1979.

PREFACE

One day I attended a book party for an older Iranian woman who had written her memoirs. She spoke for an hour about her eventful life. Although she never touched on politics, she mentioned in passing that her family was related to the family of Mohammad Mossadegh, who served as prime minister of Iran for twenty-six months in the early 1950s and was overthrown in a coup d'etat staged by the Central Intelligence Agency.

After she finished speaking, I couldn't resist the temptation to ask a question. "You mentioned Mossadegh," I said. "What do you remember, or what can you tell us, about the coup against him?" She immediately became agitated and animated.

"Why did you Americans do that terrible thing?" she cried out. "We always loved America. To us, America was the great country, the perfect country, the country that helped us while other countries were exploiting us. But after that moment, no one in Iran ever trusted the United States again. I can tell you for sure that if you had not done that thing, you would never have had that problem of hostages being taken in your embassy in Tehran. All your trouble started in 1953. Why, why did you do it?"

This outburst reflected a great gap in knowledge and understanding that separates most Iranians from most non-Iranians. In Iran, almost everyone has for decades known that the United States was responsible for putting an end to democratic rule in 1953 and installing what became the long dictatorship of Mohammad Reza Shah. His dictatorship produced the Islamic Revolution of 1979, which brought to power a passionately anti-American theocracy that embraced terrorism as a tool of statecraft. Its radicalism inspired anti-Western fanatics in many countries, most notably Afghanistan, where al-Qaeda and other terror groups found homes and bases.

These events serve as a stark warning to the United States and to any country that ever seeks to impose its will on a foreign land. Governments that sponsor coups, revolutions, or armed invasions usually act with the conviction that they will win, and often they do. Their victories, however, can come back to haunt them, sometimes in devastating and tragic ways. This is especially true in today's complex and volatile Middle East, where tradition, history, and religion shape political life in ways that many outsiders do not understand.

The violent anti-Americanism that emerged from Iran after 1979 shocked most people in the United States. Americans had no idea of what might have set off such bitter hatred in a country where they had always imagined themselves more or less well liked. That was because almost no one in the United States knew what the Central Intelligence Agency did there in 1953.

In his time, Mohammad Mossadegh was a titanic figure. He shook an empire and changed the world. People everywhere knew his name. World leaders sought to influence him and later to depose him. No one was surprised when *Time* magazine chose him over Harry Truman, Dwight Eisenhower, and Winston Churchill as its Man of the Year for 1951.

Operation Ajax, as the CIA coup against Mossadegh was code-named, was a great trauma for Iran, the Middle East, and the colonial world. This was the first time the CIA overthrew a foreign government. It set a pattern for years to come and shaped the way millions of people view the United States.

This book tells a story that explains a great deal about the sources of violent currents now surging through the world. More than just a remarkable adventure story, it is a sobering message from the past and an object lesson for the future.

ACKNOWLEDGMENTS

A small but dedicated group of scholars has devoted considerable effort to uncovering the truth about events surrounding the 1953 coup. Most persistent among them is Mark J. Gasiorowski, who has become the group's unofficial dean. Others who have accompanied him on his mission of discovery include Ervand Abrahamian, Fakhreddin Azimi, James A. Bill, Maziar Behroos, Malcolm Byrne, Richard W. Cottam, Farhad Diba, Mostafa Elm, James F. Goode, Mary Ann Heiss, Homa Katouzian, William Roger Louis, and Sepehr Zabih. Their work made this book possible.

The CIA prepared its own internal history of the coup, but it remained secret for many years. In 2000, a copy was leaked to the *New York Times*. It confirmed much of what was known about the coup and added many new details. The reporter who obtained it, James Risen, deserves much credit for his role in bringing it to light.

My research also owes much to the cooperation of librarians and archivists who freely shared their time and expertise. They include those at the public libraries in Chicago and Oak Park, Illinois; the Kent Law Library in Chicago; the Dwight D. Eisenhower Library in Abilene, Kansas, and the Harry S. Truman Library in Independence, Missouri; the National Archives in College Park,

Maryland; and the Public Records Office in Kew Gardens, Surrey, England.

Among those who read early drafts of the manuscript, in whole or in part, and made valuable comments were Janet Afary, David Barboza, Elmira Bayrasli, David Shuman, James M. Stone, and John E. Woods. They bear no responsibility for the final product but have my warm appreciation.

Most of the Iranians who helped me during my research in Iran asked not to be identified by name. They know who they are, and to them I extend deep thanks.

NOTES ON USAGE

There is no universally accepted system for transliterating Persian words into English. As a result, there are many variations in the English spellings of Iranian names and other words. English-language books and articles about Mossadegh, for example, spell his name in almost a dozen different ways.

I have chosen spellings that seem closest to the original pronunciation. For the sake of consistency I have standardized these spellings and changed alternate spellings that occur in quoted documents. I have also omitted diacritical marks that are unfamiliar to English-speaking readers.

At several points I have made minor adjustments in translation and punctuation. These have been made only to clarify meaning and do not in any case represent substantive changes.

The division of Britain's Secret Intelligence Service that conducts operations abroad is called MI6. To avoid confusion, I have referred to it by the former name throughout.

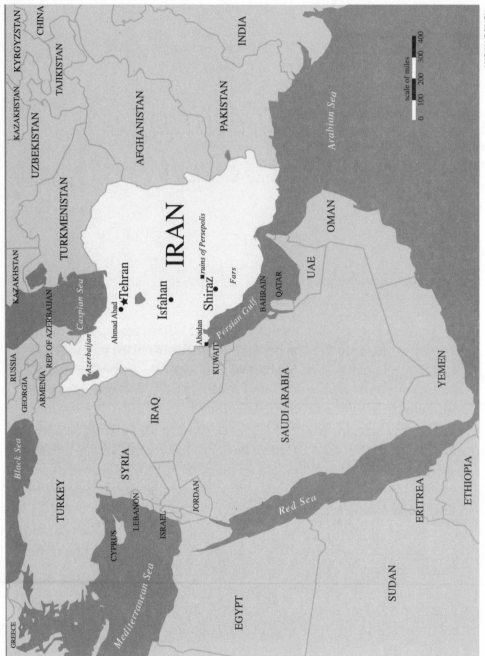

CHAPTER 1

Good Evening, Mr. Roosevelt

M ost of Tehran was asleep when an odd caravan set out through the darkness shortly before midnight on August 15, 1953. At its head was an armored car with military markings. Behind came two jeeps and several army trucks full of soldiers. The day had been exceptionally hot, but nightfall brought some relief. A crescent moon shone above. It was a fine night to overthrow a government.

Sitting in the lead car, Colonel Nematollah Nasiri, the commander of the Imperial Guard, had reason to be confident. In his pocket he carried a decree from the Shah of Iran dismissing Prime Minister Mohammad Mossadegh from office. Nasiri was on his way to present this decree to Mossadegh and arrest him if he resisted.

The American and British intelligence agents who plotted this rebellion assumed that Mossadegh would immediately call out the army to suppress it. They had arranged for no one to be on the other end of the phone when he called. Colonel Nasiri was to stop first at the home of the military chief of staff and arrest him, then move on to deliver the fateful decree.

The colonel did as he was told. When he arrived at his first stop, however, he found something most unusual. Despite the late hour, the chief of staff, General Taqi Riahi, was not at home. Neither was anyone else. Not even a servant or a doorkeeper could be found.

This might have alerted Colonel Nasiri that something was amiss, but it did not. He simply climbed back into his armored car and ordered the driver to proceed toward his main objective, Prime Minister Mossadegh's home. With him rode the hopes of two elite intelligence agencies.

Colonel Nasiri would not have been foolhardy enough to attempt such a bold mission on his own. The decree he carried was of dubious legality, since in democratic Iran prime ministers could be installed or removed only with the permission of parliament. But this night's work was the culmination of months of planning by the Central Intelligence Agency and Britain's Secret Intelligence Service. The coup they were staging had been ordered by President Dwight Eisenhower and Prime Minister Winston Churchill.

In 1953 the United States was still new to Iran. Many Iranians thought of Americans as friends, supporters of the fragile democracy they had spent half a century trying to build. It was Britain, not the United States, that they demonized as the colonialist oppressor that exploited them.

Since the early years of the twentieth century a British company, owned mainly by the British government, had enjoyed a fantastically lucrative monopoly on the production and sale of Iranian oil. The wealth that flowed from beneath Iran's soil played a decisive role in maintaining Britain at the pinnacle of world power while most Iranians lived in poverty. Iranians chafed bitterly under this injustice. Finally, in 1951, they turned to Mossadegh, who more than any other political leader personified their anger at the Anglo-Iranian Oil Company (AIOC). He pledged to throw the company out of Iran, reclaim the country's vast petroleum reserves, and free Iran from subjection to foreign power.

Prime Minister Mossadegh carried out his pledges with single-minded zeal. To the ecstatic cheers of his people, he nationalized Anglo-Iranian, the most profitable British business in the world. Soon afterward, Iranians took control of the company's giant refinery at Abadan on the Persian Gulf.

That sent Iran into patriotic ecstasy and made Mossadegh a national hero. It also outraged the British, who indignantly accused Mossadegh of stealing their property. They first demanded that the

World Court and the United Nations punish him, then sent war-ships to the Persian Gulf, and finally imposed a crushing embargo that devastated Iran's economy. Despite this campaign, many Irani-ans were thrilled with Mossadegh's boldness. So were anticolonial leaders across Asia and Africa.

Mossadegh was utterly unmoved by Britain's campaign against him. One European newspaper reported that Mossadegh "would rather be fried in Persian oil than make the slightest concession to the British." For a time the British considered launching an armed invasion to retake the oil fields and refinery, but they dropped the idea after President Harry Truman refused his support. Only two options remained: leave Mossadegh in power or organize a coup to depose him. Prime Minister Churchill, a proud product of the imperial tradition, had no trouble deciding for the coup.

British agents began conspiring to overthrow Mossadegh soon after he nationalized the oil company. They were too eager and aggressive for their own good. Mossadegh learned of their plotting, and in October 1952 he ordered the British embassy shut. All British diplomats in Iran, including clandestine agents working under diplomatic cover, had to leave the country. No one was left to stage the coup.

Immediately, the British asked President Truman for help. Tru-man, however, sympathized viscerally with nationalist movements like the one Mossadegh led. He had nothing but contempt for old-style imperialists like those who ran Anglo-Iranian. Besides, the CIA had never overthrown a government, and Truman did not wish to set the precedent.

The American attitude toward a possible coup in Iran changed radically after Dwight Eisenhower was elected president in Nov-ember 1952. Within days of the election, a senior agent of the Secret Intelligence Service, Christopher Montague Woodhouse, came to Washington for meetings with top CIA and State Depart-ment officials. Woodhouse shrewdly decided not to make the tra-ditional British argument, which was that Mossadegh must go because he had nationalized British property. That argument did not arouse much passion in Washington. Woodhouse knew what would.

"Not wishing to be accused of trying to use the Americans to pull British chestnuts out of the fire," he wrote later, "I decided to emphasize the Communist threat to Iran rather than the need to recover control of the oil industry."

This appeal was calculated to stir the two brothers who would direct American foreign policy after Eisenhower's inauguration. John Foster Dulles, the incoming secretary of state, and Allen Dulles, the incoming CIA director, were among the fiercest of Cold Warriors. They viewed the world as an ideological battleground and saw every local conflict through the prism of the great East-West confrontation. In their eyes, any country not decisively allied with the United States was a potential enemy. They considered Iran especially dangerous.

Iran had immense oil wealth, a long border with the Soviet Union, an active Communist party, and a nationalist prime minister. The Dulles brothers believed there was a serious danger that it would soon fall to communism. The prospect of such a "second China" terrified them. When the British presented their proposal to overthrow Mossadegh and replace him with a reliably pro-Western prime minister, they were immediately interested.

Soon after President Eisenhower took office on January 20, 1953, John Foster Dulles and Allen Dulles told their British counterparts that they were ready to move against Mossadegh. Their coup would be code-named Operation Ajax, or, in CIA jargon, TPAJAX. To direct it, they chose a CIA officer with considerable experience in the Middle East, Kermit Roosevelt, a grandson of President Theodore Roosevelt.

Like other members of his famous family, Kermit Roosevelt had a penchant for direct action and was known to be decisive in times of crisis. He was thirty-seven years old, chief of the CIA's Near East and Asia Division, and an acknowledged master of his clandestine trade. The Soviet agent Kim Philby described him as the quintessential quiet American, "a courteous, soft-spoken Easterner with impeccable social connections, well-educated rather than intellectual, pleasant and unassuming as host and guest. An especially nice wife. In fact, the last person you would expect to be up to the neck in dirty tricks."

CIA agents in those days shared a profound idealism, a conviction that they were doing the vital dirty work of freedom. Many combined the best qualities of the thinker and the adventurer. None epitomized that combination more fully than did Kermit Roosevelt.

At the beginning of July, ignoring a CIA doctor's order that he first submit to urgent kidney surgery, he flew off on his secret mission. He landed in Beirut and from there set out by car across the deserts of Syria and Iraq. As he entered Iran at a remote crossing, he could barely contain his excitement:

> I remembered what my father wrote of his arrival in Africa with *his* father, T. R., in 1909 on the *African Game Trails* trip. "It was a great adventure, and all the world was young!" I felt as he must have felt then. My nerves tingled, my spirits soared as we moved up the mountain road. . . . As it turned out, on July 19, 1953, we encountered an unusually listless, stupid and semi-literate immigration/customs fellow at Khanequin. In those days US passports carried, as they do not now, some brief description of any notable features of the holder. With encouragement and help from me, the guard laboriously transcribed my name as "Mr. Scar on Right Forehead." This I found a good omen.

Roosevelt spent his first two weeks in Tehran conducting business from a villa rented by one of his American agents. Decades of British intrigue in Iran, coupled with more recent work by the CIA, gave him excellent assets on the ground. Among them were a handful of experienced and highly resourceful Iranian operatives who had spent years assembling a clandestine network of sympathetic politicians, military officers, clergymen, newspaper editors, and street gang leaders. The CIA was paying these operatives tens of thousands of dollars per month, and they earned every cent. During the spring and summer of 1953, not a day passed without at least one CIA-subsidized mullah, news commentator, or politician denouncing Prime Minister Mossadegh. The prime minister, who had great respect for the sanctity of free press, refused to suppress this campaign.

Iranian agents who came in and out of Roosevelt's villa knew him only by his pseudonym, James Lockridge. As time passed, they naturally developed a sense of comradeship, and some of the Iranians, much to Roosevelt's amusement, began calling him "Jim." The only times he came close to blowing his cover were during tennis games that he played regularly at the Turkish embassy and on the campus of the French Institute. When he missed a shot, he would curse himself, shouting, "Oh, *Roosevelt!*" Several times he was asked why someone named Lockridge would have developed such a habit. He replied that he was a passionate Republican and considered Franklin D. Roosevelt to have been so evil that he used Roosevelt's name as a curse.

The plan for Operation Ajax envisioned an intense psychological campaign against Prime Minister Mossadegh, which the CIA had already launched, followed by an announcement that the Shah had dismissed him from office. Mobs and military units whose leaders were on the CIA payroll would crush any attempt by Mossadegh to resist. Then it would be announced that the Shah had chosen General Fazlollah Zahedi, a retired military officer who had received more than $100,000 from the CIA, as Iran's new prime minister.

By the beginning of August, Tehran was afire. Mobs working for the CIA staged anti-Mossadegh protests, marching through the streets carrying portraits of the Shah and chanting royalist slogans. Foreign agents bribed members of parliament and anyone else who might be helpful in the forthcoming coup attempt.

Press attacks on Mossadegh reached new levels of virulence. Articles accused him not just of communist leanings and designs on the throne, but also of Jewish parentage and even secret sympathy for the British. Although Mossadegh did not know it, most of these tirades were either inspired by the CIA or written by CIA propagandists in Washington. One of the propagandists, Richard Cottam, estimated that four-fifths of the newspapers in Tehran were under CIA influence.

"Any article that I would write—it gave you something of a sense of power—would appear almost instantly, the next day, in the Iranian press," Cottam recalled years later. "They were designed to show Mossadegh as a Communist collaborator and as a fanatic."

As the plot gathered momentum, Roosevelt faced his most serious obstacle, Mohammad Reza Shah. The thirty-two-year-old monarch, only the second shah in the Pahlavi line, was timid and indecisive by nature, and he doggedly refused to be drawn into such an audacious plot. "He hates taking decisions and cannot be relied on to stick to them when taken," one British diplomat reported. "He has no moral courage and succumbs easily to fear."

More than personality traits held the Shah back. Mossadegh had been the most popular figure in modern Iranian history, and although Britain's campaign of subversion and economic sabotage had weakened him, he was still widely admired and beloved. It was not even clear that the Shah had the legal authority to remove him. The plot could easily backfire and endanger not only the Shah's life but the monarchy itself.

None of this daunted Roosevelt. To carry out his coup, he needed signed decrees from the Shah dismissing Mossadegh and naming General Zahedi in his place. Roosevelt never doubted that he would ultimately obtain them. His battle of wits with the Shah was unequal from the start. Roosevelt was clever and well trained, and behind him lay immense international power. The Shah was weak, immature, and alone.

Roosevelt's first gambit was to send emissaries who might have special influence over the Shah. First he arranged for the Shah's twin sister, Princess Ashraf, who was as sharp and combative as the Shah was dull, to visit her brother and try to stiffen his backbone. Ashraf's tongue-lashings of her brother were legendary, including one in the presence of foreign diplomats when she demanded that he prove he was a man or else be revealed to all as a mouse. She detested Mossadegh because he was an enemy of royal power. Her attacks on his government became so bitter that the Shah had felt it best to send her out of the country. From her golden exile in Europe, she watched events in her homeland with undiminished passion.

Ashraf was enjoying life in French casinos and nightclubs when one of Roosevelt's best Iranian agents, Asadollah Rashidian, paid her a call. He found her reluctant, so the next day a delegation of American and British agents came to pose the invitation in stronger terms. The leader of the delegation, a senior British operative named Norman Darbyshire, had the foresight to bring a mink coat and a packet of cash. When Ashraf saw these emoluments, Darbyshire later recalled, "her eyes lit up" and her resistance crumbled. She agreed to fly to Tehran and landed without incident under her married name, Madame Chafik. At first her brother refused to receive her, but after being not so subtly urged to change his mind by associates who were in touch with the CIA, he relented. Brother and sister met late on the evening of July 29. Their meeting was tense. She failed to persuade him to issue the crucial decrees, and to make matters worse, news of her presence leaked out and set off a storm of protest. To everyone's relief, she quickly returned to Europe.

Next Roosevelt turned to General H. Norman Schwarzkopf, who had spent most of the 1940s in Iran leading an elite military regiment and to whom the Shah felt deeply indebted. The CIA gave Schwarzkopf a "cover mission" of meetings and inspections in Lebanon, Pakistan, and Egypt so that his visit to Iran could be explained as a simple stopover. According to one account, he arrived there carrying "a couple of large bags" into which were stuffed several million dollars in cash. He met first with Roosevelt and then with Iranian principals in the operation, to whom he distributed much money. On the first day of August he called on the Shah at Saad Abad Palace.

It was a bizarre encounter. At first the Shah refused to say a word to his guest, indicating with gestures that he suspected hidden microphones. Then he led Schwarzkopf into a large ballroom, pulled a table into the center of the room, sat down on top of it, and invited the general to join him. There he whispered that he had still not decided whether to sign the decrees Roosevelt wanted. He doubted that the army would obey any order he signed, and he did not want to be on the losing side in such a risky operation.

Even as Schwarzkopf listened, he sensed the Shah's resistance weakening. One more visitor might be enough to bring the desired result, but it would have to be Roosevelt himself. This was a dangerous proposition. If Roosevelt was seen at the palace, news of his presence in Iran might leak out and compromise the entire operation. Schwarzkopf, however, told him there was no alternative.

Roosevelt expected this advice. "I had been sure from the beginning that a personal meeting would be necessary," he wrote afterward. "Securely and alone, the Shah and I could resolve the many difficult problems confronting us. This could only be done on a person-to-person basis. In all likelihood we would have to meet not once but several times. So the sooner we got to it, the better."

To prepare the way for his visit, Roosevelt sent his trusted agent Assadollah Rashidian to see the Shah on August 2. Rashidian's message was simple: the British and the Americans were planning a coup and would not be deterred. Under these circumstances,

Rashidian observed tartly, the Shah had little choice but to cooperate. The Shah nodded in silent agreement.

Only Roosevelt, however, could close the deal. He asked an agent in the royal court who was known by the code name Rosenkrantz to approach the Shah and say that "an American authorized to speak for Eisenhower *and* Churchill desired a secret audience." In a matter of hours the overture was made, and the Shah accepted it. He would send a car to Roosevelt's villa that night at midnight.

"Two hours to wait!" Roosevelt thought to himself after receiving the message. "I considered my costume. If not appropriate for a royal audience, it did seem good for these rather peculiar circumstances. I had on a dark turtleneck shirt, Oxford-gray slacks, and a pair of black-topped *givehs,* rope-soled cloth-covered Persian footwear somewhere between shoes and bedroom slippers. Not exactly smart but suitably unobtrusive."

Roosevelt, who had interviewed the Shah six years earlier while researching a book called *Arabs, Oil and History* and had met him again during subsequent visits to Iran, waited for the appointed hour with a handful of his agents. He thought it best not to drink, though his comrades had no such scruples. When midnight finally came, he walked through the front gate and out onto the street. A car was waiting. He climbed into the back seat.

Nothing stirred on the streets as Roosevelt was driven toward the stately palace. As his car began to climb the hill on which the palace sits, he decided that he should duck out of sight. His hosts had thoughtfully left a folded blanket on the car seat, and he put it to good use, lying down on the floor and pulling it over him.

There was no trouble at the sentry's gate, just a perfunctory wave. The car continued on for a few moments and then pulled to a stop well short of the palace's broad limestone steps. Roosevelt pulled off his blanket and sat up. A slim figure was walking down the steps toward him. The man, whom he recognized immediately as the Shah, approached his car, opened the door, and slid in beside him. Discreetly, the driver withdrew into the shadows.

"Good evening, Mr. Roosevelt," the monarch said, extending his hand. "I cannot say that I expected to see you, but this is a pleasure."

Roosevelt told the Shah that he was in Iran on behalf of the American and British secret services, and that this would be confirmed by a code word the Shah would be able to hear on the BBC the next night. Churchill had arranged that the BBC would end its broadcast day by saying not "It is now midnight," as usual, but "It is now *exactly* midnight." Such assurances were hardly necessary, the Shah replied. The two men understood each other.

Still, however, the Shah was hesitant to join the plot. He was no adventurer, he told Roosevelt, and could not take the chances of one. Roosevelt's tone sharpened. He told the Shah that leaving Mossadegh in power would "lead only to a Communist Iran or to a second Korea," which Western leaders were not prepared to accept. To avoid it, they had approved a plot to overthrow Mossadegh—and, incidentally, to increase the power of the Shah. He must embrace it within a few days; if he refused, Roosevelt would leave the country and devise "some other plan."

The Shah made no direct reply. Let them meet again the following night, he suggested. Then he turned to open the car door. Before stepping out into the darkness, he looked back at Roosevelt and said, "I am glad to welcome you once again to my country."

From then on, Roosevelt met with the Shah almost every midnight, entering the palace compound under the same blanket in the back seat of the same car. Before and after each session, he conferred with his Iranian operatives. When local police became suspicious of the villa he was using, he stopped conducting business there and devised another way to hold his conferences. He obtained a Tehran taxi, and at appointed times he would drive it to a quiet corner, always with the "On Call" sign showing. There he would park and begin walking until one or another of his agents, usually hyperactive and pumped on the adrenaline of the operation, picked him up in a Chrysler or a Buick. They planned their day-to-day tactics while careening through the hilly outskirts of town.

In his conversations with the Shah, Roosevelt said he had at his disposal "the equivalent of about $1 million" and several "extremely competent, professional organizers" who could "distribute pamphlets, organize mobs, keep track of the opposition—you name it, they'll do it." He described Operation Ajax as based on "four lines of attack." First, a campaign in mosques, the press, and the streets would undermine Mossadegh's popularity. Second, royalist military officers would deliver the decree dismissing him. Third, mobs would take control of the streets. Fourth, General Zahedi would emerge triumphantly and accept the Shah's nomination as prime minister.

It was an appealing but not entirely convincing plan, and the Shah continued to agonize. His mood turned to what Roosevelt called "stubborn irresolution." But it was "hopeless to proceed without the Shah," Roosevelt cabled to his CIA superiors, so he continued turning up the pressure. Finally, inevitably, the Shah's resistance broke. He agreed to sign the *firmans,* as the royal decrees were called, but only on condition that he be allowed to leave Tehran for some safer place immediately afterward.

Mohammad Reza Shah had never been known as a courageous man, so this latest show of prudence did not surprise Roosevelt. The two men decided that the safest place for the Shah to hide was a hunting lodge that the royal family maintained near Ramsar on the Caspian coast. There was an airstrip nearby, which the Shah found reassuring.

"If by any horrible chance things go wrong," he indelicately told Roosevelt, "the Empress and I will take our plane straight to Baghdad."

The two men met for the last time in the predawn of August 9. Before bidding the Shah farewell, Roosevelt felt it correct to thank him for his decision to cooperate, reluctant though it had been. This was a historic moment, and something beyond the ordinary was appropriate. Roosevelt came up with a wonderful way to embellish his message.

"Your Majesty, I received earlier this evening a cable from Washington," he prevaricated. "President Eisenhower had asked that I convey to you this word: 'I wish Your Imperial Majesty godspeed. If the Pahlavis and the Roosevelts working together cannot solve this little problem, then there is no hope anywhere. I have complete faith that you will get this done.'"

It was agreed that a CIA courier would bring the vital *firmans* to the palace early the next morning. The Shah would sign them and then fly immediately to his refuge at Ramsar. All seemed perfectly arranged.

When Roosevelt returned to his villa with the good news, he and his agents celebrated with an exuberant drinking binge. He finally made it to bed at five o'clock. A few hours later he was awakened by the cursing of an aide. There had been a last-minute failure. The courier who was to obtain the Shah's signature had turned up late at the palace. When he arrived, the royal couple was gone.

Whether this was a simple missed connection or a last-minute attempt by the Shah to run from signing the *firmans,* Roosevelt was determined that it not be allowed to upset his plan. These *firmans* played an indispensable role in the coup he had designed. They provided not just a fig leaf of legality but the operation's central organizing principle. If the Shah was not in Tehran to sign them, they would have to be brought to wherever he was.

The man best equipped to help at this moment, Roosevelt quickly realized, was Colonel Nasiri of the Imperial Guard. He was a strong royalist, could find and fly a plane, and was on intimate terms with the Shah. The arrangements were quickly made, and this time the connection worked. Nasiri flew to Ramsar, obtained the Shah's scribbled signature on both *firmans,* and then, because bad weather prevented him from taking off, sent them to Tehran by car.

Roosevelt and his comrades spent the day waiting impatiently around their pool, with no idea of what was taking Nasiri so long. When night fell, they took to smoking, playing cards, and drinking vodka with lime. Tehran was under a nine o'clock curfew, but after that hour passed, they still hoped someone would turn up. It was almost midnight when they heard shouts at the gate. They ran to open it. Outside was a small throng of unshaven and very excited Iranians, most of whom they did not recognize. They pushed a packet to Roosevelt, who opened it gingerly. Inside were the two *firmans,* duly signed by His Imperial Majesty.

After jubilantly embracing his new friends, Roosevelt considered how quickly he could now move. He was much dismayed when his agents told him there would have to be one more delay. The weekend, which Iranians observe on Thursday and Friday, was about to begin, and Iranians do not like to conduct business, much less overthrow governments, on weekends. Roosevelt reluctantly agreed to postpone the coup until Saturday night, August 15.

Confident of their plan but acutely aware that each passing hour increased the chance of betrayal, Roosevelt and his comrades spent three excruciating days at poolside. Saturday was the hardest to bear because the moment of truth was so near. Roosevelt later wrote that on that day, time moved "more slowly than anything we had ever before lived through."

By now Roosevelt had moved his command post to a basement

in the American embassy compound. His Iranian agents visited him less frequently, but they were busier than ever at their subversive work, as a CIA report on the coup makes clear:

> At this same time the psychological campaign against Mossadegh was reaching its climax. The controllable press was going all out against Mossadegh, while [DELETED] under station direction was printing material which the station considered to be helpful. CIA agents gave serious attention to alarming the religious leaders at Tehran by issuing black propaganda in the name of the [Communist] Tudeh party, threatening these leaders with savage punishment if they opposed Mossadegh. Threatening phone calls were also made to them, in the name of the Tudeh, and one of several sham bombings of the houses of these leaders was carried out.
>
> The word that the Shah would support direct action in his behalf spread rapidly through the "colonel's conspiracy" fostered by the station. Zahedi saw station principal agent, Colonel [DELETED], and named him as liaison officer with the Americans and as his choice to supervise the staff planning for the action. . . .
>
> On 14 August the station cabled that upon the conclusion of TPAJAX the Zahedi government, in view of the empty treasury of the country, would be in urgent need of funds. The sum of $5,000,000 was suggested, and CIA was asked to produce this sum almost within hours after the conclusion of the operation.

Now, in the words of that CIA report, "there was nothing that either the station or Headquarters could do except wait for action to begin." When dusk finally began falling over Tehran on August 15, Roosevelt climbed into his Hillman-Minx taxi, flipped down the "On Call" sign, and drove to a nearby safe house where his agents had gathered to await the news of victory. As vodka flowed, they sang along with records of Broadway show tunes. Their favorite was "Luck Be a Lady Tonight" from the musical *Guys and Dolls*. By acclamation, they adopted it as the official Operation Ajax theme song:

> They call you lady luck, but there is room for doubt;
> At times you have a very un-ladylike way of running out.
> You're on this date with me, the pickings have been lush,
> And yet before the evening is over you might give me the brush.

You might forget your manners, you might refuse to stay
And so the best that I can do is pray:
Luck, be a lady tonight.

As Roosevelt drove back to the American embassy later that evening, his route took him past the residence of General Riahi, the military chief of staff. He enjoyed the coincidence. If his plan worked, General Riahi would be behind bars in a few hours.

The officer Roosevelt had chosen to arrest the chief of staff and the prime minister that night, Colonel Nasiri, seemed ideal for the operation. He believed in the primacy of royal power and loathed Mossadegh. His command of the seven-hundred-man Imperial Guard gave him control of considerable resources. By successfully obtaining the vital *firmans* at a crucial moment, he seemed to have proven his reliability.

On the night of August 15, however, Nasiri was not thinking clearly enough. It was well after eleven o'clock when he arrived at General Riahi's home and found it abandoned. He was untroubled and simply ordered his men to proceed toward Mossadegh's residence. Unbeknownst to him, another military column was also on its way there. General Riahi had learned of the coup and sent troops to foil it.

The precise identity of the informant has never been established. Most guesses center on a military officer who belonged to a secret communist cell. There may have been more than one informant. In the end, what happened was precisely what Roosevelt feared. Too many people knew about the plot for too long. A leak was all but inevitable.

In the confusing hours around midnight, Tehran was bursting with plots and counterplots. Some rebellious officers learned of the betrayal in time to abort their missions. Others, not realizing that they were compromised, went ahead. One seized the telephone office at the bazaar. Another roused Foreign Minister Hussein Fatemi from bed and dragged him away barefoot and shouting.

The future of constitutional rule in Iran depended on which column of soldiers reached Mossadegh's house first. Shortly before one o'clock in the morning, the rebel column drove up Kakh Street, passed the corner of Heshmatdowleh, and stopped. Here Mossadegh lived with his wife in a small apartment, part of a larger complex that his family had owned for many years. The gate was closed. Colonel Nasiri stepped out to demand entry. In his hand he held the *firman* dismissing Mossadegh from office. Behind him stood several files of soldiers.

Colonel Nasiri had arrived too late. Moments after he appeared at the gate, several loyal commanders stepped from the shadows. They escorted him into a jeep and drove him to general staff headquarters. There General Riahi denounced him as a traitor, ordered him stripped of his uniform, and sent him to a cell. The man who was to have arrested Mossadegh was now himself a prisoner.

Roosevelt, who had no way of knowing that any of this was happening, was at his embassy command post, waiting for Colonel Nasiri to call. Tanks clattered by several times, but the telephone never rang. Roosevelt's apprehensions deepened as dawn broke. Radio Tehran did not begin its transmissions at six o'clock as normal. Then, an hour later, it crackled to life with a burst of military music, followed by the reading of an official communiqué. Roosevelt did not speak Persian but feared the worst when he heard the announcer use the word *Mossadegh*. Then Mossadegh himself came on the air, announcing victory over a coup attempt organized by the Shah and "foreign elements."

The Shah, cowering at his seaside villa, was also listening. As soon as he grasped what had happened, he roused his wife and told her it was time to run. They quickly packed two small briefcases, grabbed what clothes they could carry in their arms, and walked briskly out toward their twin-engine Beechcraft. The Shah, a trained pilot, took the controls and set a course for Baghdad. After arriving there, he told the American ambassador that he "would be looking for work shortly as he has a large family and very small means outside of Iran."

While the Shah was fleeing, military units loyal to the government were fanning out through Tehran. City life quickly returned to normal. Several conspirators were arrested and others went into hiding. A reward was offered for the capture of General Zahedi. CIA operatives made mad dashes back to the security of the American embassy or safe houses. Jubilant crowds took to the streets chanting, "Victory to the Nation!" and "Mossadegh Has Won!"

Inside his embassy compound, Roosevelt felt himself "close to despair." He had no choice but to send a cable to Washington saying that things had gone terribly wrong. John Waller, the head of the CIA's Iran desk, read it with great disappointment. Waller feared for the lives of his agents, and he sent Roosevelt an urgent reply. No copy of it is known to exist. According to CIA lore, it was an order that Roosevelt leave Iran immediately. Many years later, though, Waller said that it was not so categorical. Its message, he recalled, was: "If you're in a jam, get out so you don't get killed. But if you're not in a jam, go ahead and do what you have to do."

Things looked bleak for the plotters. They had lost the advantage of surprise. Several of their key agents were out of action. Their anointed prime minister, General Zahedi, was in hiding. The Shah had fled. Foreign Minister Fatemi, free after several hours in rebel custody, was making fiery speeches denouncing the Shah for his collaboration with foreign agents.

"O Traitor!" Fatemi railed before one crowd. "The moment you heard by Tehran Radio that your foreign plot had been defeated, you fled to the nearest country where Britain has an embassy!"

Operation Ajax had failed. Radio Tehran reported that the situation was "well under control," and so it seemed. Shock waves reverberated through CIA headquarters in Washington.

Then suddenly, around midevening, Roosevelt cabled a most unexpected message. He had decided to stay in Tehran and improvise another stab at Mossadegh. The CIA had sent him to overthrow the government of Iran, and he was determined not to leave until he had done it.

CHAPTER 2

Curse This Fate

Rising dramatically from the desert of southern Iran, with distant mountains adding to the majesty of the scene, the spectacular ruins of Persepolis testify to the grandeur that was Persia. This was the ceremonial and spiritual capital of a vast empire, built by Cyrus, Darius, and Xerxes, titans whose names still echo through history. Giant statues of winged bulls guard the Gate of All Nations, through which princes from vassal states passed once each year to pay homage to their Persian masters. The great Apadana, or Hall of Audience, where these princes knelt together before their dead sovereign, was the length of three football fields. Its roof was supported by thirty-six towering columns, some of which still stand. Two monumental staircases leading up to the hall are decorated with intricately detailed carvings depicting the annual ritual of obedience, which was held on the day of the vernal equinox. Today they offer a vivid picture of how completely Persian emperors once dominated the richest lands on earth.

The carvings show rulers of subject states filing past their supreme leader, each bearing gifts symbolizing the wealth of his province. Archaeologists have managed to identify most of them, and the very names of their cultures evoke the richness of antiquity.

The warlike Elamites, who lived east of the Tigris River, bring a lion to symbolize their ferocity. Arachosians from Central Asia offer camels and rich furs, Armenians a horse and a delicately crafted vase, Ethiopians a giraffe and an elephant's tusk, Somalis an antelope and a chariot, Thracians shields and spears, and Ionians bolts of cloth and ceramic plates. Arabs lead a camel, Assyrians a bull, Indians a donkey laden with woven baskets. All these tributes were laid before the King of Kings, a monarch whose reign spread Persian power to the edges of the known world.

Many countries in the Middle East are artificial creations. European colonialists drew their national borders in the nineteenth or twentieth century, often with little regard for local history and tradition, and their leaders have had to concoct outlandish myths in order to give citizens a sense of nationhood. Just the opposite is true of Iran. This is one of the world's oldest nations, heir to a tradition that reaches back thousands of years, to periods when great conquerors extended their rule across continents, poets and artists created works of exquisite beauty, and one of the world's most extraordinary religious traditions took root and flowered. Even in modern times, which have been marked by long periods of anarchy, repression, and suffering, Iranians are passionately inspired by their heritage.

Great themes run through Iranian history and shape it to this day. One is the continuing and often frustrating effort to find a synthesis between Islam, which was imposed on the country by Arab conquerors, and the rich heritage of pre-Islamic times. Another, fueled by the Shiite Muslim tradition to which most Iranians now belong, is the thirst for just leadership, of which they have enjoyed precious little. A third, also sharpened by Shiite beliefs, is a tragic view of life rooted in a sense of martyrdom and communal pain. Finally, Iran has since time immemorial been a target of foreign invaders, victim of a geography that places it astride some of the world's most important trading routes and atop an ocean of oil, and it has struggled to find a way to live with powerful outsiders. All these strains combined in the middle of the twentieth century to produce and then destroy the towering figure of Mohammad Mossadegh.

Migrants from Central Asia and the Indian subcontinent began arriving in what is now Iran nearly four thousand years ago, pushed out by a combination of resource depletion and marauding tribes from the north and east. Among them were the Aryans, from whose name the word *Iran* is taken. The emperor who united these migrant bands for the first time was Cyrus, one of history's most gifted visionaries and the figure who first conceived the idea of an empire based in the region known as Pars (later Fars).

After rising to power in 559 B.C., Cyrus launched a brilliant campaign that brought other leaders on the vast Iranian plateau under his sway. Some he conquered, but many he won to his side by persuasion and compromise. Today he is remembered for his conquests but also for the relative gentleness with which he treated his subjects. He understood that this was an even surer way to build a durable empire than the more common means of oppression, terror, and slaughter.

In 547 Cyrus marched into Asia Minor and captured the majestic Lydian capital of Sardis. Seven years later he subdued the other great regional power, Babylon. Over the decades that followed, he and his successors went on to more great victories, including one by Xerxes in which Macedon, Thermopylae, and Athens were taken by an army of 180,000 men, by far the largest seen in Europe up to that time. This dynasty, known as the Achaemenians, built the greatest empire of its era. By 500 B.C. it embraced the eastern Mediterranean from Greece through modern-day Turkey, Lebanon, Israel, Egypt, and Libya and stretched eastward across the Caucasus to the banks of the Indus. Cyrus called it Persia because it sprang from his own base in Pars.

The tolerant and all-embracing approach to life and politics for which Achaemenian emperors were known sprang in part from their connection to the Zoroastrian faith, which holds that the sacred responsibility of every human being is to work toward establishing social justice on earth. Zoroastrians believe that humanity is locked in an eternal struggle between good and evil. Theirs is said to have been the first revealed religion to preach that people must face judgment after death, and that each soul will spend eternity in either paradise or perdition. According to its precepts, God makes his judgment according to how virtuous one has been in life, measured by one's thoughts, words, and deeds. The prophet Zoroaster, later known to Europeans as Zarathustra, lived sometime between the tenth and seventh centuries B.C. in what is now northeastern

Iran, and preached this creed after a series of divine visions. Zoroastrianism has had a profound effect on Persian history not simply because Cyrus used it in his audaciously successful campaign of empire-building, but because it has captured the hearts of so many believers over the course of so many centuries.

The Zoroastrian religion taught Iranians that citizens have an inalienable right to enlightened leadership and that the duty of subjects is not simply to obey wise kings but also to rise up against those who are wicked. Leaders are seen as representatives of God on earth, but they deserve allegiance only as long as they have *farr,* a kind of divine blessing that they must earn by moral behavior. To pray for it, generations of Persian leaders visited Zoroastrian temples where holy flames burned perpetually, symbolizing the importance of constant vigilance against iniquity.

Cyrus and the other kings of his line bound their vast empire together with roads, bridges, uniform coinage, an efficient system of taxation, and the world's first long-range postal service. But eventually and inevitably, the tide of history turned against them. Their empire began to shake after Darius, Persia's last great leader, lost the decisive Battle of Marathon in 490 B.C. The death blow came from no less a conqueror than Alexander, who marched into Persia in 334 B.C. and, in a rampage of destruction, sacked and burned Persepolis.

For the next ten centuries, through periods of rule by three dynasties, Persians nurtured and deepened their strong feelings of pride and nobility. They flourished by assimilating influences from the lands around them, especially Greece, Egypt, and India, reshaping them to fit within the framework of their Zoroastrian faith. In the third century A.D. they began returning to the peak of world power on a scale that recalled the glory of the early emperors, capturing Antioch, Jerusalem, and Alexandria and pushing to the walls of Constantinople. Persian armies suffered a reverse at the hands of Byzantines in 626, but the great defeat was yet to come. A few years later, an army arose on the barren Arabian peninsula and turned toward Persia. These Arabs came armed not only with the traditional weapons of war, but with a new religion, Islam.

The invasion by the Arabs, who to the cultivated Persians seemed no more than barbarians, was a decisive turning point in the nation's history. Persia's fate paralleled that of many empires. Its army had been worn down by long campaigns, its leaders had slipped from what Zoroastrian priests would call the realm of light into that of darkness, and the priests themselves had become divorced from the masses. People fell into poverty as the greedy court imposed ever-increasing taxes. Tyranny tore apart the social contract between ruler and ruled that Zoroastrian doctrine holds to be the basis of organized life. By both political and religious standards, the last of the pre-Islamic dynasties in Persia, the Sassanians, lost the right to rule. The merciless logic of history dictated that it be overrun by an ascendant people fired by passionate belief in its leaders, its cause, and its faith.

Sassanian power was centered in Ctesiphon, the luxurious capital of Mesopotamia. This was not a city of stately columns like Persepolis but one bathed in excess. Its royal palace housed fabulous collections of jewels and was guarded by statuary of solid gold and silver. The centerpiece was the king's cavernous audience hall, which featured a ninety-foot-square silk carpet depicting a flowering garden and, metaphorically, the empire's wealth and power. Rubies, pearls, and diamonds were sewn into it with golden threads. When Arab conquerors reached Ctesiphon in 638, they looted the palace and sent the magnificent carpet to Mecca, where Muslim leaders ordered it cut to pieces to show their contempt for worldly wealth. They destroyed countless treasures, including the entire royal library. In an account of this conquest written by the tenth-century Persian poet Ferdowsi, a general laments: "Curse this world, curse this time, curse this fate / That uncivilized Arabs have come to force me to be Muslim."

Later in the same epic, the *Shahnameh*, which is four times as long as the *Iliad* and took thirty-five years to compose, Ferdowsi portrays the losing Persian commander, Rustam, lamenting the misfortune he sees ahead:

> O Iran! Where are all those kings, who adorned you
> With justice, equity and munificence, who decorated
> You with pomp and splendor, gone?
> From that date when the barbarian, savage, coarse
> Bedouin Arabs sold your king's daughter in the street
> And cattle market, you have not seen a bright day, and
> Have lain hid in darkness.

By the time of the Arab conquest, Persians already had long experience in assimilating foreign cultures, and whenever they did so, they shaped those cultures to their liking or took certain parts while resisting others. So it was when they were forced to adopt Islam. They had no choice but to accept Mohammad as God's prophet and the Koran as God's word, but over a period of centuries they fashioned an interpretation of Islam quite different from that of their Arab conquerors. This interpretation, called Shiism, is based on a particular reading of Islamic history, and it has the ingenious effect of using Islam to reinforce long-standing Iranian beliefs.

About 90 percent of the one billion Muslims in the world today identify with the Sunni tradition. Of the remainder, most are Shiites, the largest number of whom are in Iran. The split between these two groups springs from differing interpretations of who deserved to succeed the prophet Mohammad as caliph, or leader of the Islamic world, after his death in 632. Shiites believe that his legitimate successor was Ali, a cousin whom he raised from childhood and who married one of his daughters. Ali was one of those to whom Mohammad dictated his revelations, which became known as the Koran, and he once slept in Mohammad's bed as a decoy to foil a murder plot. But another man was chosen as caliph, and soon Ali found himself in the position of a dissident. He criticized the religious establishment for seeking worldly power and diluting the purity of its spiritual inheritance. Economic discontent brought many to his side, and ultimately the conflict turned violent.

Ali was passed over twice more when caliphs died, and he devoted himself to preaching a doctrine of piety and social justice that won him many followers, especially among the lower classes. He finally won the supreme post in 656, but the conflict only intensified, and less than five years later he was assassinated while praying inside the mosque at Kufa, a Mesopotamian garrison town that was a cauldron of religious conflict. According to tradition, he knew he was to be murdered that day but refused to flee because "one cannot stop death." After being stabbed, he cried out, "O God, most fortunate am I!"

The mantle of resistance passed to Ali's son, Hussein, who was himself killed while leading seventy-two followers against an army of thousands in a suicidal revolt at Karbala in 680. Determined to suppress Hussein's legacy, the authorities ordered most of his family slain afterward. His body was trampled in the mud and his severed head taken to Damascus, where Shiites believe that it continued to chant the Koran even as the caliph beat it with a stick. Retelling these stories and others about Hussein, "the lord among martyrs," is what provokes the paroxysm of passion that spreads through Qom and other sacred Iranian cities every year on the anniversary of his death.

Hussein's embrace of death in a sacred cause has shaped the collective psyche of Iranians. To visit Qom during the mourning that commemorates his martyrdom is to be caught up in a wave of emotion so intense that it is hard for an outsider to comprehend. Processions of men and boys dressed in black move slowly, as if in a trance, toward the gate of the main shrine. All the while, they chant funereal verses lamenting Hussein's fate and flog themselves with metal-studded whips until their shoulders and backs are streaked with blood. In storefront mosques, holy men recount the sad tale with such passion that soon after they begin, worshipers fall prostrate with grief, weeping uncontrollably as if the most intimate personal tragedy had just crushed them. The breathtaking authenticity of this scene testifies to the success Iranian Shiites have had in formulating a set of religious beliefs that is within the Islamic tradition but still distinctly native.

Sunnis do not attribute great importance to the violent deaths of Ali and Hussein, but for Shiites, whose name comes from the phrase *Shi'at-Ali*, or "followers of Ali," they were cataclysmic events. To them, Ali and Hussein represent both the mystic spirituality of pure Islam and the self-sacrificing life that true Muslims must live. In this view, shaped by Zoroastrian tradition, the two heroes rebelled against an establishment that had become corrupt and thereby lost its *farr*. They are believed to have sacrificed themselves, as the truly pious must, on the altar of evil. By doing, so they embraced a pattern that still shapes Iran's consciousness. They bequeathed to Shiites a legacy of religious zeal and a willingness, even an eagerness, to embrace martyrdom at the hands of God's enemies. Ali remains the most perfect soul and the most enlightened leader who ever lived, excepting only the Prophet himself; Shiites still pore over his speeches and memorize his thousands of proverbs and aphorisms. Hussein epitomizes the self-sacrifice that is the inevitable fate of all who truly love Islam and humanity. His martyrdom is considered even more universally significant than that of Ali because it was inflicted by government soldiers rather than by a lone fanatic. Grasping the depth of this passion is essential to any understanding of modern Iran.

Iranian Shiites consider Ali to have been the first of twelve legitimate imams, or successors to Mohammad. The twelfth was still a youth when he passed into an occult state, apart from the world but aware of its suffering. For Iranian believers he is still vividly alive. They revere him as the Twelfth Imam, often called the Hidden Imam or the Imam of the Age, and many pray each day for his return to earth. When he does return, he will be the Mahdi, or messiah, who will right all wrongs and usher in an age of perfect justice. Until that time, it is the duty of temporal rulers to emulate his wisdom and righteousness. When they fail to do so, they trample not only on human rights but on the very will of God.

"The Imam watches over men inwardly and is in communion with the soul and spirit of men even if he be hidden from their physical eyes," the twentieth-century Shiite scholar Allamah Tabatabai has written. "His existence is always necessary, even if the time has not yet arrived for his outward appearance and the universal reconstruction that he is to bring about."

The profound hold that this tradition has on the souls of Iranian Shiites raises their beliefs above the level of traditional doctrine to what the anthropologist Michael M. J. Fischer has called "a drama of faith." They revere Mohammad but focus far more viscerally on Ali and Hussein, embracing what Fischer calls "a story expandable to be all-inclusive of history, cosmology and life's problems" and reinforcing it with "ritual or physical drama to embody the story and maintain high levels of emotional investment." Ali and Hussein gave them a paradigm that tells them not only how the moral believer should live, but also how he should die.

After Ali and Hussein met their worldly ends in the seventh century, the Arabian empire reached its peak and then began to weaken. Arabs who dominated Iran slowly melted into the country's already mixed population. As Arab power receded, Shiites gained strength, partly because their warnings about the corruption of worldly dynasties were borne out by the excesses of the conquering Seljuk Turks and the savagery of Genghis Khan's Mongol hordes, who ravaged Iran in the years after their invasion in 1220. When the Mongols began to lose control, power passed to the revolutionary Safavid dynasty, which was inspired by Shiite belief. The Safavid leader, Ismail, was a militant Shiite who sent his warriors into battle crying: "We are Hussein's men, and this is our epoch! In devotion we are slaves of the Imam! Our name is Zealot and our title is Martyr!"

After a series of victories won with the help of Shiites who flocked to his side from other lands, Ismail proclaimed himself shah, or king, in 1501. His first act after assuming the throne was to declare Shiism the official state religion. A famous miniature painting depicts the scene, with this caption: "On Friday, the exalted king went to the congregational mosque of Tabriz and ordered its preacher, who was one of the Shiite dignitaries, to mount the pulpit. The king himself proceeded to the front of the pulpit, unsheathed the sword of the Lord of Time, may peace be upon him, and stood there like the shining sun."

Far more than simply a religious act, this was the single most important step toward creating the Iranian nation. Ismail used Shiism to help him build an empire that within ten years of his coronation not only included most of modern-day Iran but extended from Central Asia to Baghdad and from the frosty Caucasus to the sands of the Persian Gulf. During Ismail's rule, today's Iran emerged not just politically but also spiritually. Iranians were already bound together by a shifting geography, a language, and a collective memory of ancient glory, but none of these ties evoked anything close to the unifying fervor of Shiism. By embracing this faith, Iranians accepted Islam but not in the way their Sunni Arab conquerors had wished. They rebelled while appearing to submit.

Perhaps most important, Iranians found an institution that would ultimately free them, at least spiritually, from the authority of the state. Ismail and the Safavid leaders who followed him thought they could control Shiism, and for most of the next two hundred years they did. But integral to Shiism, as to Zoroastrianism, is the belief that rulers may hold power only as long as they are just. Ultimately, this belief gave the Shiite masses, and by extension their religious leaders, the political and emotional power to bring temporal regimes crashing down.

By the time Ismail rose to power, Iranians had already reached

great cultural pinnacles. As early as the ninth century, their intellectuals had traveled through the Islamic world in search of the wisest
philosophers and the most learned scientists and had translated and
studied the works of Plato, Aristotle, Archimedes, Euclid, Ptolemy,
and other Greek thinkers. Artisans made breathtaking leaps forward
in architecture and ceramic arts. Persian miniaturists established
styles that were copied but never matched by masters from Constantinople to the steppes of Central Asia. Captivating poets composed works full of ecstasy and passion that are still read around the
world. Many of them, like the thirteenth-century mystic Jelaluddin
Rumi, reject orthodoxy of any kind:

> I hold to no religion or creed,
> am neither Eastern nor Western,
> Muslim or infidel,
> Zoroastrian, Christian, Jew or Gentile.
> I come from neither land nor sea,
> am not related to those above or below,
> was not born nearby or far away,
> do not live either in Paradise or on this Earth,
> claim descent not from Adam and Eve or the Angels above.
> I transcend body and soul.
> My home is beyond place and name.
> It is with the beloved, in a space beyond space.
> I embrace all and am part of all.

These cultural achievements meant that when Iranians finally
achieved political unity, they were poised to enter the modern age
confident of their creative, as well as of their military and spiritual,
power. The Safavid king who inspired them to some of their greatest achievements as a people, Abbas Shah, is still revered as a hero.
He sat on the throne for more than forty years, from 1588 to 1629.
His success in unifying his people and giving them a sense of shared
destiny was at least as profound as the success of his contempo-
raries, Elizabeth I in Britain and Philip II in Spain. He built roads
that brought European traders into Iranian cities and established
workshops to produce silk, ceramics, and other products those
traders wanted to buy. His bureaucracy collected taxes, enforced
justice, and organized life as it had not been organized since the era
of Cyrus and Darius two thousand years before.

Abbas fit the archetype of Iranian rulers not only because he was dedicated to bringing the best of the world into his kingdom. He was also typical because he imposed cruel tyranny and brooked no challenge to his absolutism. Torture and execution were commonplace during his reign. For years he locked his own sons inside the royal palace, allowing them the pleasure of concubines but denying them access to the education and training that would prepare them for future leadership—or, Abbas feared, for rebellion against his rule. He had his eldest son murdered and two other sons, two brothers, and his father blinded.

The greatest physical legacy Abbas left to posterity was his glorious capital, Isfahan, which he transformed into one of the world's most splendid cities. To this day its soaring domes, intricately designed royal residences, and magnificently tiled prayer halls inspire awe in the visitor and justify what generations of Iranians have believed: *Isfahan nesf-i-jahan* (Isfahan is half the world). Abbas brought Armenian craftsmen to help build his city, Dutch traders to expand the reach of its grand bazaar, and diplomats from around the world to give it a cosmopolitan air. Half a million people lived there, and few cities on earth could compete with its grandeur. Yet Isfahan came to symbolize not just Iran's brilliance but also the dark sides of Abbas's rule.

"Everything, from the ornamental profusion of the faience decoration of the mosques to the ponds and flower beds round the royal pavilions, bears the hallmark of an art that not only aimed at pleasing but was enhanced by the might and majesty of the sovereign," one modern author has written. "Here we can best understand the peculiar mixture of cruelty and liberalism, barbarity and sophistication, magnificence and voluptuousness, that made up Persian civilization."

Given the savagery with which Abbas Shah treated potential heirs to his throne, it is not surprising that Iran fell into disarray after his death. Neighbors began to prey on it, and in 1722 Afghan tribesmen swept down and overran it, even sacking Isfahan itself. The Afghans were finally expelled by the last of Iran's great historical leaders, Nadir Shah, a Sunni Turk who then marched on to seize Delhi. One of the treasures he looted from Delhi was the jewel-encrusted Peacock Throne, which became a symbol of Iranian royalty. Nadir was assassinated in 1747, and after a series of power struggles that lasted nearly fifty years, a new dynasty, the Qajars, came to power.

The Qajars, a Turkic tribe based near the Caspian Sea, ruled Iran from the late eighteenth century until 1925. Their corrupt, small-minded kings bear heavy responsibility for the country's poverty and backwardness. As much of the world rushed toward modernity, Iran under the Qajars stagnated.

"In a country so backward in constitutional progress, so destitute of forms and statutes and charters, and so firmly stereotyped in the immemorial traditions of the East, the personal element, as might be expected, is largely in the ascendant," the British statesman Lord Curzon wrote toward the end of the Qajar period. "The government of Persia is little else than the arbitrary exercise of authority by a series of units in a descending scale from the sovereign to the headman of a petty village."

Had Iran been governed during the nineteenth century by a strong and sophisticated regime, it might have managed to fend off the ambitions of foreign powers. The pressures, however, would have been intense in any case. Geography placed Iran in the way of that era's two great imperial powers, Britain and Russia. When the British looked at Iran, they saw a nation that straddled the land route to India, their richest and most precious colony. The Russians, for their part, saw a chance to control a large swath of land across their exposed southern border. The fact that Iran was ruled by weak and self-involved monarchs made it too tantalizing for either empire to resist. Both rushed to fill the power vacuum left by the ignorant Qajars.

Qajar kings did not seem disturbed to see Iran slipping into subservience, or if they were, they determined to take what advantage they could of its seemingly unavoidable fate. In what turned out to be a great miscalculation, they presumed that the Iranian people would accept whatever their rulers dictated. But by their corruption and especially their willingness to allow Iran to slip under the domination of foreign powers, the Qajars fell out of step with their people and ultimately lost their right to rule, their *farr*. Armed with the Shiite principle that endows the ordinary citizen with inherent power to overthrow despotism, and with the ideals of the emerging new world, Iranians rebelled in a way their forefathers never had. Their demands were as astonishing as their rebellion itself: an end to the country's domination by outside powers and a parliament to express the popular will. This was the most radical program Iranians had ever embraced. It would spell the overthrow of the Qajar dynasty and define all of Iran's subsequent history.

CHAPTER 3

The Last Drop of the Nation's Blood

Democracy dawned in Iran one day in December 1891, when the Shah's wives put aside their water pipes and vowed to smoke no more. It was no easy sacrifice. Tobacco was one of the great pleasures of harem life, and beauteous odalisques spent hours each day smoking it while reclining on lush divans. By renouncing it, they were defying the Shah, the institution of absolute monarchy, and the imperial system by which most of the world was ruled.

By the time the harem women took their fateful step, their husband, Nasir al-Din Shah, had been on the Peacock Throne for more than forty years. Like other Qajar rulers, he was famous for his excesses. His harem, where he spent much of his time, grew to sixteen hundred wives, concubines, and eunuchs. He fathered hundreds of princes, all of whom had free access to the national treasury. Garish clusters of jewels decorated his palaces. When he became bored by the pleasures of home, he would set out for Europe accompanied by a huge entourage. He demanded to be called not only Shah of Shahs but also Asylum of the Universe, Subduer of Climate, Arbitrator of His People, Guardian of the Flock, Conqueror of Lands, and Shadow of God on Earth. Those who refused to honor him were flogged, shot from cannons, buried alive, or set afire in public squares.

To support his lavish tastes, Nasir al-Din Shah sold government jobs, imposed oppressive taxes, and confiscated the fortunes of wealthy merchants. When there was no money left for him to take, he came up with the idea of raising cash by selling Iran's patrimony to foreign companies and governments. The British were his first customers. British officials were worried by native uprisings in India and wanted a telegraph line to their command posts there. In 1857 they bought a concession to build one across Iran. French, German, and Austrian groups bought a variety of other concessions. A German-born British subject, Baron Julius de Reuter, of news agency fame, won the most breathtaking one of all. In 1872, for a paltry sum and a promise of future royalties, he acquired the exclusive right to run the country's industries, irrigate its farmland, exploit its mineral resources, develop its railroad and streetcar lines, establish its national bank, and print its currency. Lord Curzon described this as "the most complete and extraordinary surrender of the entire industrial resources of a kingdom into foreign hands that has probably ever been dreamt of, much less accomplished, in history."

Many were angered by the extreme one-sidedness of the Reuter concession. Iranian patriots, of whom there were already quite a number, were naturally outraged. So were merchants and business-men, who saw their opportunities suddenly snatched away from them. Clerics feared for their status in a country so fully dominated by foreign interests. Russia, Iran's most powerful neighbor, was alarmed to see a British concern take so much power just across its southern border. Even the British government, which Reuter had not consulted in negotiating the concession, doubted its wisdom. Finally, Nasir al-Din Shah realized that he had overstepped the lim-its of the possible, and he revoked the concession less than a year after granting it.

The Shah's greed, however, did not allow him to abandon the idea of selling concessions. Over the next few years he sold three to British consortiums. One bought the mineral-prospecting rights that had briefly belonged to Reuter, another the exclusive right to establish banks, and a third the exclusive right to commerce along the Karun River, the only navigable waterway in Iran. Russia protested but was placated when the Shah sold Russian merchants the exclusive right to his caviar fisheries. Through these and other concessions, control over the nation's most valuable assets passed from the hands of Iranians to those of foreigners. The money they brought into the Iranian treasury sustained the Shah's lavish court for a while, but then, inevitably, it ran out. He raised more by borrowing from British and Russian banks.

As Iran sank ever deeper into the mire of poverty and dependence, a thirst for change gripped the population. Bazaars in large cities became hotbeds of protest. Religious reformers, Freemasons, and even socialists began spreading new and radical ideas. News about struggles for constitutional rule in Europe and the Ottoman Empire roused the literate classes. Provocative articles, books, and leaflets began to circulate.

Nasir al-Din Shah, isolated in the private world of the Qajar court, was oblivious to this rising discontent. In 1891 he sold the Iranian tobacco industry for the sum of £15,000. Under the terms of the concession, every farmer who grew tobacco was required to sell it to the British Imperial Tobacco Company, and every smoker had to buy it at a shop that was part of British Imperial's retail network.

Iran was then, as it is today, both an agricultural country and a country of smokers. Many thousands of poor farmers across the country grew tobacco on small plots; a whole class of middlemen cut, dried, packaged, and distributed it; and countless Iranians smoked it. That this native product would now be taken from the people who produced it and turned into a tool for the exclusive profit of foreigners proved too great an insult. A coalition of intellectuals, farmers, merchants, and clerics, such as had never before been seen in Iran, resolved to resist. The country's leading religious figure, Sheik Shirazi, endorsed their protest. In a shattering act of rebellion, he endorsed a *fatwa,* or religious order, declaring that as long as foreigners controlled the tobacco industry, smoking would constitute defiance of the Twelfth Imam, "may God hasten his appearance." News of his order flashed across the country through telegraph wires the British had built several decades earlier. Almost all who heard it obeyed. Nasir al-Din Shah was bewildered, frightened, and then overwhelmed by the unanimity of the protest. When his own wives stopped smoking, he realized that he had no choice but to cancel the concession. To add to the indignity, he had to borrow half a million pounds from a British bank to compensate British Imperial for its loss.

History changes course when people realize there is an alternative to blind obedience. Martin Luther's challenge to established Christianity, the storming of the Bastille during the French Revolution, and the Boston Tea Party were such moments. For Iran, the beginning of the end of absolutism came with the Tobacco Revolt. It ushered in a new political age. No longer would Iranians remain passive while the Qajar dynasty oppressed them and sold their nation's patrimony to foreigners.

After several years during which he drifted ever further from his royal duties and from reality itself, Nasir al-Din Shah was shot to death in 1896 while visiting a mosque near Tehran. Few mourned him. He left behind a country dominated by foreigners and plagued by widespread unemployment, crippling inflation, and serious food shortages. His son Muzzaffar, who succeeded him on the Peacock Throne, ignored his people's crying needs and wallowed in all the vices that led Iranians to hate the Qajars. Soon after ascending to the throne, he embarked on a lavish European tour, paid for with money borrowed from a Russian bank. Upon his return he took out another loan, this one from British financiers, and gave them in exchange a share of his customs revenue. Disgusted Iranians began denouncing him in public. When he responded by arresting some of the agitators, antigovernment riots broke out in Tehran and other cities.

Instead of trying to rally Iranians to his side, Muzzaffar al-Din Shah took a step that further inflamed them. In 1901 he sold William Knox D'Arcy, a London-based financier, the "special and exclusive privilege to obtain, exploit, develop, render suitable for trade, carry away and sell natural gas [and] petroleum . . . for a term of sixty years." It would be nearly a decade before D'Arcy struck oil and even longer before his concession turned into a blunt instrument of British imperial policy. Simply by granting it, however, Muzzaffar al-Din Shah shaped all of subsequent Iranian history.

In the decade since the Tobacco Revolt, the political consciousness of Iranians had grown enormously. Their belief that God requires leaders to rule justly, a central tenet of Shiite doctrine, led

many to embrace the ideals of popular sovereignty that were cours-
ing through society. By the time the twentieth century dawned,
some had even begun to doubt the very principle of monarchy.
Secret societies dedicated to subversion were formed in several
cities. Books about the French Revolution, including several that
glorified Danton and Robespierre, began passing from hand to
eager hand. A sense of unlimited possibility gained strength with
news that the supposedly invincible British were losing battles to
upstart Boers in South Africa. It was reinforced by the turmoil of
1905 in Russia, where military defeat at the hands of Japan led to a
revolt that forced Czar Nicholas II to accept a parliament. The stage
was set for revolution in Iran. All that was needed was a spark to set
the nation ablaze.

The spark came in December 1905, when a handful of merchants in Tehran were arrested in a dispute over sugar prices. They
were subjected to the *bastinado,* a favorite Qajar punishment in
which victims were hung by their wrists and thrashed on the soles
of their feet. The bazaar erupted in protest. At first, the rioters
demanded only dismissal of the local governor who had ordered
the beatings. Then, sensing their rising power, they began calling
for reduced taxes. Finally, at one of their climactic meetings, they
added an astonishing new demand: "In order to carry out reforms
in all affairs, it is necessary to establish . . . a national consultative
assembly to insure that the law is executed equally in all parts of
Iran, so that there can be no difference between high and low, and
all may obtain redress of their grievances."

This demand soon subsumed all others. With his people on the
brink of revolt, Muzzaffar al-Din Shah had no choice but to accept
the idea that Iran should have a parliament. After agreeing, however, he began to stall and for several months did nothing to bring
the idea to fruition. The protest movement swelled anew. Islamic
clerics took a leading role. Some invoked the authority of the Shiite
martyr Hussein, vowing to defend the poor even if it meant expos-
ing themselves, as he did, to the sword of evil. Thrilled by this
rhetoric, throngs of people took to the streets in the summer of
1906. Emotions reached a feverish pitch, and several hundred radicals, seeking to organize themselves in a place where troops could
not attack them, decided to take *bast,* or refuge, on the grounds of a
diplomatic mission. They chose the British Legation, a sprawling

compound with lands covering the space of sixteen city blocks. Most of the Legation staff was away on summer holiday, and its secretary told the protesters that although he wished they would find another sanctuary, he would not, "in view of the acknowledged custom in Persia and the immemorial right of *bast* . . . use, or cause to be used, force to expel them if they came." Before long, fourteen thousand Iranians were inside the compound. They lived in tents according to their guilds and ate from great cauldrons of food prepared in a common kitchen.

This assemblage quickly turned into a school at which the principles of democracy formed the core curriculum. Every day, articles from reformist newspapers were read aloud to the multitude, agitators gave speeches about social progress, and foreign-educated intellectuals translated the works of European philosophers. The Shah, disconcerted but still failing to grasp the intensity of the movement, offered to name a council that would help run the justice ministry. That was not nearly enough to satisfy the protesters. They wanted a Majlis, or parliament, with true power, not simply an advisory council.

"The law must be what the Majlis decides," they declared in one statement. "Nobody is to interfere in the laws of the Majlis."

The Shah finally agreed, although without enthusiasm and with the proviso that laws passed by the Majlis would require his signature before taking effect. This was a climactic moment, comparable in some ways to the signing of the Magna Carta in England seven centuries before. One British diplomat cabled his amazement back to London: "One remarkable feature of this revolution here—for it is surely worthy to be called a revolution—is that the priesthood have found themselves on the side of progress and freedom. This, I should think, is almost unexampled in the world's history. If the reforms which the people, with their help, have fought for become a reality, all their power will be gone."

Having won the Shah's reluctant assent, jubilant protesters left their sanctuary and set to work laying the groundwork for what many believed would be a new Iran. They produced a draft constitution based on Belgium's, which was considered the most progressive in Europe, and convoked national elections for a two-hundred-seat Majlis. Some members were directly elected and others chosen from guilds, one each for the grocers, blacksmiths, printers, butchers, watchmakers, doctors, tailors, and so on. They assembled for their historic first session on October 7, 1906.

A host of troubles faced the new Majlis. The haste with which the new system had been designed and the inexperience of those who now sought to help rule Iran threw it into discord. Many deputies were uneducated, and there were no political parties to forge them into blocs. Debates over the proposed constitution faltered because no one was quite sure how to divide the powers of government. To make matters worse, it had to be written in great haste because Muzzaffar al-Din Shah was dying and his crown prince, Mohammad Ali, was known to detest the very idea of democratization. It was finally adopted on December 30, 1906, setting Iran on what would be a century of highly uneven progress toward democracy. A week later Muzzaffar al-Din Shah died.

The new monarch, Mohammad Ali Shah, ridiculed and ignored the Majlis. Several deputies demanded that he be deposed if he continued his resistance. Monarchists bitterly counterattacked, and violent debate, often echoed by clashes in the streets, shook the capital. Regional and tribal factions, encouraged by bribes and corrupt arrangements, staged protests that greatly weakened the constitutional movement. Ordinary people began to associate the word *constitution* with upheaval and conflict.

Worst of all, the tenuous alliance between clerics and secular reformers began to unravel. Mullahs who had supported the reform movement became alarmed by the demands of radicals who they said had "thrown out the law of the Prophet and set up their own law instead." The Qajar court played adroitly on their concerns and managed to persuade many of them that their true interests lay with the monarchy.

"It is not advisable for the government of Iran to be constitutional, for in constitutional government all things are free, and in this case there must also be freedom of religion," one courtier asserted in a speech to the Majlis. "Certain persons will insist upon religious freedom, which is contrary to the interests of Islam."

Many clerics shared these fears. When the Majlis debated a bill to legalize secular schools, one asked, "Will entry into them not lead to the overthrow of Islam? Will lessons in foreign languages and the study of chemistry and physics not weaken the students' faith?" Others questioned the very premise of the reform movement: "By the use of two enticing words, justice and consultation, the freedom seekers have deceived our brothers into making common cause with atheists. . . . Islam, the most complete, the most perfect, took the world by justice and consultation. What has happened that we must bring our regulation of justice from Paris, and our plan of consultation from England?"

This clash between clerics and secular reformers would resonate through modern Iranian history. So would another clash that emerged during this period, the one that split the religious class itself. Some clerics believed that received religion was compatible with modern ideas, but others saw a contradiction and abandoned the reform movement. This debate reflected Iran's age-old conflicts: ancient versus modern, religious versus secular, faith versus reason. It pitted, in the words of one historian, "the Persian trait of openness and assimilation against the Islamic trait of insularity and traditionalism."

Confident that most of the country's religious leaders were with him, Mohammad Ali Shah began a campaign of terror and violence against the Majlis. In June 1908 his men assembled a gang of thugs and sent them rampaging through Tehran shouting, "We want the Koran! We do not want a constitution!" Then he ordered his elite Cossack Brigade to bombard and sack the building where the Majlis was meeting. Iranians rose up in protest in several cities, and many were killed in street fighting. For a time it seemed that full-scale civil war might break out, and at one point the Shah even took *bast* at the Russian Legation.

Both of the imperial powers that sought to dominate Iran, Britain and Russia, realized that the reform movement now threatened their dominant position in the country and encouraged the Shah to continue resisting it. Still the Majlis pressed on. One of its most decisive steps was its vote to hire an American banker, Morgan Shuster, as Iran's treasurer-general. Shuster arrived with a zealot's energy and set out to dismantle the elaborate systems of tax exemptions and back-room deals through which British and Russian syndicates were looting Iran. The governments of both countries demanded that he be removed, and in the fall of 1911 the Russians sent troops to enforce their will. When the Majlis defiantly refused to dismiss him, the royal court, immeasurably strengthened by the presence of foreign soldiers, shut it down and arrested many of its members. Iran's tumultuous five-year Constitutional Revolution, the first concerted attempt to synthesize Iranian tradition with modern democracy, was over.

The experience of these years profoundly reshaped Iran's collective psychology. Unlike the Tobacco Revolt, which had the narrow aim of defeating a single arbitrary law, the Constitutional Revolution aimed to establish an entirely new social and political order. It was crushed with the decisive help of foreign powers, but only after it had laid the foundation for a democratic Iran. A constitution had been written and adopted, and under its provisions there would be regular elections, which meant political campaigns and at least the semblance of open debate. In the years to come, Iranian rulers could and would ignore, overrule, and act against public opinion, but they would never manage to extinguish the people's conviction that they were endowed with rights no government could take from them. The lessons they learned during this burst of reformist passion shaped the peaceful revolution that Mohammad Mossadegh led nearly half a century later.

Iranians had flocked to the banner of democracy because they believed that establishing the rule of law in their country would help pull them out of poverty. They were also driven by mounting anger directed at two targets. One was the Qajar court, as exemplified first by the execrable Mohammad Ali Shah and then by his obese son, Ahmad, who ascended to the throne in 1909 at the age of twelve. The other was the suffocating role that foreign powers— Britain and Russia in particular—had come to play in Iran.

During the Constitutional Revolution, reformers tried repeatedly to pull Iran out of the orbit of foreign powers. At one point the Majlis went so far as to refuse a loan offered by Russian bankers. Soon afterward it voted to establish a national bank run by Iranians. These efforts, however, were in vain. Iran fell ever more deeply into bondage as the Qajars continued selling the country's assets.

In 1907 Britain and Russia signed a treaty dividing Iran between them. Britain assumed control of southern provinces, while Russia took the north. A strip between the two zones was declared neutral, meaning that Iranians could rule there as long as they did not act against the interests of their powerful guests. Iran was not consulted but was simply informed of this arrangement after the treaty was signed in St. Petersburg. What had long been informal foreign control of Iran now became an explicit partition, backed by the presence of Russian and British troops. When the treaty formalizing it came before the British Parliament for ratification, one of the few dissenting members lamented that it left Iran "lying between life and death, parceled out, almost dismembered, helpless and friendless at our feet."

As Russia was consumed by civil war and revolution, its influence in Iran waned. After the Bolsheviks seized power in 1917, they renounced most of their rights in Iran and canceled all debts that Iran had owed to Czarist Russia. The British, now at the peak of their imperial power, moved quickly to fill the vacuum. Oil was the new focus of their interest. The newly formed Anglo-Persian Oil Company, which grew out of the D'Arcy concession, had begun extracting huge quantities of it from beneath Iranian soil. Winston Churchill called it "a prize from fairyland beyond our wildest dreams."

Realizing the immense value of this new resource, the British in 1919 imposed the harsh Anglo-Persian Agreement on Ahmad Shah's impotent regime, assuring its approval by bribing the Iranian negotiators. Under its provisions the British assumed control over Iran's army, treasury, transport system, and communications network. To secure their new power, they imposed martial law and began ruling by fiat. Lord Curzon, who as foreign secretary was one of the agreement's chief architects, argued its necessity in terms that crystallized a century of British policy toward Iran:

> If it be asked why we should undertake the task at all, and why Persia should not be left to herself and allowed to rot into picturesque decay, the answer is that her geographical position, the magnitude of our interests in the country, and the future safety of our Eastern Empire render it impossible for us now—just as it would have been impossible for us any time during the last fifty years—to disinherit ourselves from what happens in Persia. Moreover, now that we are about to assume the mandate for Mesopotamia, which will make us coterminous with the western frontiers of Asia, we cannot permit the existence between the frontiers of our Indian Empire and Baluchistan and those of our new protectorate, a hotbed of misrule, enemy intrigue, financial

chaos and political disorder. Further, if Persia were to be alone, there is every reason to fear that she would be overrun by Bolshevik influence from the north. Lastly, we possess in the southwestern corner of Persia great assets in the shape of oil fields, which are worked for the British navy and which give us a commanding interest in that part of the world.

The Anglo-Persian Agreement removed the last vestiges of Iran's sovereignty, but it also infused the nationalist movement with new passion. Iranian patriots were inspired by the emergence of anti-colonial forces in other countries, including several under British rule. Radicals in northern provinces established a Communist party, and after Soviet troops landed on the Caspian coast and declared the surrounding area an "Iranian Soviet Socialist Republic," it seemed possible that two world powers might soon be waging war on Iranian soil. In much of the country, millions of people were living in worse conditions than they had ever known. Separatist movements gained force in several provinces. Iran was on the brink of extinction. Conditions were ripe for the rise of a charismatic leader. In 1921 he burst into the nation's consciousness, a rough man on horseback named Reza.

Born in the remote Alborz Mountains near the Russian border, Reza left home as a teenager to follow the family tradition of military service. Rather than join the private army of a local chief, he chose to enlist in the Cossack Brigade, the only unit in the country that was modern, disciplined, and well commanded. It had been founded by Russian officers dispatched by the Czar and served principally as a private guard for the interests of foreigners and the Qajar kings who served them. Reza signed on as a stable boy but was soon given a uniform and began rising through the ranks as Reza Khan. He was six feet four inches tall, as fierce a fighter with his scimitar as with his machine gun, and much admired for his bravery. Profane and hot-tempered, his face deeply pockmarked as a result of smallpox in childhood, he cut a fearsome figure.

During his years as a soldier, Reza had the chance to travel through Iran and see the misery in which most of its people lived. He participated in many operations against the tribes, gangs, and bandits who controlled much of the countryside. "Whenever an expedition was sent to any part of the country to round up brigands or quell a disturbance," one British diplomat reported, "he seems to have taken part in it."

Reza quickly came to share his people's disgust with their Qajar rulers. That made him a logical tool for the British, who had tired of dealing with mercurial tribal leaders and wanted a stronger central government. They saw in the Cossack Brigade the means to impose it. To seize control of the brigade and oust its Russian officers, they resolved to stage a coup and replace the Shah's prime minister with one of their choosing. Their candidate was a fiery ex-journalist, Sayyed Zia Tabatabai. To provide Sayyed Zia with the military power he needed, they approached Reza. He was willing. On the evening of February 20, 1921, he and a handful of his fellow officers led two thousand men to the outskirts of Tehran. He roused them with a passionate speech: "Fellow soldiers! You have offered every possible sacrifice in the defense of the land of your fathers. . . . But we have to confess that our loyalty has served merely to preserve the interests of a handful of traitors in the capital. . . . These insignificant men are the same treacherous elements who have sucked the last drop of the nation's blood."

The fervor in camp was intense, and Reza, not a patient man, seized on it. Before dawn the next morning, his soldiers entered Tehran and arrested the prime minister and every member of his cabinet. To the dissolute Ahmad Shah, Reza made two demands: Sayyed Zia must be named prime minister and he himself commander of the Cossack Brigade. The Shah had neither the will nor the means to resist. Within the space of a few hours, with almost no resistance, the coup had succeeded. It was a testament to the power of the British, the weakness of the dying Qajar dynasty, and the bold self-confidence of Reza Khan.

Cossack regiments immediately set about pacifying the country and suppressing tribal armies. Power flowed into Reza's hands. He dismissed Sayyed Zia just three months after the coup and then forced him to leave the country. Soon afterward he persuaded the Shah himself to leave, ostensibly on a temporary trip for health reasons. Soon this ambitious soldier was prime minister, army commander, and effective head of the resurgent Iranian state.

Reza had proclaimed himself a nationalist, but he recognized the power of his British backers and the debt he owed them. One study of the coup concluded: "There can be no doubt about the involvement of British army officers. . . . The day before the march to Tehran, Sayyed Zia had paid 2,000 tumans to Reza Khan and distributed 20,000 among his 2,000 men. No Iranian could have raised such a substantial amount of cash over a short period of time."

Once he had completed his drive to power, Reza had to choose a political framework in which to rule. He fervently admired the Turkish reformer Kemal Atatürk and for a time considered following Atatürk's example by declaring Iran a republic and installing himself as president. That idea terrified the religious class, which had been deeply shocked by Atatürk's decisions to abolish the sultanate and the Islamic caliphate. They insisted that Reza preserve the monarchy, and finally won him to their side.

Although Reza was uneducated and barely literate, he had a deep understanding of the Iranian style of politics. A couple of years after his coup, he conceived a theatrical drama that he correctly calculated would carry him to the pinnacle of power. He retired to a small village, supposedly to reflect and meditate, and resigned from all his government posts. Before departing, he had arranged to be bombarded by demands that he return to power. For a time Reza pretended to resist, but then, as he had hoped, the hated Ahmad Shah announced his intention to return home. The Majlis, which had reconstituted itself after the debacle of 1911 but never managed to accumulate any real power, was horrified at this prospect. United in rebellion, it pronounced the Qajar dynasty dead and offered the Peacock Throne to Reza. He assumed it on April 25, 1926, and proclaimed himself Reza Shah. His new dynasty, he announced, would be known by the family name Pahlavi, after a language that Persians spoke before the Muslim conquest.

Reza Shah was not averse to denouncing the British in public, but he and they had fundamental interests in common. He was the strongman they had sought, a reliable figure with whom they could bargain and whom they could, if necessary, depose. "The old Persia was a loose-knit pyramid resting on its base," observed the always-perceptive British diplomat Harold Nicholson. "The new Persian pyramid is almost equally loose, but resting on its apex; hence, it is much easier to overthrow."

It was impossible for Reza Shah to pull his country out of the orbit of foreign powers, especially the all-powerful British, but after consolidating his power, he worked steadily to limit their influence.

He accepted no loans from foreign financiers, banned the sale of property to non-Iranians, revoked a concession that gave the British-owned Imperial Bank of Iran the exclusive right to issue Iranian currency, and even forbade officials of his foreign ministry to attend receptions at foreign embassies. When the British insisted that he hire European engineers to build the rail line that was one of his grandest dreams, he did so on the condition that the engineers and their families agree to stand beneath each bridge they built when a train passed over it for the first time.

Subduing the vast expanse of Iran by military force would have required an enormous army. Instead, Reza Shah imposed his will by exemplary terror. Stories of his ruthlessness terrified and then pacified his people.

In 1935 religious leaders called a protest against Reza Shah's ban of the veil for women and his order that men wear billed caps that would prevent them from touching the floor with their foreheads during prayer. They gathered with several hundred believers in the sacred Khorasan mosque. As soon as Reza Shah learned of their assembly, he ordered soldiers to storm the mosque and massacre them. More than one hundred were killed. There were no further protests against his religious reforms.

Time and again, Reza Shah resolved problems with this brand of brutal decisiveness. Once during a visit to Hamedan in western Iran, for example, he is said to have learned that people there were going hungry because bakers were hoarding wheat in order to drive up prices. He ordered the first baker he saw thrown into an oven and burned alive. By the next morning, every bakery in town was filled with low-priced bread.

Many Iranians were appalled by stories like these, but many others, remembering that their country had enjoyed glory only when it was ruled by a powerful leader, remained silent or applauded. None could deny Reza Shah's achievements. He began by wiping out gangs of bandits that terrorized many parts of Iran. Then he embarked on a huge construction program that gave the country new avenues, plazas, highways, factories, ports, hospitals, government buildings, railroad lines, and schools for both boys and girls. He created the country's first civil service and the first national army it had known for centuries. He introduced the metric system, the modern calendar, the use of surnames, and civil marriage and divorce. Ever ready to scorn tradition, he restricted traditional clothing and forbade camel caravans to enter cities. He promulgated legal codes and established a network of secular courts to enforce them. In 1935 he announced that he would no longer tolerate references to his country as *Persia,* a word used mainly by foreigners, and would insist on *Iran,* the name by which its own citizens knew it. With typical resolve, he ordered that any mail from abroad addressed to Persia be returned unopened.

Yet for all Reza Shah's reformist passion, he did not manage a true social transformation. Under his rule, newspapers were strictly censored, labor organizing forbidden, and opposition figures murdered, jailed, or forced to flee. He forced nomadic tribes, which he considered relics of the past incompatible with a modern state, into barren settlements where thousands suffered and died. Commerce was centralized in the hands of the state and a small cadre of loyal entrepreneurs. The Shah himself became enormously wealthy by extracting bribes from foreign businesses and extorting money from tribal leaders. He confiscated so much land that at the peak of his power, he was the country's largest landowner.

"Reza Shah eliminated all the thieves and bandits in Iran," one member of the British Parliament observed, "and made his countrymen realize that henceforth there would be only one thief in Iran."

In 1934 Reza Shah traveled to Turkey to meet Atatürk. The two men got along famously, but as they toured the Turkish countryside, the Shah became depressed and frustrated as he realized how quickly Turkey was progressing toward modernity and secularism. He returned home determined to redouble his campaign to transform Iranian society. In his zeal, he charged ahead without regard to the country's long-established social patterns or its religious beliefs. Utterly lacking Atatürk's statesmanship and political skill, he turned much of the population against him.

Reza Shah was fascinated by the fascist movements that emerged in Europe during the 1930s. Mussolini, Franco, and Hitler seemed to him to be embarked on the same path he had chosen, purifying and uniting weak, undisciplined nations. He launched an oppressive campaign to obliterate the identity of minority groups, especially Kurds and Azeris, and he established a Society for Public Guidance to glorify his ideas and person. Baldur von Schirach, head of Hitler Youth, led a stream of Nazi dignitaries who visited Iran and spoke glowingly of the emerging German-Iranian alliance.

"The cardinal goal of the German nation is to attain its past glories by promoting national pride, creating a hatred of foreigners, and preventing Jews and foreigners from embezzlement and treason," one of the Shah's newspapers declared. "Our goals are certainly the same."

Partly because he needed a foreign friend who shared his growing enmity toward Britain and the Soviet Union, Reza Shah developed great sympathy for the German cause. When World War II broke out, he declared a policy of neutrality that tilted decidedly toward Germany. He allowed hundreds of German agents to operate in Iran. Many worked to build support networks among regional warlords. Western leaders feared that the Nazis were planning to use Iran as a platform for an attack across the Soviet Union's southern border that would greatly complicate the Allied war effort. To prevent that, British and Soviet troops entered Iran on August 25, 1941. Their planes dropped leaflets over Tehran. "We have decided that the Germans must go," they said, "and if Iran will not deport them, then the English and the Russians will."

Some Iranians must have appreciated the irony of these two countries positing themselves as Iran's friends and protectors, but there was little they could do. Iran's army yielded in a matter of days. After seizing strategic points around the country, Allied commanders demanded that Reza Shah sever his government's ties to Germany and allow the free use of his territory by their forces. If he had not alienated himself from almost every segment of Iranian society, and if he had kept a cadre of wise advisers around him instead of systematically exiling or murdering them, he might have been able to resist. Instead he found himself alone, his dreams shattered by his own narrow-mindedness, corruption, and boundless egotism.

Reza Shah did not wish to work for the Allies, and they had no use for him either. He abdicated on September 16, 1941. The next day his eldest son, twenty-one-year-old Mohammad Reza, was sworn in to succeed him. No more was heard from Reza, who died in Johannesburg three years later.

Although Reza Shah imagined himself a modernizing visionary, in fact he reinforced the tradition of *istibdad,* or absolute rule, that lies at the heart of Iranian history. His reforms were superficial and, because of the brutality with which they were imposed, deeply resented by his subjects. He made no progress toward creating the sense of shared enterprise and civic responsibility that is at the heart of successful societies. His efforts to rid Iran of foreign influence were praiseworthy in theory but disastrous in effect. In the end, his dictatorial impulses brought him down by driving him toward an alliance with fascist powers. His departure left Iran in the hands of foreigners and a weak, confused young king. Monarchy had once again failed to resolve the country's continuing crisis of development and identity. When World War II ended, Iranians were desperate for a new kind of leader.

CHAPTER 4

A Wave of Oil

Years in the rocky Iranian desert, where smallpox raged, bandits and warlords ruled, water was all but unavailable, and temperatures often soared past 120 degrees, might have driven lesser men than George Reynolds to madness or worse. Reynolds, however, was one of those legendary figures whose persistence and audacity have changed world history. He was a self-taught geologist and a petroleum engineer with several expeditions in the Sumatran jungle to his credit. During the first decade of the twentieth century, already in his fifties, he crisscrossed the barren wastelands of Iran in search of oil. To help him pull his wagonloads of equipment and dig his wells, he had at his service a ragged band that included a handful of Polish and Canadian drillers, a comically incompetent Indian doctor, and several dozen tribesmen who had trouble even understanding what oil is. "A more helpless crew I seldom saw," he lamented in one letter home.

Home for Reynolds was London, and there his patron, the millionaire dandy William Knox D'Arcy, waited anxiously for good news. D'Arcy had made a fortune prospecting for gold in Australia but was not satisfied. He sensed that oil would prove even more valuable than gold and knew that Iran was, in the words of one geologist who had surveyed its terrain, "unquestionably petrol-iferous territory." In 1901 he signed an agreement with the Shah of Iran, Muzzaffar al-Din, under which he assumed the exclusive right to prospect for oil in a vast tract of Iranian territory larger than Texas and California combined. To secure it, he gave the Shah, whom the British minister in Tehran described as "merely an elderly child," the sum of £20,000, an equal amount in shares of his company, and a promise of 16 percent of future profits.

D'Arcy, an elegantly mustachioed lion of London society known for extravagant gestures like hiring Enrico Caruso to sing at private parties in his Grosvenor Square mansion, never considered travel-ing to Iran himself. He hired Reynolds instead, and month after month, year after year, he wrote checks to support their venture. His spirits soared in January 1904 when Reynolds finally struck oil but crashed a few months later when the well ran dry. Bit by bit, his fortune slipped away. Finally he was forced to sell most of his rights to a Glasgow-based syndicate, the Burmah Oil Company, that was even wealthier than he was.

The Scottish financiers who took charge of the drive to find oil in Iran recognized that an epochal change was about to reshape Britain and the world. Internal combustion engines would soon revolutionize every aspect of human life, and control over the oil needed to fuel them would henceforth be the key to world power. Oil had been discovered around the Caspian Sea, in the Dutch East Indies, and in the United States, but neither Britain nor any of its colonies produced or showed any promise of producing it. If the British could not find oil somewhere, they would no longer be able to rule the waves or much of anything else.

By 1908 D'Arcy and his Scottish partners had sunk more than half a million pounds into their Persian venture and had come up with nothing. Finally they concluded that they must abandon their explorations and begin looking elsewhere. At the beginning of May they sent Reynolds a telegram telling him that they had run out of money and ordering him to "cease work, dismiss the staff, dismantle anything worth the cost of transporting to the coast for re-shipment, and come home."

It must have been a crushing moment for Reynolds, who had spent years in some of the most trying conditions imaginable looking for a treasure he knew could reshape the world. Desperate to buy whatever time he could, he told his men that in such a remote region, telegrams could not be trusted. They must continue working until the message was confirmed by post.

Reynolds was sleeping in his tent near an outpost in western Iran called Masjid-i-Suleiman when, at four o'clock on the morning of May 26, 1908, rumbling noises and wild shouting awakened him. He bolted up, ran across a stony plain, and saw oil spurting high above one of his derricks. In what might have been one of his last attempts, he had drilled into the greatest oil field ever found.

It did not take long for British leaders to grasp the scope and implications of this find. In the autumn of 1908 they arranged for a group of investors to organize a new corporation, the Anglo-Persian Oil Company, to absorb the D'Arcy concession and take control of oil exploration and development in Iran. Five years later, at the urging of First Lord of the Admiralty Winston Churchill, who saw world war on the horizon and knew he would need oil to power the ships that would win it, the British government spent £2 million to buy 51 percent of the company. From that moment on, the interests of Britain and the Anglo-Persian Oil Company became one and inseparable. "Mastery itself was the prize of the venture," Churchill asserted.

During its first few years in existence, Anglo-Persian drilled scores of wells, laid more than a hundred miles of pipeline, and extracted millions of barrels of oil. It established a network of filling stations throughout the United Kingdom and sold oil to countries across Europe and as far away as Australia. Most impressive of all, it began construction of what would for half a century be the world's largest oil refinery on the desert island of Abadan in the Persian Gulf.

Abadan, at the Gulf's northern end, had come slowly into existence over a period of a thousand years, built up by silt running from the rivers that meet to form the Shatt-al-Arab waterway. The first engineer Anglo-Persian sent there, twenty-eight-year-old R. R. Davidson, wrote home in 1909 that it was a place of "sunshine, mud and flies," totally flat and without a single stone bigger than a man's hand. It was also among the hottest places on earth. Nonetheless, within a couple of years Davidson had more than a thousand tribesmen at work building piers, barges, and brick buildings. Soon

Abadan boasted a power-generating station, several stores and workshops, a water filtration plant, and even a small railway. In 1911 the first pipeline from Fields, as the oil-producing region was called, was completed, and the next year oil began to flow.

Before long, Abadan was a bustling city with more than one hundred thousand residents, most of them Iranian laborers. From its private Persian Club, where uniformed waiters served British executives, to the tight-packed Iranian workers' quarters and the water fountains marked "Not for Iranians," it was a classic colonial enclave. Almost all of the technicians and administrators were British, and many enjoyed handsome homes with terraces and manicured lawns. For them and their families, Abadan was an idyllic place.

Life was much different for the tens of thousands of Iranian laborers. They lived in slums and long dormitories with only primitive sanitation. Shops, cinemas, buses, and other amenities were off limits to them. With their British employers, however, they shared life amid networks of giant pipes, beneath cavernous holding tanks, and in the shadow of towering smokestacks from which plumes of flame leapt up day and night. The air was heavy with sulfur fumes, a constant reminder of the vast wealth that was pouring from Iranian soil into Anglo-Persian's coffers.

Any doubts about the value of this new resource were resolved by the experience of World War I, in which, as Lord Curzon put it, the Allies "floated to victory on a wave of oil." Over the years that followed, the amount of oil flowing from Abadan increased steadily, from less than three hundred thousand tons in 1914 to five times that amount in 1920. Anglo-Persian gave first priority to the Royal Navy, which bought its oil at a great discount. What remained was sold to industrial customers and drivers in Britain and then, as supplies increased, to others around the world.

Oil could have made Qajar kings rich and powerful. They did not have the resources to find or exploit their deposits without foreign help, but with more foresight they could have struck a far better deal with their British partners. Instead they sold their birthright for a pittance. Iran's royalty payment for 1920, set according to the concession agreement at 16 percent of the company's net profit, was £47,000. Ahmad Shah considered it manna from heaven, but it was a small sum compared to what was pouring into the oil company's coffers.

The next year brought the fall of Qajar power and the rise of Reza Khan. As Reza consolidated his rule over Iran, he cast a scornful eye on Anglo-Persian and the D'Arcy concession that was its central asset. The company's profits were reaching astronomical levels, the means by which it calculated Iran's 16-percent royalty were becoming more questionable, and the gap between the living conditions of its British and Iranian employees widened steadily. In 1928 Reza, who was by then Reza Shah, directed his ministers to seek a new and more equitable accord with the company. The British did not take him seriously. For four years they turned aside his demands with a combination of refusals and delays. While he stewed, the worldwide depression spread and the royalties Anglo-Persian paid to Iran began to shrink. Finally and inevitably, Reza Shah exploded in anger. At a cabinet meeting on November 26, 1932, he cursed his ministers for their failure and then demanded to be shown the file of documents covering the four years of talks. When it was brought to him, he cursed some more and then threw the entire file into a blazing stove. The next day, he notified Anglo-Persian that he had canceled the D'Arcy concession.

This act, if allowed to stand, would have meant the end of Anglo-Persian's operations in Iran and, in effect, the death of the company. British officials were in turn shocked, outraged, and desperate. They appealed to the League of Nations, only to be met with a scathing counterattack from Iranian representatives who charged that Anglo-Persian had systematically falsified its accounts and cheated Iran out of its legitimate royalties. Sir John Cadman, Anglo-Persian's chairman, realized that he had to negotiate directly with Reza Shah, whose coronation he had attended eight years earlier. Cadman flew to Tehran, and the two old friends took only a few days to reach a compromise. Under its terms, the area covered by the D'Arcy concession was reduced by three-quarters, Iran was guaranteed payments of at least £975,000 annually, and the company agreed to improve working conditions at Abadan. In return, Reza Shah extended the concession, which was to expire in 1961, for an additional thirty-two years. It was also agreed that since the Shah did not like the name Persia, the company would henceforth be known as the Anglo-Iranian Oil Company.

"Am personally satisfied," Cadman wired home, "that new

Concession in every respect will open new era in our relations with Persia."

The 1933 accord stabilized the oil company's position for the rest of Reza Shah's reign. When the British forced him to abdicate eight years later, however, they removed the one leader who was strong enough to impose his rule by fiat on an increasingly restive country. Discontent over the company's privileged position grew steadily during the war years as the amount of oil it extracted rose from six and a half million tons in 1941 to sixteen and a half million tons in 1945.

In March 1946, less than a year after the guns finally fell silent, laborers at Abadan did something they would never have dreamed of doing in Reza Shah's time: they went on strike. Marching through the teeming streets, they carried signs and chanted slogans demanding better housing, decent health care, and a commitment by employers to abide by Iranian labor laws. Accustomed by long experience to challenges from restless natives, the British not only refused to negotiate but chose the path of active resistance. They organized ethnic Arabs and separatist tribesmen from nearby regions into a bogus union of their own and sent it to confront the strikers. Bloody rioting broke out, leaving dozens dead and more than one hundred injured. It ended only after Anglo-Iranian's directors grudgingly agreed to begin observing Iranian labor law. They never did, and to remind Iranians of their power, they arranged for two British warships to stage threatening maneuvers within sight of Abadan. With this show of force, they believed they had resolved the crisis. In fact, they had further inflamed public opinion and taken another step toward the abyss.

The Iranian labor movement was not the only long-dormant institution that came back to life after Reza Shah's departure. So did the Majlis. It had never ceased to exist, but Reza Shah had not allowed it to function freely. Now, angered like the rest of Iran by the rioting at Abadan, it began asserting itself. In 1947 it passed a bold law forbidding the grant of any further concessions to foreign companies and directing the government to renegotiate the one under which Anglo-Iranian was operating.

This law was the first blow in a long battle. It set Iran on the course of cataclysmic confrontation with Britain. The deputy who wrote it and pushed it through the Majlis had been an active nationalist in the early years of the century but was forced out of politics by Reza Shah and had lived in obscurity for twenty years. Now he was back, as fervent a defender of Iranian interests as ever. His name was Mohammad Mossadegh.

Two central beliefs shaped Mossadegh's political consciousness. The first was a passionate faith in the rule of law, which made him an enemy of autocracy and, in particular, Reza Shah. The second was a conviction that Iranians must rule themselves and not submit to the will of foreigners. That made him the nemesis, the tormentor, the implacable foe of the Anglo-Iranian Oil Company. In mid-twentieth-century Iran, he and the company faced off in an epic confrontation. Fate bound them together. The story of one cannot be told without the story of the other.

From the moment of his birth on May 19, 1882, Mossadegh had advantages that few of his countrymen enjoyed. His mother was a Qajar princess from a family that had produced governors, cabinet ministers, and ambassadors. The man she married came from the distinguished Ashtiani clan and served for more than twenty years as Nasir al-Din Shah's finance minister. He died when their son was still a child, but according to custom, young Mohammad was schooled in his father's profession. At the tender age of sixteen he was named to his first government post. It was no sinecure; he was chief tax auditor for Khorasan, his home province. This post introduced him not only to the complexity of public finance but also to the corruption and chaos that were eating away at the Qajar dynasty. By all accounts he performed brilliantly. A visitor who met Mossadegh soon after he assumed his post estimated that he was in his mid-twenties. The visitor wrote presciently in his journal:

> Among men of intelligence and learning, his decorum cannot be surpassed. He speaks, behaves, and receives people with respect, humility and courtesy, but without undermining his own eminence and dignity. He may at times have treated his colleagues, including high officials and finance ministers, with a measure of contempt, but in his dealing with other people he has shown warm human feeling, courtesy and humility. Such an impressive young man is bound to become one of the great ones.

Mossadegh came of age during a tumultuous time in Iranian history. He was eight years old when the Tobacco Revolt broke out, and considering how precocious he was and how involved his parents were in public life, it is safe to assume that he followed its course carefully. Several of his relatives, including his uncle, the formidable Prince Farman Farma, played important roles in the Constitutional Revolution. When elections for the first Majlis were convoked in 1906, Mossadegh became a candidate and won a seat from Isfahan. He could not assume it because he had not yet reached the legal age of thirty, but his political career was under way.

In those early years, Mossadegh developed more than a political perspective. He also began showing extraordinary emotional qualities. His boundless self-assurance led him to fight fiercely for his principles, but when he found others unreceptive, he would storm off for long periods of brooding silence. He did this for the first time in 1909, when Mohammad Ali Shah launched his bloody assault on the Majlis. Rather than stay and fight alongside his fellow democrats, he concluded that Iran was not ready for enlightenment and left the country. Like many Iranians of his class, he considered Paris the center of the civilized world, and he made his way there to study at l'Ecole de Sciences Politiques.

During his stay in France, Mossadegh suffered from illnesses that would plague him all his life. No one could precisely identify them. They were certainly real and periodically flared up to cause ulcers, hemorrhaging, stomach secretions, and other symptoms. But they also had a nervous component that led to fits and breakdowns. Neither purely medical nor psychosomatic, they both reflected and became a part of Mossadegh's persona. He was as dramatic a politician as his country had ever known. At times he became so passionate while delivering speeches that tears streamed down his cheeks. Sometimes he fainted dead away, as much from emotion as from any physical condition. When he became a world figure, his enemies in foreign capitals used this aspect of his personality to ridicule and belittle him. But in Iran, where centuries of Shiite religious practice had exposed everyone to depths of public emotion unknown in the West, it was not only accepted but celebrated. It seemed to prove how completely he embraced and shared his country's suffering.

The onset of illness forced Mossadegh to give up his studies in

France after a year and return to Iran. There he was able to rest, partly because the ruler he detested so viscerally, Mohammad Ali Shah, had been forced from the throne. After his recovery he returned to Europe, this time to the Swiss town of Neuchâtel, accompanied by his wife, their three small children, and his beloved mother. He entered the university there, earned his doctorate of law in 1914—the first Iranian to win such a degree from a European university—and decided to apply for Swiss citizenship. First, though, he would travel home to complete research for a book about Islamic law.

Mossadegh returned to a country ablaze with conflict. The Constitutional Revolution had given Iranians a taste of the forbidden fruit of democracy, and they were anxious for more of it. Qajar rule was crumbling. Most important, the outbreak of World War I had thrown all political certainties into question and made everything seem possible. Britain and Russia, having effectively divided Iran between them in 1907, still held the reins of true power, but resentment over their role was leading many Iranians to sympathize with the Kaiser's Germany. A group of intellectuals centered around Hasan Taqizadeh, who had been a key figure in the Constitutional Revolution, went so far as to set up a "liberation committee" in Berlin that published a radical newspaper and aimed ultimately to seize power in Tehran. Mossadegh was much encouraged by these developments, and instead of returning to Switzerland, he joined the faculty of the Tehran School of Law and Political Science, which was becoming Iran's first modern university. His book *Iran and the Capitulation Agreements* argued that Iran could develop modern, European-style legal and political systems if it took one vital step. It must impose the law equally on everyone, including foreigners, and never grant special privileges to anyone.

After Mossadegh had been home for less than a year, his uncle, Farman Farma, who had become prime minister, asked him to join the cabinet as minister of finance. Mossadegh declined because he did not want to be accused of rising to power through family connections. In 1917 he suffered an attack of appendicitis and was operated on in Baku, and while recovering, he received another offer, this time to become deputy finance minister. By this time his uncle was no longer prime minister, and at his mother's urging he accepted the offer. He upset his new colleagues by unearthing a series of corrupt schemes and insisting that the wrongdoers be punished, and after less than two years in office he was dismissed. Once again he decided that Iran did not deserve his services, and he returned to Neuchâtel. By doing so he showed, as he would show repeatedly throughout his life, that he was a visionary rather than a pragmatist, preferring defeat in an honorable cause to what he considered shameful compromise.

Mossadegh was in Neuchâtel when he received news of the infamous 1919 Anglo-Persian Agreement that effectively reduced Iran to the status of a British protectorate. He was outraged and did all he could to protest, as an Iranian biographer reported:

> He talked and corresponded with other prominent Iranians in Europe, published leaflets, and wrote to the League of Nations protesting against the agreement. He even traveled to Bern for the sole purpose of having a rubber stamp made for the Comité de Résistance de Nations in whose name the anti-agreement statements were issued. Anger, frustration and loneliness must have taken their toll on his nerves, for it is unlikely that, as he suspected, he was being watched by British agents—one of them in the shape of the "chic, pretty and bouncy" woman next door who called from her balcony, "Est-ce que vous voulez fumer ce soir?" and was disappointed when Mosaddegh answered, "Pardon, madame. Je suis malade. Je suis très occupé. Je suis fatigué. Excusez-moi. Je n'ai pas le temps."

Mossadegh was devastated by his countrymen's failure to rise up in righteous anger against the Anglo-Persian Agreement. The cause of Iranian patriotism, he concluded after a few months, was lost forever, and so there was no place for him in his homeland. He resolved to file his application for citizenship in Switzerland and spend the rest of his days practicing law there. Unfortunately Swiss immigration laws had been tightened since he had last considered this option, and his application was delayed. He came up with the idea of opening an import-export firm and decided to travel to Iran to make arrangements with merchants there. As soon as he set foot on his native soil, he found himself caught up again in politics. On his way to Tehran he passed through the southern province of Fars, and when local dignitaries learned of his presence, they offered him a large sum of money to stay there and become governor. He agreed, though he turned down the financial offer and even insisted on serving without salary.

After Reza Khan came to power in 1921, he tried to make use of Mossadegh's evident talents. Theirs was a short and unhappy partnership. Mossadegh first became minister of finance, a post for which he was eminently qualified, but upon taking office he launched an anticorruption campaign that threatened Reza and his friends, and was soon forced to resign. Next he was named governor of Azerbaijan province, where the Soviets were trying to stir up a separatist rebellion, but quit when Reza refused to give him authority over troops stationed there. Then he served for a few months as foreign minister. Finally he concluded that Reza shared neither his democratic instincts nor his anti-imperialist creed. He quit the foreign ministry, ran for a seat in the Majlis, and was elected easily. He was now a free agent, and soon he emerged as one of Reza's sharpest opponents.

By the time Mossadegh entered the Majlis in 1924, he was already a thoroughly political man. He had developed a deep understanding of his country, its political system, and above all its backwardness, much of which he attributed to the rapacity of foreign overlords. Yet he was never truly part of any establishment, political or otherwise. Many rich and influential Iranians considered him a class traitor because of his insistence on judging them by the letter of the law. Even some of his supporters chafed at the intense self-confidence that often led him to dismiss his critics as either rogues or fools.

Mossadegh's appearance was as strikingly unusual as his character. He was tall, but his shoulders slumped down as if they were bearing a heavy weight, giving him the image of a condemned man marching stoically toward execution. His face was long, marked by sad-looking eyes and a long, very prominent nose that his enemies sometimes compared to a vulture's beak. His skin was thin and pasty white. But for all that, he moved through life with a determination that many of his countrymen found impressive to the point of inspiration. In intellect and education he towered above almost all of them, a drawback for a politician in some countries but not in Iran, where those who do not live the life of the mind have always admired those who do. His arrival in the Majlis marked the beginning of a new stage in his remarkable career, as one of his cousins recalled in a memoir:

> With his droopy, basset-hound eyes and high patrician forehead, Mossadegh did not look like a man to shake a nation. . . . To his mind the parliament was the only mouthpiece of the people of Iran. No matter how rigged the election or how corrupt its members, it was the only body that did not depend for its power either on outside influence or on the [royal] court, but on the authority of the constitution. The Majlis became his soapbox. Elected to it time and again by the people of Tehran, he used it to denounce the misconduct of the British and the Russians, and later the Americans. When he said, "The Iranian himself is the best person to manage his house," he was stating not only a conviction but a policy that he was to pursue with unwavering purpose until his picture had appeared on the cover of *Time* magazine and he had thoroughly shaken the foundations of the world's oil establishment.
>
> Although Mossadegh championed Iranian self-determination, he had little faith in his fellow deputies, and few escaped the lash of his tongue. He accused them of cowardice, of lacking initiative, and worst of all being unpatriotic. His fulminations at the podium were both frightening and theatrical. Gesturing wildly, his hand unconsciously wiping away the famous tears that sprung unbidden from his eyes at times of nervousness or rage, he pilloried his listeners with the righteousness of a priest who suffers with his victims even as he unmasks them. . . . Distinguished, highly emotional, and every inch the aristocrat, he believed so totally in his own country that his words reached out and touched the common man. Mossadegh was Iran's first genuinely popular leader, and he knew it.

If Iran had faced only domestic problems, Mossadegh might still be remembered only as a vigorous advocate of reform and modernization. The country's main dilemma, however, centered around its relationship with outside powers, especially Britain and most especially the Anglo-Iranian Oil Company. Many Iranians resigned themselves to the imposition of these powers, but Mossadegh never did.

During his first few months in the Majlis, Mossadegh rose often to speak. He addressed topics ranging from military corruption to the need for new industries in Iran, but his central themes were always democracy and self-reliance. "If bringing prosperity to the country through the work of other nations were of benefit to the people," he asserted in one speech, "every nation would have invited foreigners into its home. If subjugation were beneficial, no subjugated country would have tried to liberate itself through bloody wars and heavy losses."

On October 29, 1925, the Majlis received one of the most far-reaching proposals it had ever considered. It was from supporters of Reza, asking that the Qajar dynasty be abolished and that Reza be named Shah. Mossadegh was horrified. When his turn came to speak on the proposal, other deputies fell into a hush. He began by producing a copy of the Koran and demanded that everyone in the chamber rise to acknowledge that they had sworn upon it to defend the constitutional system. All did so. Then, in the day's longest and most emotional speech, Mossadegh paid tribute to Reza's achievements but said that if Reza wanted to govern the country, he should become prime minister, not Shah. To centralize royal and administrative power in the hands of one man would be "pure reaction, pure *istibdad*," a system so perverse that it "does not exist even in Zanzibar." Darkly, Mossadegh warned of Reza's authoritarian tendencies and predicted that elevating him to the throne would lead the country back to absolutism.

"Was it to achieve dictatorship that people bled their lives away in the Constitutional Revolution?" he demanded. "If they cut off my head and mutilate my body, I would never agree to such a decision."

Mossadegh was under no illusion that he could prevent Reza from taking the throne. Reza was the rising power in a country that had been on the brink of extinction, and just two days after Mossadegh's fiery speech, the Majlis recognized that fact by agreeing to his coronation. At the ceremony, Reza placed the plumed and jeweled crown on his own head as Napoleon had done, symbolizing his determination to govern as he pleased. For a few months he ruled alone and then, having secured his power, named a prime minister and directed him to offer Mossadegh the post of foreign minister. It was an astute move. Mossadegh had a base of popular support and impeccable nationalist credentials that would serve the new regime well. To no one's surprise, however, he declined the offer. He enjoyed being a free agent and undoubtedly realized that his abhorrence of dictatorship would soon place him in conflict with the new Shah. Not satisfied with refusing an offer to join the cabinet, he denounced it when it was finally formed. In his speech he called two of the incoming ministers traitors for their role in negotiating the Anglo-Persian Agreement.

Over the months that followed, Reza Shah approached Mossadegh several more times with offers of high government posts, including chief justice and even prime minister. Mossadegh rejected them all. After he was reelected to the Majlis at the end of 1926, he went so far as to refuse to take his oath of office because it included a vow to respect the Shah's authority. That should have prevented him from taking his seat, but given the power of his presence and the force of his will, no one challenged him.

The Majlis, like every other institution in Iran, was soon reduced to the role of a rubber stamp for Reza Shah. He outlawed opposition parties and banned their leaders from public life. Once this repressive campaign began, there was no doubt that Mossadegh would soon be among the victims. When the 1928 election approached, Reza Shah ordered that votes be counted in such a way that no one who opposed him would win. Mossadegh was among the losers. At the age of forty-five, his political career seemed over.

Several possible courses lay open to the deposed statesman. He could soften his opposition to Reza Shah and try to work within the regime, but given the strength of his principles this was impossible. He could defy the regime by launching a campaign of subversion, which might have led to his murder; even several of Reza Shah's longtime allies suffered this fate when he began to suspect their loyalty. The remaining option fit best not only with the times but with Mossadegh's own personality. He simply dropped out of sight, retiring to his country estate at Ahmad Abad, sixty miles west of Tehran, and devoting himself to study and experimental farming. His name disappeared from the press and from public discourse. As Reza Shah's power grew, Mossadegh's image faded and then all but disappeared. Most Iranians presumed that his moment had passed. He believed so himself.

After the first few years of his self-imposed exile, weighed down by the travails of isolation and devastated by news of the 1933 accord under which Reza Shah reaffirmed Anglo-Iranian's right to run the country's oil industry, Mossadegh fell ill. He bled so profusely from his mouth that in 1936 he traveled to Germany to consult specialists; they could find no cause for his condition. Even in his weakened state, however, Reza Shah feared him. One day in 1940 soldiers appeared at his house in Ahmad Abad, ransacked it in search of evidence that might implicate him in subversion and then, although finding nothing, placed him under arrest. At the local police station, he protested indignantly to the chief, citing a law under which prisoners had to be charged with a crime or released within twenty-four hours. The chief replied that the only law he knew was Reza Shah's will and that Reza Shah had ordered Mossadegh imprisoned indefinitely without charge. This sent Mossadegh into a rage. He had to be dragged into the car that was waiting to take him to prison. On the way he took an overdose of tranquilizers, apparently a suicide attempt, but succeeded only in falling into a coma. In his cell he showed evidence of what his jailer called "chronic hysteria," trying to cut himself with razor blades and at one point embarking on a hunger strike. After several months, through the intercession of Ernest Perron, a Swiss-born friend of the Shah who had once been cured of an illness at a hospital endowed by Mossadegh's mother, he was allowed to return to Ahmad Abad under house arrest.

For twenty years, part of it spent in active politics and the rest in obscurity, Mossadegh saw Reza Shah and his regime as Iran's great enemy. Then, suddenly, Reza Shah was gone. That changed everything, both for the nation and for Mossadegh himself. The election of 1943 was the first free one in many years. Mossadegh emerged from his retreat, ran for his old seat in the Majlis, and was elected with more votes than any other candidate. But although his old enemy had been dethroned, a new and even more powerful one stood in the way of his dream for Iran. The British, and in particular the Anglo-Iranian Oil Company, dominated the country as never before. Now Mossadegh would turn his sights on them.

CHAPTER 5

His Master's Orders

During the late 1940s, when Iran was being torn by separatist rebellion and bled dry by the Anglo-Iranian Oil Company, the young Mohammad Reza Shah concentrated his attention on sports cars, race horses, and women. He became a fixture of the international party set, favoring London nightclubs and carrying on a string of affairs with second-level movie actresses like Yvonne De Carlo, Gene Tierney, and Silvana Mangano. Several times he tried to consolidate his shaky position at home through repression and vote-rigging, but succeeded only in making himself a figure of ridicule. Newspapers called him a lackey of the British. Public rallies were held to denounce him. He was blissfully unaware of the contempt in which many Iranians held him, however, and did not imagine he was in any danger when he visited the University of Tehran to attend an anniversary celebration.

Snow was falling on that day, February 4, 1949. The Shah had just stepped out of his car and was approaching a staircase when a young man posing as a photographer pulled out a pistol and began shooting at him. Just six feet separated the two, but the gunman proved a very poor shot. His first three bullets hit only the Shah's military cap. In a reflexive response, the Shah turned toward him, and as he turned, a fourth shot tore a hole in his right cheek. Body-guards, generals, and police officers, apparently not considering the Shah's life worth saving, dove for cover, leaving the two men facing each other for a second. The Shah ducked as a fifth shot rang out. It grazed his shoulder. With just one bullet left, the shooter pointed directly at the monarch's chest and pulled the trigger. There was only a light click. The pistol had jammed.

With the danger past, security agents jumped up and quickly clubbed and shot the would-be assassin to death. Mohammad Reza Shah, then twenty-nine years old, took a few minutes to recover. Still breathing heavily, he announced that he had been saved by divine intercession. He may have believed it. The next day he sent his bloodstained uniform to the Officers Club and ordered that it be placed in a display case. Soon afterward, he decided that it was time for him to impose his will on Iran as his father had done.

Iran had entered a new era when Reza Shah abdicated in 1941. Many of his former subjects were thrilled to see him gone, among them thousands of tribal families who immediately abandoned the wretched settlements into which he had herded them and returned to their ancestral mountains and nomadic life. Others, even some who had chafed under his harsh rule, feared that they had lost their country's only bulwark against chaos and the rule of foreigners. Most felt the mixture of relief and apprehension that rowdy school-children feel when a strict teacher suddenly takes ill. Newspapers, political parties, labor unions, and social organizations blossomed, but so did criminal gangs. The fear of authority that Reza Shah had instilled in people melted away. When one upper-class woman rep-rimanded her chauffeur for turning the wrong way into a one-way street, he replied, "Oh! It does not matter, now Reza Shah has gone."

After forcing the feared strongman to abdicate, the British had first considered restoring the discredited Qajar dynasty. Only after discovering that the pretender, who lived in London, spoke no Per-sian, did they decide to allow Mohammad Reza to take the throne. Immediately after his coronation, they directed him to appoint a pro-British politician, Mohammad Ali Furughi, as prime minister. Through Furughi they effectively ruled Iran. To secure their power, they revived the old formula under which the country was divided into three sectors. Soviet troops controlled the north, while the British held southern provinces that embraced oil fields, the refinery at Abadan, and the land route to India. Iranians were allowed to continue governing Tehran and the rest of the country's midsection, always under the occupiers' watchful eyes.

The Allies made good use of Iran during the war, not only extracting huge amounts of its oil but also building several large supply bases from which they launched military operations across the Middle East and North Africa. Ordinary Iranians, however, saw their standard of living fall precipitously. Much food was diverted from civilian to military use. Trucks and railroads were used mainly for military purposes. Prices rose as speculators thrived, and poor harvests left many people hungry. Furughi was dismissed when he became the target of public anger, but his successors fared no better.

As long as the war was on and Iran was under military occupation, dissent was muted. Slowly, however, political life resumed. Everyone understood that war and occupation were only temporary conditions. Once they were over, there would be a new nation to build.

Neither the young Mohammad Reza Shah nor his various prime ministers managed to capture the public imagination during the 1940s. The only figure who did was a flamboyant American soldier, General H. Norman Schwarzkopf, who arrived in 1942 as head of a military mission. Schwarzkopf was a West Point graduate who had become chief of the New Jersey State Police. He reached celebrity status while directing the investigation of the Lindbergh kidnapping and later spent several years as the voice of the radio drama *Gang Busters.* When World War II broke out, he rejoined the army and was sent to Iran. Allied commanders assigned him to transform the country's ragged rural police force into a crack unit, and he took to the task with gusto. For six years, including difficult periods when bread riots and other protests shook the country, he and his Imperial Iranian Gendarmerie turned up wherever trouble broke out. At the same time he quietly trained a secret security squad that became the scourge of leftists and other dissidents. He struck many Iranians as a larger-than-life figure, a fearsome avenger who carried the Shah's power into every corner of the country. In a remarkable quirk of history, his son, also General H. Norman Schwarzkopf, returned to the region as commander of Operation Desert Storm in 1990–1991 and also left a lasting imprint on its history.

□ □ □

Iranians in the mid-twentieth century were searching for new solutions to their old problems of poverty and underdevelopment, and like their counterparts in other countries, some embraced the emerging ideology of communism. During the 1930s, Reza Shah had imprisoned several dozen left-leaning professors and political organizers, and while they were behind bars together they spent much time discussing politics. When they were released after Reza's abdication, they constituted themselves as the Group of Fifty-Three and began searching for a new political platform. Some of them joined with a loose group of liberals, reformers, and social activists to form Iran's first real political party, called Tudeh (Masses). At its founding convention, held in 1942, Tudeh adopted a progressive program based on the principle that government should protect ordinary people from exploitation by the rich. It advocated sweeping reform, though not revolution or one-party rule. Young, patriotic, and idealistic, it seemed a promising movement. The British allowed it to function, and Soviet commissars, pleased by the presence of communists in its ranks, actively supported it.

For a time, Tudeh thrived as the party of modernity and European ideas. Its pro-Soviet faction, however, grew steadily stronger and finally, in 1944, seized control. Tudeh turned decisively toward Marxism and launched an intensive organizing campaign among the urban poor. It was so successful that on May Day 1946, it was able to fill the streets of Tehran and Abadan with tens of thousands of enthusiastic demonstrators. Several of its leaders won election to the Majlis that year and went on to help pass laws limiting child labor, establishing a forty-eight-hour workweek, guaranteeing maternity leaves, and setting a minimum wage.

Tudeh's growing power tempted the Soviet Union to make a daring strike against Iran. During World War II, the three Allied powers had agreed that they would withdraw their occupation forces from Iran six months after the end of hostilities, but when that deadline came in early 1946, Stalin ignored it. Citing vague threats to Soviet security, he declared that the Red Army would remain in Iran's northern province of Azerbaijan. When Tudeh activists there proclaimed a People's Republic of Azerbaijan, he ordered his troops to prevent Iranian soldiers from entering the province to reestablish their authority. Soon a local militia emerged, flush with weapons from Moscow. For a time it seemed that Azerbaijan might secede entirely, perhaps to join the Soviet Union or serve as a jumping-off point for a Soviet move against Turkey. But Azerbaijanis remembered Reza Shah and rebelled at the prospect of another dictatorship. Prime Minister Ahmad Qavam, an exceptionally talented statesman, traveled to Moscow and managed to persuade Stalin to step back from the brink of confrontation. He withdrew his soldiers as General Schwarzkopf's gendarmes marched into Tabriz, the provincial capital. The People's Republic of Azerbaijan passed into history. Jubilant Azerbaijanis celebrated by summarily executing all the Tudeh leaders they could find.

Mohammad Reza Shah rightly feared Tudeh, which was strongly antimonarchist, but for several years after the Azerbaijan episode he could find no way to act against it. After the assassination attempt of 1949 he came up with one. All evidence suggested that the failed assassin was a religious fanatic, but the Shah ignored it and accused Tudeh of organizing the attempt. He banned it and imprisoned dozens of its leaders.

Seizing on the public sympathy that the shooting had generated, the Shah also took several other steps to increase his power. He ordered the creation of a second legislative chamber, the Senate, which had been authorized by the 1906 constitution but never established; he liked the provision that gave him the right to appoint half the senators. Then he persuaded the Majlis to pass a bill allowing him to dissolve both chambers and call new elections at his pleasure. Finally and perhaps most important, he won from the Majlis a change in the way prime ministers were appointed. Under the constitution, the Majlis chose them and the Shah gave his assent. Now the system would work the other way, with the Shah choosing and the Majlis voting afterward to confirm or reject his nominee.

Mohammad Reza Shah took all of these steps with the discreet advice and support of the British. For many years, British officials had taken it as a matter of simple logic that since they had such a vital commercial stake in Iran, they must keep it stable and friendly. Without their assent, Mohammad Reza would not have been able to ascend the throne, and he fully understood the debt he owed them. When violent protests broke out at their refinery in 1946, they came to collect.

The riots that shook Abadan led many Iranians to rally to the workers' cause, partly out of instinctive sympathy but also because of the grossly unequal terms under which the Anglo-Iranian Oil Company operated. In 1947, for example, the company reported an after-tax profit of £40 million—the equivalent of $112 million dollars—and gave Iran just £7 million. To make matters worse, it never complied with its commitment under the 1933 agreement with Reza Shah to give laborers better pay and more chance for advancement, nor had it built the schools, hospitals, roads, or telephone system it promised. Manucher Farmanfarmaian, who in 1949 became director of Iran's petroleum institute, was appalled by what he found at Abadan:

> Wages were fifty cents a day. There was no vacation pay, no sick leave, no disability compensation. The workers lived in a shantytown called Kaghazabad, or Paper City, without running water or electricity, let alone such luxuries as iceboxes or fans. In winter the earth flooded and became a flat, perspiring lake. The mud in town was knee-deep, and canoes ran alongside the roadways for transport. When the rains subsided, clouds of nipping, small-winged flies rose from the stagnant waters to fill the nostrils, collecting in black mounds along the rims of cooking pots and jamming the fans at the refinery with an unctuous glue.
>
> Summer was worse. It descended suddenly without a hint of spring. The heat was torrid, the worst I've ever known—sticky and unrelenting—while the wind and sandstorms whipped off the desert hot as a blower. The dwellings of Kaghazabad, cobbled from rusted oil drums hammered flat, turned into sweltering ovens. . . . In every crevice hung the foul, sulfurous stench of burning oil—a pungent reminder that every day twenty thousand barrels, or one million tons a year, were being consumed indiscriminately for the functioning of the refinery, and AIOC never paid the government a cent for it.
>
> To the management of AIOC in their pressed ecru shirts and air-conditioned offices, the workers were faceless drones. . . . In the British section of Abadan there were lawns, rose beds, tennis courts, swimming pools and clubs; in Kaghazabad there was nothing—not a tea shop, not a bath, not a single tree. The tiled reflecting pool and shaded central square that were part of every Iranian town, no matter how poor or dry, were missing here. The unpaved alleyways were emporiums for rats. The man in the

grocery store sold his wares while sitting in a barrel of water to avoid the heat. Only the shriveled, mud-brick mosque in the old quarter offered hope in the form of divine redemption.

Under the leadership of Sir William Fraser, a famously obstinate Scotsman who hated the idea of compromise, Anglo-Iranian rejected every appeal to reform. Fraser's militancy and that of the British government were easy to understand. Britain had risen to world power largely because of its success in exploiting the natural resources of subject nations. More than half of Anglo-Iranian's profits went directly to the British government, which owned 51 percent of the shares. It paid millions of additional pounds each year in taxes and also supplied the Royal Navy with all the oil it needed at a fraction of the market price. Foreign Secretary Ernest Bevin was not exaggerating when he observed that without oil from Iran, there would be "no hope of our being able to achieve the standard of living at which we are aiming in Great Britain."

Iranians, of course, found it difficult to generate much sympathy for the British. Members of the Majlis began demanding that the oil company offer Iran a better deal, and in 1949 ten of them went so far as to submit a bill that would revoke its concession. Their pressure and the evident threat of continued violence at Abadan became too intense for the British to ignore. They needed a new framework to relegitimize their position in Iran.

Three months after the attempt on the Shah's life, Fraser arrived in Tehran to make his offer. The contract he proposed became known as the Supplemental Agreement, since it was intended to supplement the one Reza Shah signed in 1933. It offered Iran several improvements: a guarantee that Anglo-Iranian's annual royalty payments would not drop below £4 million, a reduction of the area in which it would be allowed to drill, and a promise that more Iranians would be trained for administrative positions. It did not, however, offer Iranians any greater voice in the company's management or give them the right to audit the company's books. The Iranian prime minister took this proposal as a basis for discussion and invited Fraser to negotiate their differences. Fraser dismissed him, declared that his offer was final, and flew back to London aboard his private plane.

"The British want the whole world," Finance Minister Abbasgholi

Golshayan lamented after Fraser stormed out of Tehran. But Mohammad Reza Shah, who knew he must do what Britain wanted, ordered the cabinet to accept the Supplemental Agreement, and on July 17, 1949, it did so. To take effect, however, it had to be approved by the Majlis, which was beyond the Shah's control.

Many members of the Majlis publicly denounced the Supplemental Agreement even before the cabinet accepted it. Others turned against it when Finance Minister Golshayan, whose position should have made him a faithful servant of the British, presented a fifty-page report he had commissioned from Gilbert Gidel, a renowned professor of international law at the University of Paris, that documented the accounting tricks by which Anglo-Iranian was cheating Iran out of huge sums of money. One outraged deputy, Abbas Iskandari, gave an impassioned speech denouncing the agreement that finished with a warning so far-reaching that even he may not have grasped its implications. Iskandari demanded that Anglo-Iranian begin splitting its profits with Iran on a fifty-fifty basis, as American oil companies were doing in several countries. If it refused, he warned, Iran would "nationalize the oil industry and extract the crude itself."

The Majlis's term was expiring and elections were approaching. Many deputies did not want to anger the Shah by voting against the Supplemental Agreement, but given the highly agitated state of public opinion they could hardly vote in favor. They chose to filibuster. For four days the Majlis chamber echoed with long denunciations of both the agreement and the generalized perfidy of Albion. Finally the clock wound down. The Supplemental Agreement was left to the next Majlis.

Mohammad Reza Shah was not amused by this turn of events, and he resolved to do whatever necessary to assure that the next Majlis would heed him. Using a variety of techniques ranging from the recruitment of royalist candidates to bribery and blatant electoral fraud, he managed to secure the election of many pliable deputies. His presumption that he could cheat voters as his father had, however, proved quite mistaken. Iranians were thirsty for democracy and could no longer be terrorized into silence. Several cities exploded in protest. Outrage was strongest in Tehran, where nationalist candidates led by the hugely popular Mohammad Mossadegh were declared losers.

Mossadegh issued a statement inviting all who believed in fair elections to gather in front of his home on October 13. Thousands turned up, and he led them through the streets to the royal palace. When they reached the gate, he turned to face them, delivered a fiery speech, and declared that he would not move until the Shah agreed to hold new and fair elections. He kept his word. For three days and nights he and several dozen other democrats sat on the palace lawn. Finally the Shah, who was about to embark on a tour of the United States and was anxious to avoid embarrassment, gave in.

By choosing to travel to the United States, the Shah was recognizing the emergence of a new world power, one whose will would shape Iranian history more decisively than anyone could have then imagined. President Truman hoped to use the visit, which stretched over several weeks in November and December of 1949, to persuade the young monarch that he must devote himself above all to improving the daily lives of his people. He was convinced that only social reform, not military power, would keep Iran safe from communism.

Truman sent his personal plane, the *Independence,* to bring the Shah to Washington and put him up at Blair House. Later the Shah went on to New York, where he was feted at the Metropolitan Museum of Art, and to a variety of destinations not usually on the itinerary of foreign dignitaries, among them Idaho, Kentucky, Arizona, and Ohio. Companies like Lockheed and General Motors held lavish dinner parties for him. The State Department arranged for him to be honored at Princeton and the University of Michigan. He attended a football game between Georgetown and George Washington, and before the game he was made an honorary captain of the George Washington team. At West Point and Annapolis he was welcomed with twenty-one-gun salutes.

Behind the scenes, however, the Shah's visit did not go well. In meetings with Truman, Secretary of State Dean Acheson, and General Omar Bradley, the chairman of the Joint Chiefs of Staff, he insisted repeatedly that what Iran needed most was a bigger army and more weapons. He asked for tanks, antitank weapons, trucks, and large stores of ammunition, as well as money to pay for tens of thousands of more soldiers and advanced training for a greatly expanded officer corps. His single-mindedness was understandable.

Under the Iranian constitution he controlled the military but nothing else, so a strong army was the key to his personal power. When his hosts tried to steer their conversations to the subject of Iran's social needs, he lost interest. Acheson warned him to pay attention to what had happened in China, where the Nationalist leader Chiang Kai-shek had enjoyed vast military superiority but lost power to ragtag Communists because he had sought "a purely military solution." The two sides could not come to an understanding. In the end, Truman sent his guest home without the military aid he had sought. The joint communiqué issued as the Shah departed said only that the United States would "bear in mind" his request for military aid.

After failing to persuade the Americans to pay for the military buildup that was his most fervent desire, the Shah returned to Iran to find his adversaries better organized than ever. His agreement to cancel the results of his rigged election had shown the limits of his power. It also had another, more far-reaching effect. After leaving the palace grounds following their successful sit-in, twenty of the triumphant protesters had met at Mossadegh's house and made a historic decision. They resolved to build on their victory by forming a new coalition of political parties, trade unions, civic groups, and other organizations devoted to strengthening democracy and limiting the power of foreigners in Iran. They christened it the National Front and by unanimous vote chose Mossadegh as its leader. With a formal organization behind him for the first time and aroused public opinion at his side, the sixty-seven-year-old patriarch now had all the tools he needed to launch his shattering challenge to the political order.

Mossadegh and six other founders of the National Front were elected to the Majlis in the new election they had forced the Shah to call. Their victories marked the arrival of something new in Iranian politics: an organized, sophisticated opposition bloc fired with nationalist zeal and confident of broad public support. Its emergence posed a considerable obstacle both to the Shah's immediate goal, which was to secure approval of the Supplemental Agreement, and to his longer-term project of reestablishing royal power. Two opposing visions of Iran's future were now in sharper conflict than ever before.

The Shah preferred weak prime ministers because he could bend them to his will, but at the beginning of 1950 he and the

British needed one strong enough to force the Majlis to approve the Supplemental Agreement. His first choice, Mohammad Saed, was decidedly unenthusiastic about the agreement and refused even to present it for a vote. After two months the Shah replaced him with a more strongly pro-British figure, Ali Mansur, but Mansur also proved unwilling to fight for the agreement. The British became impatient. In April they sent a new ambassador to Tehran, Sir Francis Shepherd, whose diplomatic experience had been in countries run by tyrants or foreign powers: El Salvador, Haiti, Peru, the Belgian Congo, and the Dutch East Indies. In one of his first cables back to the Foreign Office, Shepherd reported that although the Shah had ordered Mansur "to secure as soon as possible the passage of Supplemental Oil Agreement," Mansur seemed to have "no intention of carrying out his master's orders."

It did not take long for both the Foreign Office and Anglo-Iranian to conclude that Mansur was not their man. They needed a tougher prime minister. Their candidate was not a civilian, as was traditional in Iran, but General Ali Razmara, who had been one of General Schwarzkopf's most trusted officers and had then become chief of staff of the army. Only a man with his fierce determination, they believed, would be strong enough to face down Mossadegh and the National Front.

On June 20 the Majlis voted to create an eighteen-member committee to study the Supplemental Agreement. The British took this as an act of defiance and advised the Shah that he must respond by sacking Prime Minister Mansur and naming General Razmara to succeed him. Such advice could not be ignored.

Razmara's slight stature and ingratiating smile belied his energy, intelligence, and relentless ambition. He was a career soldier, forty-seven years old, known as ruthless and cold-blooded. Like most Iranian officers he had taken advantage of many corrupt opportunities, but he was also a man of unmistakable talent. His hero was the late Reza Shah, with whom he shared the belief that Iran could rise to greatness only under the rule of a harsh, unforgiving tyrant. Unlike Reza, however, he was a sophisticated cosmopolitan, educated at the French military academy and intimately aware of how important it was for Iranian leaders to placate foreign powers. He rose to power by winning their support. To the British, he promised quick passage of the Supplemental Agreement; to the Russians, freedom for Tudeh leaders imprisoned by Mohammad Reza Shah after the attempt on his life; and to the Americans, who were becoming more interested in the Middle East, a sympathetic ear and support in their anticommunist crusade.

The Majlis met at the end of June to debate Razmara's nomination. No one was surprised when Mossadegh delivered a blistering speech denouncing him as a tool of foreign powers and a dictator in the making. Nor was there any surprise when, after the speeches were over, Razmara was confirmed by a comfortable margin. He had used his power to help the campaigns of more than half the deputies, and they were repaying their debts.

Razmara took office convinced that destiny had chosen him to lead Iran back to greatness. Mossadegh believed the same about himself. So did the Shah. Only one of the three could emerge victorious from the coming confrontation.

Razmara's first days in office during that summer of 1950 would have discouraged a less formidable man. The arrival of a new American ambassador, Henry Grady, sparked an outbreak of rioting in which several people were killed; no one had anything against Grady personally, but politicized Iranians had become so angry at foreign interference in their country's affairs that the mere appearance of what seemed to be a new proconsul was enough to send thousands onto the streets. Prime Minister Razmara had to take this rising nationalism into account as he planned his political strategy. He told his British patrons that he could win approval of their Supplemental Agreement, but only if they revised it. Let Anglo-Iranian sweeten its offer, he suggested, by agreeing to open its books to Iranian auditors, train Iranians for managerial jobs, and make some of its royalty payments in advance as a sign of support for national development.

This was a shrewd proposal. By accepting it, Anglo-Iranian might well have undercut the National Front and stabilized its own position for years to come. Much to Razmara's dismay, however, the British rejected it out of hand. Ambassador Shepherd told him the company's offer was final and that the only sweetener it would accept "was perhaps free medical treatment of certain hysterical deputies who continued to denounce the Supplemental Agreement." By failing to recognize that the colonial era was ending and that they could maintain their world power only by working with the rising forces of nationalism, the British passed up a historic opportunity.

Razmara had no choice but to reconcile himself to the will of the Shah, the Foreign Office, and Anglo-Iranian. He named a finance minister known for pro-British views and resumed his campaign for ratification of the Supplemental Agreement. One of his key allies was a radio celebrity named Bahram Sharogh, who had risen to fame as a Nazi propagandist. During the early 1940s, Sharogh had been chief of Radio Berlin's Persian service, and his was the enthusiastic voice that brought Iranians their daily diet of news about Axis victories and the glorious future of German–Iranian relations. His broadcasts were filled with anti-British vitriol, and they fueled the hatred of British imperialism that spread through Iran. When the tide of the war turned, he mysteriously lost his job; some Nazi security officers suspected him of being a British agent. Not long afterward, to the astonishment of his listeners, he turned up at Radio Tehran and began broadcasting lavishly pro-British commentaries. Razmara named him director of "radio and propaganda," and he embraced Anglo-Iranian's cause with a fervor every bit as intense as that he had shown for the Nazis a decade earlier. Besides broadcasting streams of passionate reports himself, he helped Anglo-Iranian single out and bribe pliable newspaper columnists and editors.

By this time the Majlis had named the members of its oil committee. Mossadegh was of course among them, and at the committee's first meeting he was elected chairman. The committee met twice a week. Many of its members were no more interested in finding a compromise than Anglo-Iranian was. Manucher Farmanfarmaian, the director of Iran's petroleum institute, attended many of the sessions and later wrote about them:

> The committee was ostensibly set up to investigate the Supplemental Agreement and find grounds for settlement, but the technical and economic aspects of the agreement were rarely raised. The deputies were not well versed in oil and were interested in it only insofar as it related to politics. Instead, they fixated on the human costs. . . . Mossadegh dominated the proceedings. He criticized everything with great sarcasm, a technique he'd mastered

in the twenty-five years in which he'd done nothing but carp and bestow blame.... Mossadegh did not care about dollars and cents or numbers of barrels per day. He saw the basic issue as one of national sovereignty. Iran's sovereignty was being undercut by a company that sacrificed Iranian lives for British interests. This is what infuriated him about the government's willingness to compromise—and it was what made him decide unequivocally that AIOC had to go.

As the weather cooled in Tehran that autumn, the temperature of public opinion rose steadily. The British, by their refusal to compromise, had managed to unite a broad cross-section of the politically active population against them. They even pushed religious groups committed to Islamic law into a coalition with Mossadegh and other secular liberals. A few mullahs, including the young Ruhollah Khomeini, who thirty years later would emerge as the country's supreme leader, refused to join this coalition because they believed that Mossadegh and his allies had forsaken Islam. Most of the important ones, however, entered into a tactical alliance with the National Front. The most influential among them was the flamboyant and impassioned Ayatollah Abolqasem Kashani, who had never been considered a great religious scholar but who became a central figure in Iran's anti-imperialist movement. Kashani's father had been killed fighting the British in Mesopotamia during World War I, and he himself was held in a British prison camp during the Allied occupation of Iran in World War II. After his release, he quickly emerged as an incendiary popular leader. Mohammad Reza Shah tried to silence him by sending him into exile after the 1949 assassination attempt, but from Beirut he ran for a seat in the Majlis and won. Popular pressure forced the Shah to allow him to return, and hundreds of thousands turned out to welcome him. In his speech to the multitude, he hailed Mossadegh and the National Front as Iran's truest patriots.

Kashani was fiercely anti-Western, hated liberal ideas, and believed that Muslims should obey secular laws only if they were in harmony with the Islamic legal tradition known as *sharia*. If he was a nationalist, it was only in a limited sense; he wanted Iranians to control their own affairs but also imagined that once the infidels were pushed out, Iran would become part of a pan-Islamic commonwealth that would challenge both the Western and communist blocs. Yet like mullahs who had supported the Constitutional Revolution nearly half a century before, he saw the anti-British campaign as a sacred duty. In pursuit of that duty he plunged into politics, building his own faction in the Majlis and working tirelessly to mobilize the masses to Mossadegh's cause. "Islam warns its adherents not to submit to a foreign yoke!" he thundered at one rally.

With the bearded holy man Kashani and the Swiss-educated aristocrat Mossadegh stoking the anti-British fire, opinion in the Majlis turned ever more strongly against the Supplemental Agreement. Prime Minister Razmara tried to make a speech there in October appealing for its ratification but was drowned out by a stream of invective. After he took his seat, more than a dozen deputies rose to reply. All condemned Anglo-Iranian as a rapacious monster and Razmara as its lackey. Mossadegh was the most passionate. He denounced the Supplemental Agreement as an instrument of bondage and then, in an inspired coda, turned dramatically to Razmara and told him: "If you endorse this Agreement, you leave yourself with a disgrace which you will never be able to wash away."

On November 25 Mossadegh brought the Supplemental Agreement to a vote in his parliamentary committee. The committee assembled as usual in an anteroom at the Majlis. Bright sun shone on a light snow cover outside. Mossadegh and the four other committee members who belonged to the National Front proposed the radical option of nationalizing Anglo-Iranian, but the rest of the committee was not ready to go that far. On the question at hand, though, there was no dissent. The committee voted unanimously to recommend rejection of the Agreement.

Events now began to take on a momentum of their own. Iranian politics was moving into uncharted territory, and there was no steady hand at the tiller of state. Every day positions grew more polarized. No faction believed in the goodwill of any other. Discourse was conducted by insult and tirade.

At the end of December, news reached Tehran that the Arabian-American Oil Company, known as Aramco, had reached a new deal with Saudi Arabia under which it would share its profits with the Saudis on a fifty-fifty basis. Ambassador Shepherd immediately dispatched a cable to London urging that Anglo-Iranian make a similar offer to Iran. Both the Foreign Office and the oil company rejected the idea. By doing so, they lost another chance to resolve the looming crisis before disaster struck. Anglo-Iranian's manager in Tehran, E. G. D. Northcroft, advised the home office not to "attach much importance" to the nationalist movement.

The British position was so far removed from reality that Northrop's assistant, Mostafa Fateh, the company's highest-ranking Iranian employee and for decades its faithful servant, felt compelled to protest. He wrote an impassioned twenty-three-page letter to a member of Anglo-Iranian's board of directors, Edward Elkington, whom he had known when Elkington was posted in Iran. The letter was an eloquent warning that the company needed to recognize the "awakening nationalism and political consciousness of the people of Asia" and show "breadth of vision, tolerance for other people's views and clear thinking to avoid disaster." It described Anglo-Iranian's alliance with "corrupt ruling classes" and "leech-like bureaucracies" as "disastrous, outdated and impractical." Fateh said there was still enough support in the Majlis to ratify the Supplemental Agreement if the company would revise it to include a fifty-fifty profit share and shorten its term; otherwise the Agreement was doomed, since the company's policies had "alienated the liberal and progressive classes from Britain." His eloquent cri de coeur went unheeded. Fateh "is not to be trusted far," sniffed one British diplomat to whom Elkington showed it.

Confrontation now seemed inevitable. The prospect thrilled Iranian nationalists, who believed that history was finally giving them a chance to pull their country out from under the rule of British imperialists. In January 1951 they called a rally to launch a mass-based campaign aimed at forcing the nationalization of Anglo-Iranian. A huge crowd turned out. The first speakers were from the National Front, and they were duly cheered as they laid out their case. That was just the beginning. After the politicians were finished, a succession of mullahs came to the podium to proclaim that every good Muslim had a sacred duty to support nationalization. The last of them read a *fatwa* asserting that from his place in paradise, the Prophet Mohammad himself had condemned the Razmara government for selling Iran's birthright to infidel foreigners. Neither the secularists of the National Front nor the religious fundamentalists who followed Ayatollah Kashani were comfortable in alliance with each other, but they put aside their very deep differences in the interests of the great cause.

Poor Razmara was now in an impossible position. The masses had long since decided that he was at best a pawn of the British and at worst a traitor. He replied by insisting time and again that protesters, both inside the Majlis and outside, were pursuing a mad dream, and that the country's interest required it to make a deal with the British. But although he worked feverishly to salvage the British position, neither Anglo-Iranian nor the Foreign Office gave him a shred of support. Ambassador Shepherd went so far as to send him a letter advising that he take "a strong line" against ingrates who did not appreciate "the immense service to mankind of the British people in recent times."

Razmara soldiered bravely on. On March 3 he appeared before Mossadegh's oil committee and once again explained his opposition to the idea of nationalization. He said it would be illegal, would drive the British to unpredictable retaliation, and would devastate Iran's economy. That night Ambassador Shepherd cabled home that he himself had written "the gist" of Razmara's speech.

Iranians suspected as much and reacted with another outburst of protest. At a mass rally on March 7, calls for nationalization were replaced with chants of "Death to the British!" Razmara was out of time. Even the Shah knew it. Quietly, he had begun asking politicians of various stripes whom they would suggest as a new prime minister. Each gave the same answer: Mossadegh.

Everyone recognized that Razmara's days were numbered, but few anticipated how violently his career would end. On the same day that thousands of demonstrators gathered in Tehran to shout their hatred for Britain, Razmara and a friend of the Shah named Assadollah Alam drove to a Tehran mosque for the funeral of a religious leader. A young man with a pistol stepped from the crowd and fired. Razmara fell dead. Police officers seized the gunman, a carpenter named Khalil Tahmasibi who was a member of a religious terror group called Fedayeen-i-Islam.

"If I have rendered a humble service," he told interrogators, "it was for the Almighty in order to deliver the deprived Muslim people of Iran from foreign serfdom."

The circumstances of Razmara's assassination were never clarified. Evidence emerged to suggest that the fatal shot had been fired not by Tahmasibi but by a soldier acting on behalf of the Shah or members of his inner circle, and that Assadollah Alam had knowingly driven him to his fatal rendezvous. Years later a retired Iranian colonel wrote in his memoir that the fatal shot had come from a Colt revolver, available only to soldiers.

"An army sergeant, in civilian clothes, was chosen for the deed," he asserted. "He had been told to shoot and kill Razmara with a Colt, the moment Tahmasibi began to shoot. . . . Those who had examined the wounds in Razmara's body were in no doubt that he had been killed by a Colt bullet, not by the bullet of a weak gun."

Razmara had represented the last hope for conciliation. His cause was all but lost even before his assassination, and the day after the fatal shots were fired, Mossadegh's oil committee took the fateful step toward which it had been marching. By unanimous vote, it recommended that the Majlis nationalize the Anglo-Iranian Oil Company.

The next day, thousands of people gathered at a festive rally to hear Ayatollah Kashani applaud the committee vote and demand that the Majlis act quickly. No public figure could now oppose nationalization without fear of provoking the ire of the masses or worse. Even the newly named prime minister, Hussein Ala, a British-educated diplomat who understood the difficulties that nationalization was sure to bring, dared not speak against it.

At the British embassy, Ambassador Shepherd still believed that he had a chance to hold back the flood. He launched a campaign to persuade Majlis members to stay home on the day of the nationalization vote, thereby preventing a quorum. First he sent a message to the Shah urging him to "use all his influence" with monarchist and conservative deputies. Then he met with Prime Minister Ala and informed him curtly that "the company's operations cannot be legally terminated by an action such as nationalization." He suggested for the first time, though, that Anglo-Iranian might now be ready to consider the idea of a fifty-fifty profit split.

"A fifty-fifty arrangement might have been accepted a little while ago," Ala replied, "but now something more would be required."

The Majlis met on March 15 to cast its historic vote. Ninety-six deputies turned up, including several who had promised the Shah they would stay away. Every one voted in favor of nationalization.

Five days later the largely ceremonial Senate, which had come into existence only a few years earlier and half of whose members were appointed by the Shah, also voted its unanimous approval.

Mossadegh was now a hero of epic proportions, unable even to step onto the streets without being mobbed by admirers. Tribal leaders in the hinterlands celebrated his triumph, Ayatollah Kashani lionized him as a liberator on the scale of Cyrus and Darius, and even the communists of Tudeh embraced him. Over the next few weeks the Majlis voted overwhelmingly for every bill he presented. He was so clearly the man of the moment that Prime Minister Ala found no reason to remain in office, and in mid-April he resigned.

The British government, however, had no intention of surrendering. Its resolve was stiffened when Foreign Secretary Bevin, who had shown some sympathy for the Iranian position, resigned for health reasons and was replaced by the colossally unprepared Herbert Morrison. Morrison had spent thirty years working his way up through Labor Party ranks and had never claimed expertise in world affairs. His proudest achievements were building a new Waterloo Bridge and reorganizing London's transit system. He considered the challenge from Iran a simple matter of ignorant natives rebelling against the forces of civilization. In one of his first public statements as foreign secretary, he urged that British troops be moved toward Iran and stand "ready if necessary to intervene in Persian oil fields."

At Morrison's urging, top-level policymakers from the Foreign Office, the Admiralty, the Bank of England, and the Ministry of Fuel and Power joined to form a "Working Party on Persia." It commissioned several studies to use as background in dealing with the crisis, including one on the psychology of Iranians. The author, a British diplomat, asserted that the typical Iranian was motivated by

> an unabashed dishonesty, fatalistic outlook, [and] indifference to suffering. . . . The ordinary Persian is vain, unprincipled, eager to promise what he knows he is incapable or has no intention of performing, wedded to procrastination, lacking in perseverance and energy, but amenable to discipline. Above all he enjoys intrigue and readily turns to prevarication and dishonesty when-

ever there is a possibility of personal gain. Although an accomplished liar, he does not expect to be believed. They easily acquire a superficial knowledge of technical subjects, deluding themselves into the belief that it is profound.

To deal with such people on an equal or respectful basis would, of course, be absurd. Instead, the Foreign Office devised a three-pronged strategy to bring them back under control. First, Mohammad Reza Shah should be persuaded to dissolve the Majlis. Second, he should appoint Sayyed Zia, the aging British favorite who had helped Reza Shah come to power thirty years earlier, as prime minister. Third, the Truman administration in Washington should be urged "at least not to indicate any disagreement or divergence from our point of view." As this policy was being formulated, Anglo-Iranian decided to prove its resolve by reducing the living allowances it paid to Iranian workers. Thousands walked off the job in protest.

Soon afterward, the British began sending warships to the waters off Abadan. By mid-April three frigates and two cruisers were lurking within sight of the refinery. This raised tensions even higher. Oil workers poured defiantly onto the dusty streets, and a series of brawls left six Iranians, two British oil workers, and a British sailor dead. Some Iranians concluded that the British had embarked on a deliberate campaign of provocation in order to provide a pretext for military intervention.

Ambassador Shepherd believed he could bring the situation back under control if Iran had a new and more decisively pro-British prime minister. He insisted that the Shah nominate Sayyed Zia, and the Shah dutifully agreed. The Majlis scheduled a vote on his nomination for April 28. That morning, Shepherd issued a statement asserting that His Majesty's government would not negotiate anything under the threat of nationalization. With this show of strength and his friend Sayyed Zia at the head of government, he calculated, events would begin moving in a different direction. It was a highly unrealistic scenario and showed once again how completely the British had misjudged Iran's mood.

Not even the most fervent nationalist, however, could have predicted what happened when the Majlis assembled to debate Sayyed Zia's nomination. All eyes were, of course, on Mossadegh, the hero of the hour. Everyone expected him to lead the opposition with one of his withering tirades against the British and their traitorous errand-boys. But when the speaker asked who wished to begin the debate, Mossadegh sat quietly and expressionless. A prominent right-wing deputy named Jamal Emami, who was on the British payroll, took the floor instead. Emami did not even mention Sayyed Zia. Instead he launched into a bitter attack on Mossadegh, pillorying him for having plunged the Majlis into immobility and paralyzed the country with his constant carping. If the old man wanted a real challenge, Emami said scornfully, he should try being prime minister himself and see how difficult the job was. Mossadegh had several times turned aside suggestions that he take over the government, and Emami said he knew the reason why: Mossadegh was one of those irresponsible windbags who delight in making speeches about how wrong everyone else is, but never offer anything positive.

The chamber fell silent as Emami finished. Mossadegh waited for a long moment and then rose to his feet. Speaking slowly and deliberately, he said that he was honored and grateful for the suggestion that he become prime minister and would in all humility accept. Everyone was stunned, Emami most of all. Soon the shock turned to pandemonium. A formal motion was made that Mossadegh be named prime minister, and the speaker called for an immediate vote. It passed by a margin of seventy-nine to twelve.

Sensing the power he held at that moment, Mossadegh said that he would serve as prime minister only if the Majlis also voted to approve an act he had drawn up to implement the nationalization of Anglo-Iranian. Under its provisions, a parliamentary committee would audit Anglo-Iranian's books, weigh the claims of both sides for compensation, begin sending Iranians abroad to learn the skills of running an oil industry, and draw up articles of incorporation for a new National Iranian Oil Company. The Majlis approved it unanimously that very afternoon.

The unthinkable had now happened. Mossadegh, the symbol of Iranian nationalism and resistance to royal power, had suddenly arrived at the pinnacle of power. It was a moment of exhilaration but also of profound uncertainty. Everyone understood that a clash of titans was approaching. No one dared to guess what it might mean for Iran and the rest of the world.

CHAPTER 6

Unseen Enemies Everywhere

On the morning of June 26, 1950, millions of Iranians and millions of Americans gathered apprehensively around their radios. All knew they would hear news that might reshape their lives forever. Most were grave and fearful. The crisis that was gathering in Iran, however, had nothing to do with the one suddenly gripping the United States.

That day in Iran, the Shah announced that he would nominate General Ali Razmara, the ill-fated army commander, as prime minister. In shops, factories, and tea houses across the country, people huddled to ask one another what this might mean. Would Razmara be able to strike a last-minute deal with the British? If not, what would happen? Might British troops invade Iran? Would there be a revolution? Was the nation headed toward redemption or catastrophe?

Americans were preoccupied with very different news. Communist soldiers had just poured across the thirty-eighth parallel in Korea and were racing southward. The United Nations Security Council met in emergency session and warned the invaders that if they did not withdraw, war would follow. Since both of the world's superpowers had nuclear arsenals, many Americans feared that Armageddon was at hand.

The huge gap between what preoccupied Iranians and what preoccupied Americans on that June day reflected the obsessions that gripped their countries as the second half of the twentieth century began. Iranians were marching toward a thrilling but also terrifying confrontation with Great Britain and its Anglo-Iranian Oil Company. Americans faced a prospect no less sobering. The war in Korea was final proof that their country was now locked in a worldwide struggle against a fearsome adversary.

In ways that neither nation yet understood, these two crises would ultimately become one. The United States, challenged by what most Americans saw as a relentless communist advance, slowly ceased to view Iran as a country with a unique history that faced a unique political challenge. Its duel with Britain became subsumed in the East–West conflict.

A great sense of fear, particularly the fear of encirclement, shaped American consciousness during this period. Allied leaders who met at Potsdam two months after the end of World War II pledged to cooperate "on a democratic and peaceful basis," but behind their generous words lay deep mistrust. Soviet power had already subdued Latvia, Lithuania, and Estonia. Communist governments were imposed on Bulgaria and Romania in 1946, Hungary and Poland in 1947, and Czechoslovakia in 1948. Albania and Yugoslavia also turned to communism. Greek communists made a violent bid for power. Soviet soldiers blocked land routes to Berlin for sixteen months. In 1949 the Soviet Union successfully tested a nuclear weapon. That same year, pro-Western forces in China lost their civil war to communists led by Mao Zedong. From Washington, it seemed that enemies were on the march everywhere.

In response to this changing international climate, President Truman approved the creation of the Central Intelligence Agency in 1947. Its vague original mandate, which was to carry out "functions and duties related to intelligence affecting the national security," was expanded a year later to include "sabotage, anti-sabotage, demolition and evacuation measures . . . subversion [and] assistance to underground resistance movements, guerrillas and refugee liberation movements, and support of indigenous anti-communist elements in threatened countries of the free world." In January 1950 the National Security Council prepared a seminal document, known as NSC-68, that asserted the need for the United States to confront communist movements not only in regions of vital security interest but wherever they appeared.

"The assault on free institutions is worldwide now," it concluded, "and in the context of the present polarization of power, a defeat of free institutions anywhere is a defeat everywhere."

The Cold War drove the United States to recognize not only the power of its enemies but also the vital importance of its friends. In 1949 it brought eleven of them together into a potent military alliance, the North Atlantic Treaty Organization (NATO). Solidarity between the United States and Britain was the bedrock of this new alliance. Differences over how to deal with countries like Iran could not be allowed to weaken it.

President Truman was among many who believed that the Soviets wished to draw Iran into their orbit. The day after North Koreans invaded South Korea, he told one of his aides that Korea was not the only country worrying him. He walked to a globe near his desk in the Oval Office, placed his index finger on Iran, and said, "Here is where they will start trouble if we aren't careful."

Britain and Russia had trampled on Iranian sovereignty for more than a century, and many Iranians naturally came to detest them both. For the United States, however, most felt only admiration. The few Americans they had come to know were generous and self-sacrificing, interested not in wealth or power but in helping Iran.

The American best-known to ordinary Iranians was an earnest young schoolteacher named Howard Baskerville, who was killed in 1909 while fighting alongside his Iranian friends in the Constitutional Revolution. He was revered as a martyr and called "the American Lafayette." Many took his sacrifice as proof of how much more admirable Americans were than other foreigners.

At the time Baskerville was shot down by royalist soldiers, a visionary American educator, Samuel Jordan, was beginning a forty-three-year stay in Tehran. His Alborz College was among the first modern secondary schools in the country, and thousands of its graduates went on to shape Iranian life. The Presbyterian mission for which Jordan worked also ran a hospital and one of the country's only schools for girls.

"Americans were regarded with nearly universal admiration and affection," one of its graduates wrote years later. "The American contribution to the improvement and, it was felt, the dignity of our impoverished, strife-torn country had gone far beyond their small numbers. . . . Without attempting to force their way of life on people or convert us to their religion, they had learned Persian and started schools, hospitals and medical dispensaries all over Iran."

The dedication of these exemplary men and women was not the only reason many Iranians admired the United States. American officials had spoken out to defend Iran's rights. The United States sharply criticized the 1919 Anglo-Persian Agreement through which Britain acquired colonial powers in Iran. That same year at Versailles, President Woodrow Wilson was the only world leader who supported Iran's unsuccessful claim for monetary compensation from Britain and Russia for the effects of their occupation during World War I. In the mid-1920s an American envoy in Tehran was able to report that "Persians of all classes still have unbounded confidence in America."

Until the outbreak of World War II, the United States had no active policy toward Iran. After the war, however, American power began reaching every corner of the world. The crucial role that oil played in the Allied victory led policymakers in Washington to focus especially on the Middle East. They sharpened their interest as the Cold War intensified.

A giant figure in American diplomatic history, Dean Acheson, directed United States policy toward Iran during this period. Acheson sympathized with the forces of Third World nationalism. With his gaunt frame, pin-striped suits, homburg, and jaunty mustache, he looked every inch the patrician, although in fact he had not been born into wealth. In his youth a Republican who admired Theodore Roosevelt, he later became a Democrat and served in Franklin Roosevelt's administration. Truman recognized him as a kindred spirit and, after winning the 1948 election, named him secretary of state. Both men were determined to show people in poor countries that the United States, not the Soviet Union, was their true friend.

Soon after taking office, Acheson named an energetic and liberal-minded Texan, George McGhee, as his assistant secretary for Near Eastern, South Asian and African affairs. McGhee was just thirty-eight years old when he assumed the influential post. He had studied geology at the University of Oklahoma and had gone on to win a Rhodes scholarship to Oxford. When he finished his studies, the Anglo-Iranian Oil Company offered him a job as a geophysicist in Iran, but he declined, returned to the United States, and started his own oil company. Its success made him wealthy enough to work for the State Department without pay. His background in the oil industry, however, led some in the British Foreign Office to mistrust him. They suspected him of trying to weaken Anglo-Iranian so that American oil companies, perhaps some in which he had a hidden interest, could take its place in Iran.

McGhee attended many of the meetings that Mohammad Reza Shah held with American officials during his visit to Washington at the end of 1949 and was put off by the young monarch's "grandiose and unrealistic" military ambitions. Soon afterward, he invited officials of Anglo-Iranian to a meeting. He told them that he had read their company's most recent annual report and was impressed with how much profit they were making. Perhaps it was time, he suggested, for the company to begin sharing its wealth more equitably with Iran. His guests scorned the idea. One of them went so far as to say that if Anglo-Iranian began giving in to Iran's demands, it would soon be left with "nothing in the till."

This debate sharpened over the next months. McGhee repeatedly warned directors of Anglo-Iranian that if they hoped to save Prime Minister Razmara and persuade the Majlis to approve their Supplemental Agreement, they must make concessions. At one point, angered by the company's insistence that it could not afford to pay Iran more, he asked the State Department's petroleum expert, Richard Funkhouser, to prepare a report on its operations. The report concluded that Anglo-Iranian was an "exceptionally profitable" company, that it sold its oil for between ten and thirty times the cost of producing it, and that its arrogance had made it "genuinely hated in Iran."

McGhee, deeply worried about what he saw as a looming disaster, decided to travel to London to press his case in person. He arrived there in September of 1950 to a frosty welcome. Senior officials of both the British government and Anglo-Iranian resolutely rejected his pleas for compromise. They told him that the company would not train more Iranians for supervisory positions, would not open its books to Iranian auditors, and would not offer Iran more money for its oil. "One penny more and the company goes broke," said the chairman, Sir William Fraser. That astonishing piece of mendacity made clear to McGhee that more talks were fruitless. He packed up and returned home.

British officials, steeped in the world's most fully developed colonial tradition, were baffled by what they saw as the Truman administration's refusal to agree that Britain should benefit from the work it had done in foreign countries. What seemed like rapacious imperialism to the Americans—and even more so to the Iranians—seemed only common sense to the British. They insisted that they were doing the world a great service by their work in Iran, as Sir Donald Fergusson, the permanent undersecretary at the Ministry of Fuel and Power, wrote in one memorandum:

> It was British enterprise, skill and effort which discovered oil under the soil of Persia, which has got the oil out, which has built the refinery, which has developed markets for Persian oil in thirty or forty countries, with wharves, storage tanks and pumps, road and rail tanks and other distribution facilities, and also an immense fleet of tankers. This was done at a time when there was no easy outlet for Persian oil in competition with the vastly greater American industry. None of these things would or could have been done by the Persian government or the Persian people.

The chasm between American and British perceptions of the gathering crisis in Iran was vividly symbolized by the new ambassadors both countries sent to Tehran in 1950. Henry Grady, the American, was an economist with firsthand experience in Greece and India, two countries where politics was being reshaped by nationalism. Grady believed that if the United States did not align itself with nationalist forces in the developing world, those forces would turn toward Marxism and the Soviet Union. He was a fervent anticommunist but an equally fervent anti-imperialist.

In both temperament and politics, Grady was the polar opposite of his British counterpart in Tehran, the fire-breathing Sir Francis Shepherd. The reports these two ambassadors sent back to their respective capitals were so different that they hardly seemed to be portraying the same country. Grady saw an impoverished land long exploited by the British, who sucked the country's lifeblood and treated the pitiful Shah like a servant. Shepherd, however, considered Anglo-Iranian a wise and paternal company that had brought

Iran nothing but good. He had no use for ungrateful Iranians—or meddling American diplomats—who believed otherwise.

In February 1951 George McGhee summoned all American ambassadors in the Middle East to a meeting in Istanbul. One of the main agenda items was the friction that had developed between the United States and Britain over the question of Iran. The gathered diplomats concluded that Anglo-Iranian's militancy was "one of the greatest political liabilities affecting the United States/United Kingdom interests in the Middle East." The company's "reactionary and outmoded policies," they declared in a secret memorandum, were not only creating a dangerously explosive situation but constituted "a handicap in the control of Communism in Iran." This consensus guided American policy through the Truman administration.

The Iranian crisis deepened over the next few weeks. Prime Minister Razmara was assassinated on March 7, and on March 15 the Majlis took its historic vote, "accepting the principle that oil should be nationalized throughout Iran." Some deputies may have believed that the British would find a way to live with this vote because the British Parliament itself had recently nationalized key British industries. As it did so, Foreign Secretary Ernest Bevin had mused, "What argument can I advance against anyone claiming the right to nationalize the resources of their country? We are doing the same thing here with our power in the shape of coal, electricity, railways, transport and steel." Bevin was out of office by the time the Iranian crisis exploded, however, and those he left behind in government agreed unanimously that although nationalization might be a wise path at home, it could not be abided abroad.

Immediately after the Majlis voted to nationalize Anglo-Iranian, McGhee flew to Tehran. He arrived on March 17 to find Ambassador Shepherd in a foul mood. Shepherd blamed the vote on Americans, specifically on Aramco, the Arabian-American Oil Company. Aramco's announcement that it would begin splitting its profits with the Saudi Arabian government on a fifty-fifty basis, Shepherd complained, had "thrown a wrench" into Britain's negotiating position. McGhee replied that he had warned Anglo-Iranian months earlier that the fifty-fifty deal was forthcoming. The company, he told Shepherd, had brought its troubles on itself by being "too rigid and too slow to recognize that a new situation had been created in Iran which required a new approach."

That evening McGhee called on the Shah. Their meeting was most disconcerting, as McGhee wrote afterward:

> I had been with the Shah about a year and a half earlier during his much-publicized official visit to Washington. He had then been a proud, erect young man, insistent that his requests be taken seriously. As I saw him in the darkened audience chamber in which he received me, lounging on a sofa, he was a dejected, almost broken man. I sensed that he feared he too might be assassinated. . . . Did he think with our support he could avert nationalization?
>
> The Shah said he couldn't do it. He pleaded that we not ask him to do it. He couldn't even form a government. Everyone was afraid. There were unseen enemies everywhere. . . . He looked lost, as if he thought the whole affair hopeless. I left him alone in his darkened room. I will always remember his sad, brooding face. . . . The specter of death and impending chaos hung gloomily over Tehran like a dark cloud. I was sad when I said goodbye.

On his way home, McGhee stopped in London and met there with Sir William Fraser, the Anglo-Iranian chairman, and Foreign Secretary Morrison. The meetings were so stormy that Morrison decided to send a delegation to Washington to present Britain's case. He named Sir Oliver Franks, the British ambassador in Washington, who had been McGhee's tutor in morals at Oxford, as its chairman.

The meetings stretched over nine days. British emissaries argued that allowing Iran to nationalize the oil company "would be widely regarded as a victory for the Russians" and would also "cause a loss of one hundred million pounds per annum in the United Kingdom's balance of payments, thus seriously affecting our rearmament program and our cost of living." Franks insisted that Iran had "no solid grievances" against either Britain or the oil company, whereas Britain was vitally concerned about losing "a prime strategic necessity." He described Anglo-Iranian as a crucial asset to the West "not only because of its magnitude as an element of our balance of payments . . . but also because of the power it gave us to control the movement of raw materials." Iranian oil was vital "to our common defense," and losing it would cripple "our ability to rearm."

McGhee listened for several days in quiet frustration. When he finally spoke, it was to warn once again that the British must compromise with Iran or face disaster. He urged them to start splitting their profits with Iran on a fifty-fifty basis, "which had an aura of fairness understandable to the ordinary man." The British would not be persuaded. "In the end," he wrote later, "I was, with great regret, forced to advise Franks in our final meeting on April 18 that their proposals did not, in the case of accommodation to nationalization, meet the requirements we saw for success."

Soon after the talks in Washington ended, Iran set out on its brave new course. On May 1, 1951, Mohammad Reza Shah signed the momentous law revoking Anglo-Iranian's concession and establishing the National Iranian Oil Company to take its place. The next day Britain demanded that the law be suspended. On May 6 Mohammad Mossadegh submitted his cabinet to the Majlis. It was immediately approved, and on that same day Mossadegh took office as prime minister.

Historic as Mossadegh's rise to power was for Iranians, it was at least as stunning for the British. They were used to manipulating Iranian prime ministers like chess pieces, and now, suddenly, they faced one who seemed to hate them. "All of Iran's misery, wretchedness, lawlessness and corruption during the last fifty years," the state-controlled Radio Tehran declared in a broadcast soon after Mossadegh took office, "has been caused by oil and the extortions of the oil company."

For a brief moment, Prime Minister Attlee seemed disposed to compromise. Attlee was a socialist who had helped draft the plans under which Britain had nationalized some of its own basic industries. At one cabinet meeting he suggested that Britain might make a public statement accepting nationalization of Anglo-Iranian, thereby giving Mossadegh "an opportunity of saving face," and then arrange some sort of complicated deal under which the company would retain most of its privileges. Herbert Morrison vigorously objected. He warned Attlee that any concessions to Iran would set an intolerable precedent and encourage nationalists everywhere. Attlee allowed himself to be persuaded and signed off on a cable to Ambassador Franks in Washington. It directed him to tell Acheson that "Persian oil is of vital importance to our economy, and that we regard it as essential to do everything possible to prevent the Persians from getting away with a breach of their contractual obligations."

Acheson, however, believed that Mossadegh represented "a very deep revolution, nationalist in character, which was sweeping not only Iran but the whole Middle East." He and others in the Truman administration never stopped urging their British counterparts to turn away from their policy of confrontation and to offer Mossadegh a legitimate compromise. They did this despite realizing that Mossadegh would not be easy to deal with, as a profile in the *New York Times* made clear:

> The tidal wave of nationalistic fervor that engulfed the Anglo-Iranian Oil Company in the space of a few weeks has now unexpectedly cast one of Iran's most redoubtable demagogues, the aged Mohammad Mossadegh, upon the pinnacle of power. In the popular view, the new Premier represents a figure of retributive justice who galvanized the impressionable Parliament and led it to victory over the dragon, Anglo-Iranian, which, in the eyes of many, had for years been feeding upon the vitals of the country. . . .
>
> A foreign diplomat, admitted recently to the new Premier's presence, asked Dr. Mossadegh to explain exactly how he intended to proceed with the expropriation of Anglo-Iranian. For half an hour Dr. Mossadegh described the misdeeds of British imperialism over the past 100 years. When he had finished, the diplomat repeated the question. Again the Premier denounced British imperialism. The interview ended there.
>
> What will Dr. Mossadegh do next? The question remains open and the answer is anybody's guess.

Messages that flew between Washington and London during mid-1951 did nothing to narrow differences between the two allies over how to deal with Mossadegh. On May 18 the State Department issued a public statement declaring that Americans "fully recognize the sovereign rights of Iran and sympathize with Iran's desire that increased benefits accrue to that country from the development of its petroleum." Morrison read it with dismay and in a cable to Ambassador Franks that afternoon said that he was "really rather annoyed at the American attitude of relative indifference to a situation which may be most grave to us all."

Soon afterward, Morrison sent a message to Acheson in which he sought to lay out the British position in the clearest possible terms. The issue Britain faced in Iran, he wrote, "concerns *the* major asset which we hold in the field of raw materials. Control of that asset is of supreme importance. . . . Parliamentary and public feeling in England would not readily accept a position where we surrender effective control of an asset of such magnitude."

The Americans were unmoved. On May 31 Truman sent a note to Attlee urging that negotiations "be entered into at once" to prevent a worsening of the "explosive situation" in Iran. Attlee replied that allowing Iran to get away with nationalization would have "the most serious repercussions in the whole free world." He realized, however, that given Truman's insistence, the British would have to make at least a show of engaging Mossadegh.

At Attlee's suggestion, Anglo-Iranian sent a delegation of officials led by the company's deputy chairman, Basil Jackson, to Tehran for negotiations. Mossadegh welcomed them by arranging for Iranian gendarmes to take over the Anglo-Iranian office at the western town of Kermanshah on the day they arrived. As if that were not enough to set the tone, Ambassador Grady restated the American position in an interview with the *Wall Street Journal.*

"Since nationalization is an accomplished fact, it would be wise for Britain to adopt a conciliatory attitude," Grady asserted. "Mossadegh's National Front party is the closest thing to a moderate and stable political element in the national parliament."

Iranians at the negotiating table said that they were willing to talk, but only after the visitors from London accepted nationalization of the "former company" as a fait accompli. Jackson refused, insisting that Iran was bound by the 1933 accord and could not renounce it until its sixty-year term expired. He had a counteroffer. Anglo-Iranian would pay Iran £10 million and another £3 million monthly while negotiations proceeded; it was also willing to transfer its assets to the newly created National Iranian Oil Company, but only if it could establish a new company that would have "exclusive use of those assets." This was a not-so-subtle declaration that Britain still did not accept the fact of nationalization. It reflected the Foreign Office's unaltered position, which was that the British "can be flexible in profits, administration or partnership, but not in the issue of control." To no one's surprise, Iranian negotiators rejected the offer.

On June 20 Mossadegh named a French-educated engineer, Mehdi Bazargan, as the managing director of the National Iranian

Oil Company. Bazargan flew immediately to Abadan, where British administrators were still running the refinery, and declared himself their new boss. His first order was that captains of British tankers must henceforth provide him with receipts before they sailed, listing the amount of oil they were carrying so he could keep track of how much was being exported.

The British considered this intolerable. They believed, as their United Nations ambassador asserted, that the oil was "clearly the legal property of the Anglo-Iranian Oil Company." When tanker captains refused to provide receipts, Bazargan threatened to have Anglo-Iranian's general manager, Eric Drake, arrested for sabotage. As that crime would carry the death penalty under a bill pending in the Majlis (it was later withdrawn), Ambassador Shepherd advised Drake to leave Iran. He did so and began running the company from an office in Basra, across the Shatt-al-Arab in Iraq. From there, he continued to refuse the demand for receipts. When the Iranians insisted, Sir William Fraser issued an order of his own from London. Tanker captains were to pump back all the oil in their holds and leave Abadan empty.

Iran had until that moment been the world's fourth largest oil exporter, supplying 90 percent of Europe's petroleum. Now, since it owned not a single tanker, it could not export a drop. That was fine with Fraser, who still believed he could bend the Iranians to his will. "When they need money," he predicted, "they will come crawling to us on their bellies."

For Fraser and his colleagues at Anglo-Iranian, as well as for officials of the British government, the very idea that Iran would nationalize its oil industry seemed absurd and impossible, even as it was happening. They had trouble taking it seriously. In their view the entire campaign was most likely a monumental bluff, a ploy to squeeze more money out of London, or, if not that, then simply a petulant outburst that would end when the consequences became clear.

"At no time before a year or two before 1951 did anyone contemplate that we would not stay there forever," Eric Drake recalled afterward. "We were there by an international agreement between the government of Iran and the Anglo-Iranian Oil Company, so there was no reason it should ever come to an end as far as we could see."

Britain's press enthusiastically jumped aboard the anti-Mossadegh bandwagon. The London *Times* blamed "irresponsible Persian politicians" for stirring up the country's uneducated masses. The *Economist* declared that Anglo-Iranian had become a "monumental scapegoat" and asserted: "No Persian with any common sense really believes that the Anglo-Iranian Oil Company is responsible for the horrifying poverty of the masses." The *Observer* described Mossadegh as a "Robespierre fanatic" and a "tragic Frankenstein" who was "obsessed with one xenophobic idea."

Across the Atlantic, the tone was quite different. The *Washington Post* asserted that most Iranians saw the oil company as "a thriving state within a stricken state—as a symbol of their poverty." The *New York Times* said that many Middle East specialists considered Mossadegh a liberator comparable to Thomas Jefferson or Thomas Paine. The *Chicago Daily News* reported that even many Britons were disturbed by the way their government was handling the issue. "British critics do not think that McGhee was really responsible for the Iranian crisis," its London correspondent wrote. "They agreed that the whole affair was badly handled by the Anglo-Iranian Oil Company with the connivance, by default, of the Foreign Office."

There was indeed dissent in Britain. Anglo-Iranian's own labor adviser, Sir Frederick Leggett, wrote to a friend in the Foreign Office that the company was in its "deplorable position" because it had "failed to make a gesture of recognition of Persian national aspirations." Minister of State Kenneth Younger complained in a memo to Morrison about "the short-sightedness and the lack of political awareness shown by the Anglo-Iranian Oil Company" and asserted that it "never even seriously tried" to make a "proper estimate" of the situation. Earl Mountbatten told his superiors at the Admiralty that instead of listening to the "notoriously bellicose" Herbert Morrison's advice on how to "cow these insolent natives," Britain should realize that "economic and military threats could only make things worse."

Even some British diplomats were sending contrary reports to the Foreign Office. The labor attaché in Tehran filed a cable describing conditions at Abadan as deplorable, saying that workers there lived in "cottages made of mud bricks, with no electricity, without outside water supply and sanitary arrangements . . . in other words, in veritable slums." And from Tel Aviv, the British minister forwarded a *Jerusalem Post* report that he said convinced him that Anglo-Iranian "deserved what happened." It was written by an Israeli who had spent several years working at Abadan alongside Iranians he described as "the poorest creatures on earth."

> They lived during the seven hot months of the year under the trees. . . . In winter times these masses moved into big halls, built by the company, housing up to 3,000–4,000 people without walls of partition between them. Each family occupied the space of a blanket. There were no lavatories. . . . In debates with British colleagues we often tried to show them the mistake they were making in treating the Persians the way they did. The answer was usually: "We English have had hundreds of years of experience on how to treat the Natives. Socialism is all right back home, but out here you have to be the master."

On June 28 Mossadegh issued an appeal to British technicians and managers at Abadan. He told them that Iran was "anxious to benefit" from their expertise and promised that if they stayed at their jobs, "our country will welcome you warmly." Fraser, determined that Iran not be able to run the refinery by itself, responded by ordering most of the company's British employees to leave Iran.

With Iranians already in control of the Anglo-Iranian office in Kermanshah, the next step was for them to take over the Abadan and Tehran offices. They did so during the last days of June. The head of the Abadan office had wisely moved his sensitive papers to the local British consulate, which Iranians could not enter. Richard Seddon, head of the Tehran office, was not as quick. When a delegation of Iranians arrived to search his home, they found many files still there, including some burning in the fireplace. An official of Iran's foreign ministry who was present that night summarized what they found:

> Although compromising documents had allegedly been removed, enough papers were left behind to make it easy for Mossadegh to prove that AIOC had interfered in all aspects of Iranian political life. The documents revealed that the company had influenced senators, Majlis deputies and former cabinet ministers, and that those who had opposed it had been subtly forced out of office. Newspapers had been paid to publish articles alleging that many

of the National Front's leaders were actually paid stooges of AIOC....

Among the documents was evidence that former Prime Minister Ali Mansur had begged AIOC to allow him to remain in office, promising in return to appoint a new finance minister more agreeable to the company. Another set of letters revealed that AIOC had helped Bahram Sharogh to become director of Iran's Radio and Propaganda Department, and that on a trip to London he had been recruited to serve the company. There were also directives and reports on influencing guilds, through the Mayor of Tehran, to rise against those in the bazaar who supported the National Front.

The government quickly made these documents public, and many Iranians took them as further proof of the oil company's perfidy. Mossadegh said they proved that Anglo-Iranian had engaged in a "sinister and inadmissible" campaign to subvert Iranian democracy. Majlis deputies were driven to new levels of anticolonial outrage. So were news commentators, one of whom wrote in a Tehran paper: "Now that the curtain is lifted and the real identity of traitors posing as newspaper men, Majlis deputies, governors and even prime ministers is laid bare, these men should be riddled with bullets and their carcasses thrown to the dogs."

President Truman, still hoping to find a solution to the crisis, called a meeting of his National Security Council at the end of June. The facts laid before him were alarming. George McGhee's attempts to sway the Foreign Office and the Anglo-Iranian Oil Company had failed utterly. Anglo-Iranian had begun evacuating its employees from Abadan, and a complete shutdown of the refinery there was a real possibility. British warships were patrolling ominously offshore. Middle East experts on the National Security Council staff warned in a report that if the oil conflict could not be resolved, "the loss of Iran to the free world is a distinct possibility." Their report asserted that the British were seriously considering invading Iran and warned that such an invasion "might split the free world, would produce a chaotic situation in Iran, and might cause the Iranian Government to turn to the Soviet Union for help."

This left Truman more worried than ever. His fears were heightened by two messages he received in the next few days. The first, from Mossadegh, made clear that Iran and Britain remained on a collision course. Mossadegh complained about Britain's efforts to sabotage his nationalization project and added ominously, "There is no danger whatever to the security of life and property of the British nationals in Iran. Any spreading of false rumors on the part of the agents of the former oil company might, however, cause anxieties and disturbances."

Mossadegh's warnings arrived in blunter terms on July 1 from Ambassador Grady. In an anguished cable he warned Truman that Iran was in "a most explosive situation" and reported for the first time that Britain was looking for ways to overthrow Mossadegh. "The British, led by Mr. Morrison, seem to be determined to follow the old tactics of getting the government out with which it has difficulties," he wrote. "Mossadegh has the backing of 95 to 98 percent of the people of this country. It is utter folly to try to push him out."

What Grady considered "utter folly" was indeed what the British were planning. They had abandoned all hope of bringing Mossadegh around to their way of thinking and were not prepared to make the concessions he wanted. Ambassador Shepherd wrote in a cable to London that "the moment has come for us to try and get him out," so that Iran would once again have a prime minister who was "reasonable and friendly" rather than "rigid and impractical."

News from The Hague on July 5 further complicated matters. The International Court of Justice, acting at Britain's request, issued an "indication" recommending that Iran allow the oil company to continue functioning as before while negotiations proceeded. Iran had refused to participate in the case. The Court was empowered to adjudicate only disputes between nations, and Iranian officials asserted that since the 1933 oil accord was a deal between Iran and a private company, it had no right to intervene. The Iranian minister at The Hague dismissed its recommendation as "null and void" and "an intervention in our internal affairs."

That steeled Foreign Secretary Morrison's resolve. He marched to the House of Commons and took the floor to declare that the situation in Iran was "becoming intolerable." To assure that Mossadegh understood the intensity of his indignation, he added that the Royal Navy was "lying close to Abadan" and would be ordered into action "should the Persians fail to discharge their responsibilities."

Truman now saw greater peril than ever. To him, the question of who would control Iranian oil was only secondary. He was more worried that the argument between the United States and Britain over how to deal with Mossadegh might spiral out of control and split the Atlantic alliance. Determined to make a last effort at compromise, he wrote to Mossadegh suggesting direct American mediation:

> This matter is so full of dangers to the welfare of your own country, of Great Britain and of all the free world, that I have been giving the most earnest thought to the problems involved. . . . I have watched with concern the breakdown of your discussions and the drift toward a collapse of oil operations with all the attendant losses to Iran and the world. Surely this is a disaster which statesmanship can find a way to avoid. . . .
>
> I lay great stress on the action of the [World] Court. . . . Therefore, I earnestly commend to you a most careful consideration of its suggestion. I suggest that its utterance be thought of not as a decision which is or is not binding depending on technical legal considerations, but as a suggestion of an impartial body dedicated to justice and equity and to a peaceful world. . . .
>
> I have a very sincere desire, Mr. Prime Minister, to be as helpful to you as possible in this circumstance. I have discussed this matter at length with Mr. W. Averell Harriman, who as you know is one of my closest advisors and one of our most eminent citizens. Should you be willing to receive him, I should be happy to have him go to Tehran as my personal representative to talk over with you this immediate and pressing situation.

Averell Harriman was an accomplished diplomat who had served as ambassador to Britain, ambassador to the Soviet Union, and director of the Marshall Plan in Europe. He also knew Mohammad Reza Shah and was thought to have some expertise in matters Iranian. Immediately after Truman told him of his new mission, Harriman received an illustrious delegation at his Washington home: Secretary of State Acheson, Assistant Secretary George McGhee, two other State Department officials, and the British ambassador, Sir Oliver Franks. All agreed that the situation in Iran had become exceedingly dangerous. A small incident at Abadan, they feared, could lead the British to intervene militarily, which might in turn lead Mossadegh to seek Soviet help. Even if that did not happen, closing the refinery was sure to set off a wave of social and political turmoil.

Harriman's mission faced challenges even before it began. The British disapproved of the whole idea. In an impatient note to Acheson, Foreign Secretary Morrison said that Britain was "in grave difficulties" and needed not more negotiations but "whole-hearted support" from the United States. "I must tell you that one of our main difficulties in dealing with this intractable problem has arisen from a belief persistently held by many Persians that there is a difference of opinion between the American and British over the oil question," he wrote. "An approach by a representative of the President would, I fear, merely encourage Dr. Mossadegh in this belief."

This message confirmed Acheson's view that Morrison, as he wrote later, "knew nothing of foreign affairs and had no feel for the situation." He had even less use for Britain's hard-line ambassador in Tehran, Sir Francis Shepherd, whom he considered an "unimaginative disciple of the 'whiff of grapeshot' school of diplomacy." Their dislike was mutual. As soon as Shepherd learned that Acheson was sending an emissary to Tehran to interfere in what he considered his business, he called a news conference to express his "astonishment and chagrin" at the temerity of the Americans.

"What is the use of Harriman flying here?" he asked. "We are not inviting mediation in this matter." This was a highly undiplomatic outburst, and under instructions from the Foreign Office, Shepherd retracted it the next day.

It was in this climate that Ambassador Grady visited Mossadegh to deliver Truman's letter. He wore a white suit and a jaunty tropical hat and waved happily to photographers as he arrived. The bedside meeting, however, did not go well. At Mossadegh's request Grady read the letter aloud, and when he reached the passage in which Truman urged him to accept the Court's advice, Mossadegh broke out into a thirty-second fit of convulsive laughter. When he finally stopped, there was a long moment of silence. Mossadegh finally told Grady that Iran believed the World Court had no jurisdiction in this case. Then he launched into a long and increasingly angry denunciation of the United States, which he said had once upheld moral principles but was wilting in the face of British pressure. His tirade was so vitriolic that Grady did not even see the point of pressing Harriman's possible visit.

Acheson was much irritated when he received news of this encounter. He sent Grady a sharp note telling him that the Harriman mission was

> the one new positive element contained in the President's proposal and is the step to which the President and I attach greatest significance. I cannot believe that Mossadegh's initial reaction will, upon reflection, be his final one. Considerations of courtesy will lead him, I am convinced, to give President's message full consideration, and to receive President's personal rep who can give both you and Mossadegh the benefit of great thought which President has put to this matter and receive any suggestions which Mossadegh may have. Therefore request that you see Mossadegh again as speedily as possible and in tactful way, which I know you will employ, urge these considerations upon him.

Grady did as he was told, and Acheson's faith in his persuasive powers turned out to have been justified. He convinced Mossadegh that the Harriman mission was in everyone's interest. Harriman arrived in Tehran on July 15, 1951. His welcoming committee consisted of ten thousand enraged Iranians shouting, "Death to Harriman!"

CHAPTER 7

You Do Not Know How Evil They Are

Averell Harriman's first hours in Tehran were not auspicious. His limousine had to take a round-about route from the airport in order to avoid angry mobs. He made it safely to the guest palace that had been prepared for him but had to dine while the sound of gunfire echoed through the air. Mounted police and soldiers in armored cars were firing at protesters. By midnight the city was awash in blood and tear gas. More than twenty people lay dead and another two hundred were wounded.

Why did the protest end with such awful carnage? The next day's newspapers blamed Mohammad Reza Shah and General Fazlollah Zahedi, the hard-line interior minister, who, they said, had intentionally provoked violence in order to give Harriman the impression that Iran was in chaos. Prime Minister Mossadegh was furious and fired Zahedi before the day was out.

That afternoon, Harriman paid his first call on Mossadegh. It was a meeting different from any in Harriman's long diplomatic career. He was ushered into an upstairs bedroom in Mossadegh's modest home. There Mossadegh was reclining in bed, dressed in a camel-hair cloak. He welcomed Harriman weakly and said that he hoped during their talks to learn whether the United States was truly a friend of the oppressed or merely a puppet of the vile British. Harriman replied that he had lived in London and knew that there were good Britons as well as bad ones. Mossadegh demurred. "You do not know them," he mumbled. "You do not know them."

Mossadegh never saw any contradiction between his boundless respect for Britain's constitutional tradition and his contempt for its government and imperial history. During one of his meetings with Harriman, he mentioned a grandson on whom he doted. Harriman asked where the grandson was studying. "Why, in England, of course," Mossadegh replied. "Where else?"

In his cables back to Washington, Harriman described Mossadegh as "completely rigid" and "obsessed with the idea of eliminating completely British oil company operations and influence within Iran." His impression of the old man, as related by a biographer, reflected his frustrations:

> Caught in deception, as he often was, [Mossadegh] would respond with disconcerting, childlike laughter or a heart-rending confession, often followed by a repeat of the devious tactic with an ill-concealed new twist. He projected helplessness; and while he was obviously as much a captive as a leader of the nationalist fanatics, he relented on nothing. Under pressure, he would take to his bed, seeming at times to have only a tenuous hold on life itself as he lay in his pink pajamas, his hands folded on his chest, eyes fluttering and breath shallow.
>
> At the appropriate moment, though, he could transform himself from a frail, decrepit shell of a man into a wily, vigorous adversary. He would arrive at the entrance of Harriman's guest palace shuffling slowly along while leaning heavily on his cane; but once inside, he would throw the cane aside and sometimes forget where it was. The first time he was presented to Marie Harriman, he took hold of her hand and didn't stop kissing until he was halfway to her elbow. Later, he could be caught stealing glances at her, sometimes losing his train of thought altogether.

Harriman had brought a petroleum expert, Walter J. Levy, with him to Iran, and Levy accompanied him to several of his meetings with Mossadegh. Again and again, Levy enumerated the obstacles that Mossadegh's government would face if it tried to run the Abadan refinery by itself. There were almost no Iranians trained for senior administrative and technical positions, and even if by some miracle a way could be found to keep the oil flowing, Iran had no tankers to bring it to market. Loss of Anglo-Iranian's royalty payments, which in 1950 had reached nearly £10 million, would destabilize Iran and possibly lead to Mossadegh's overthrow and replacement by a Tudeh government controlled from Moscow. That in turn might provoke Western military intervention.

None of these arguments moved Mossadegh in the slightest. Foreign intervention, he insisted, was the root of all Iran's troubles, and "it all started with that Greek Alexander," who had burned Persepolis twenty-four centuries before. Whenever Levy paused after making what he thought was an especially trenchant point about how much Iran would suffer if it failed to reach an accord with the British, Mossadegh would roll his eyes and reply simply, "Tant pis pour nous." Too bad for us.

Harriman and his aides, accustomed to the give-and-take of traditional diplomacy, were driven to distraction by Mossadegh's maddening style of negotiation. "Dr. Mossadegh had learned to take one step forward in order to take two backward," the American interpreter, Vernon Walters, wrote afterward. "After a day's discussion, Mr. Harriman would bring Mossadegh to a certain position. The next day when we returned to renew the discussion, not only was Mossadegh not at the position where he was at the end of the previous day, he wasn't even at the position where he had been the day before that. He was somewhere back around the middle of the day before yesterday."

Walters was then a lieutenant colonel in the United States Army. His language skills had brought him to the attention of superiors and would help carry him through a stellar career that culminated with appointments as deputy CIA director and ambassador to Germany. He had an irreverent wit, once remarking that Mossadegh's nose "made Jimmy Durante look like an amputee." More important, he knew when to interpret literally and when to reshape indiscreet comments. On one occasion, for example, Ambassador Grady's wife greeted the Iranian leader by saying, "Dr. Mossadegh, you have a very expressive face. Every time you are thinking of nothing, I can tell by the blank stare on your face." Walters rendered this comment into French as: "Dr. Mossadegh, you have a very expressive face. Every time you are thinking deep thoughts, I can tell by the look of concentration on your face."

Mossadegh's talks with Harriman did not falter because of Mossadegh's negotiating style or his failure to grasp the intricacies of the oil industry. The real reason was the fundamental difference in the way the two men perceived the dispute. To Harriman, it was a matter of practicalities, a set of technical challenges that could be resolved by rational analysis, discussion, and compromise. Mossadegh saw it from an entirely different perspective. He believed that Iran was at the sublime moment of liberation. Imbued with the Shiite ideal, he was determined to pursue justice even to the point of martyrdom. Details about refinery management or tanker capacity seemed to him laughably irrelevant at such a transcendent moment.

When Harriman insisted that there must be a way for Mossadegh to build a new relationship with the British, the old man shook his head. "You do not know how crafty they are," he said. "You do not know how evil they are. You do not know how they sully everything they touch."

Most Iranians shared this view, as Walter Levy realized when he struck up a conversation with a group of people he met on a Tehran street. Their colloquy, as Levy later related it, went like this:

Levy: You realize that if the British technicians leave Abadan you
    will have to try to run the industry by yourselves?
Iranians: Yes.
Levy: You realize that you will fail to run the industry without the
    British?
Iranians: Yes.
Levy: So Iranian oil will no longer be produced for the world
    market?
Iranians: Yes.
Levy: And if Iranian oil is no longer produced, there will be no
    money in the Iranian treasury?
Iranians: Yes.
Levy: And if you have no money there will be a financial and eco-
    nomic collapse which will play into the hands of the Commu-
    nists?
Iranians: Yes.

Levy: Well, what are you going to do about it?
Iranians: Nothing.

Unable to move Mossadegh through persuasion, Harriman decided to try influencing him indirectly. First he asked the Shah for help, but the Shah told him frankly that in the face of public opinion, there was no way he could say a word against nationalization. Then he called Iranian reporters to a news conference, and when they arrived, he began reading a statement that called on Iran to confront the crisis with "reason as well as enthusiasm." As soon as those words were out of his mouth, one journalist jumped to his feet and shouted, "We and the Iranian people all support Premier Mossadegh and oil nationalization!" The others began cheering and then marched out of the room. Harriman was left alone, shaking his head in dismay.

In pondering the question of who could influence Mossadegh and the masses, Harriman next came up with an outlandish idea: he would call on Ayatollah Kashani, the firebrand mullah who had become one of Iran's most powerful public figures. It is difficult to imagine two more different men. Harriman came from one of the world's richest families. He was a Skull-and-Bones man at Yale, a skier and a polo player who had spent his life in the highest society. Kashani had fought in the desert against the British, had been imprisoned by them, and was later sent into foreign exile at the Shah's order. He had a long black beard and wore a turban to match. His world was centered around a small, carpeted chamber where he sat for most of every day, meditating, praying, and plotting. Several times a week he emerged to visit a mosque or deliver a thunderous denunciation of imperialism to crowds of the faithful, who considered him a near-deity.

Harriman arrived at Kashani's door and was brought into a darkly curtained room where the holy man sat motionless. After removing his shoes, seating himself on a carpet, and expressing his respect, he said he hoped Kashani agreed that the oil crisis could be resolved only by some kind of agreement between Iran and Britain. Perhaps, he ventured, Kashani could help persuade Mossadegh to accept a British emissary. As soon as these first few sentences were translated, Kashani erupted with a stream of invective, the gist of which was that no self-respecting Iranian would ever meet with

British "dogs" and that the United States had turned itself into Iran's enemy by suggesting it. As for Iran's oil, it could remain in the ground for all he cared. "If Mossadegh yields," he concluded, "his blood will flow like Razmara's."

Not satisfied with that threat, the Ayatollah had another for Harriman himself. He asked if Harriman had heard of a Major Embry, and when Harriman said he had not, Kashani explained, "He was an American who came to Iran in 1911 or 1912. He dabbled in oil, which was none of his business, and aroused the hatred of the people. One day, walking in Tehran, he was shot down in the street, but he was not killed. They took him to the hospital. The enraged mob followed him to the hospital, burst into the hospital and butchered him on the operating table. Do you understand?"

With some effort Harriman managed to control his temper. "Your Eminence," he replied coldly, "you must understand that I have been in many dangerous situations in my life and I do not frighten easily." Kashani shrugged and said, "Well, there was no harm in trying."

Kashani's contempt for the idea of compromise, which was even more visceral than Mossadegh's, was not all that frustrated Harriman. The British disgusted him just as much, as he told Acheson in one cable:

> In spite of the fact that the British consider oil interest in Iran their greatest overseas asset, no minister has visited Iran as far as I can find out, except Churchill and Eden on wartime business. Oil company directors have rarely come. Situation that has developed here is tragic example of absentee management combined with world-wide growth of nationalism in undeveloped countries. There is no doubt Iranians are ready to make sacrifices in oil income to be rid of what they consider to be British colonial practices. Large groups are in mood to face any consequences to achieve this objective. It is clear that British reporting and recommendations from here have not been realistic, and it seems essential that member of British government find out for himself what is going on here.

For a time it seemed that despite all the obstacles, some solution might be reached. Harriman finally managed to persuade Mossadegh to issue a statement saying that he would negotiate with a British envoy if "the British government on behalf of the former Anglo-Iranian Oil Company recognizes the principle of nationalization of the oil industry in Iran." To his immense irritation, however, the Foreign Office rejected this overture. He decided to fly to London himself to plead for reason. There he met for three hours with the British cabinet. Its members were divided. Some argued for a continued hard line, but others agreed that it might be wise to send an emissary to Tehran. Prime Minister Attlee decided to dispatch the Lord Privy Seal, Sir Richard Stokes, a wealthy member of the British elite with no experience in the Middle East.

Stokes was instructed to tell Mossadegh that the oil company would accept the principle that Iran's oil belonged to Iran, and also that it was now willing to share its profits on a fifty-fifty basis. The British must, however, remain in control of all drilling, refining, and export operations. This was in essence the same offer that Basil Jackson had brought to Tehran six weeks earlier, though Stokes was told not to admit this fact. He was to remain within the limits of Jackson's offer but could "dress it up and present its main points in different order, together with trimmings or sweetenings as might be required."

The first question Mossadegh asked Stokes when the two men met for the first time was whether he was Roman Catholic. When Stokes replied that he was, Mossadegh told him that he was unsuited for his mission because Catholics do not believe in divorce and Iran was in the process of divorcing the Anglo-Iranian Oil Company. Stokes was not amused. What Mossadegh was doing to Anglo-Iranian, he replied, was closer to murder than divorce.

That exchange set the talks off on a sour note. They were further complicated by Anglo-Iranian's decision on July 31 to shut the Abadan refinery. Company officials said they had no alternative. Storage tanks were full, and tankers could not sail since their captains had been instructed not to sign the receipts Iran was demanding. It was a shattering step that reflected how deep the crisis had become.

Stokes knew full well that he was offering Mossadegh a deal that the prime minister had already rejected. In a cable home, Stokes said that the essence of his offer was to keep Anglo-Iranian operating as before but "under a new name" and lamented that he had tried "a number of devices by which we could disguise this hard fact, but found nothing that was not either dangerous or too transparent for even the Persians to accept." For his part, Mossadegh declared himself willing to negotiate three points only: the continued sale of Iranian oil to Britain to meet its domestic needs, the transfer of British technicians to the service of the new National Iranian Oil Company, and the amount of money Iran should pay for Anglo-Iranian's nationalized assets.

As the talks ground on toward inevitable failure, Stokes and Harriman flew to Abadan for a look around. The different ways they occupied themselves reflected their vastly different approaches to the crisis. Stokes was quickly caught up in a diplomatic flap when the British consul first tried to expel Iranian officials from Abadan and then flew into a rage when an Iranian car drove ahead of his in the caravan escorting Stokes from the airport. The consul wrote an angry letter to the local governor demanding assurances that "in the future, the representative of His Majesty's Government is not subjected to such indignities." Iran's foreign ministry responded by expelling him from the country. Before departing, he cabled London to suggest that he wait in Basra so that he could be of assistance "in the event of a military action."

Harriman made better use of his time. He toured Abadan and sent a cable to Truman reporting that the slums he saw were "shocking for housing of employees of a large Western oil company." In later cables he complained that the British held "a completely nineteenth-century colonial attitude toward Iran." Instead of negotiating seriously, they issued only "rash statements" and "impulsive expressions of resentment" about what they considered the theft of their property in Iran. "I frankly feel that if the British government does not cooperate," he concluded, "it will make the success of my mission extremely doubtful if not impossible."

Harriman's nerves were further frayed by an attack of intestinal disorder and the sweltering midsummer heat. The palace where he was staying in Tehran was lavish but had only a few languid fans to stir the oppressive air. Desperate for relief, he began taking long flights to provincial capitals aboard his official plane, which was air conditioned. He ordered that the cabin be made as cold as possible, and he and his aides wrapped themselves in blankets while they enjoyed the chill. When Vernon Walters suggested that using a plane that burned eight hundred gallons of fuel per hour in order to cool off was a bit excessive, Harriman bristled in reply: "If you had seen my income taxes over a period of years, you would know that I have bought a number of these for the United States government."

Mossadegh met several more times with Stokes and at one point handed him a memorandum that seemed to offer a glimmer of hope. If the British would accept the right of Iranians to control their oil industry, he wrote, he would "fully and fairly" negotiate the oil company's "just claims" for compensation. Stokes was intrigued and cabled the Foreign Office, asking permission to explore what seemed to him a promising offer. The reply was stern, containing two brusque orders: there were to be "no further concessions," and Stokes was to break off the talks and return forthwith to London.

On August 22 the British cabinet imposed a series of economic sanctions on Iran. They prohibited the export of key British commodities, including sugar and steel, to Iran; directed the withdrawal of all British personnel from Iranian oil fields and of all but a "hard core" of about three hundred administrators from Abadan; and blocked Iran's access to its hard currency accounts in British banks. The next day Stokes left Tehran.

"The result is nothing," Mossadegh admitted at a news conference. "It is no good. Everything is finished."

As Stokes departed, Prime Minister Attlee sent a triumphant cable to Truman. "I think you'll agree breakdown in talks entirely due to Persian side," he wrote. "Only course now is, we hope, for complete U.S. public support of His Majesty's Government's position."

His appeal fell on deaf ears. Truman was mightily disappointed by the failure of Harriman's mission but placed much of the blame on Britain's intransigence. In a reply cable, he insisted that neither the British nor the Americans should take any steps that "would appear to be in opposition to the legitimate aspirations of the Iranian people."

Harriman paid a call on the Shah before leaving Tehran, and during their meeting he made a discreet suggestion. Since Mossadegh was making it impossible to resolve the crisis on a basis acceptable to the West, he said, Mossadegh might have to be removed. Harriman knew the Shah had no way of removing Mossadegh at that moment. By bringing up the subject, however, he foreshadowed American involvement in the coup two years later.

"It was a mission unlike any other," Vernon Walters wrote afterward. "There was an Alice in Wonderland quality to it which led me after three days to write back to Mr. Harriman's secretary in Washington to ask her to send me a copy of that book so I would know what was next on the program. It was in a sense a mission that failed, but it was a mission that cast a long shadow ahead on the great problems that the Western world was to have with oil two and a half decades later. These Dr. Mossadegh was not to live to see, yet in a way their true origin led back to him."

After the failure of these last attempts at negotiation, Foreign Secretary Morrison and Ambassador Shepherd intensified their efforts to depose Mossadegh. Shepherd broached the idea with his Iranian friends, and Mossadegh learned of these discussions almost immediately. On September 6 he made a speech to the Senate condemning them and warned that if the British did not cease their plotting, he would expel all remaining British citizens from Abadan in two weeks. Prime Minister Attlee responded by ordering the Royal Navy to strengthen the flotilla of warships hovering off Iran's coast.

For at least a year, the British had been considering the possibility of landing troops in Iran to secure what they considered to be their refinery and oil fields. In the autumn of 1950 Ambassador Franks had told American officials in Washington that his government believed that "the dispatch of a small U.K. force to southern Iran would have a steadying and not a provocative influence." The following April Sir George Bolton, the executive director of the Bank of England, passed to the Foreign Office a report from his Middle East adviser saying that the political tempo in Iran "is such that the possibility of direct intervention by taking over by force the fields and refinery must be considered." Minister of Defense Emanuel Shinwell told the cabinet that tolerating nationalization of Anglo-Iranian would set a terrible precedent and that "we must be prepared to show that our tail could not be twisted interminably." Anglo-Iranian officials predicted in a memorandum to the Foreign Office that if British troops landed at Abadan, "the Persians would probably climb down" and the company could import "thousands of colored men from East Africa to do labor that Iranians might refuse to perform."

In May 1951, two months before Harriman's arrival, the British drew up two detailed plans for the invasion and occupation of Iran. The first, code-named at different stages Buccaneer and Plan Y, contemplated the use of seventy thousand troops in a "seaborne assault combined with the arrival of the maximum possible forces by air" that would "seize and secure" the refinery and oil fields. A more limited alternative, Operation Midget, envisioned the seizure of only the refinery, either for a two-week period while tankers removed the oil in storage there or indefinitely, so that it could be used to refine oil from elsewhere in the Gulf. Advocates of these plans argued that they would not only keep oil flowing to Britain but would also send a patriotic thrill through the country. Lord Fraser, First Lord of the Admiralty, said that a bold military strike would dispel Britain's "dumps and doldrums" and prove that it would not tolerate "being pushed around by Persian pip-squeaks."

Some British officials doubted the wisdom of these plans, but sentiment for invasion was strong and might have carried the day had it not been for implacable opposition from the Truman administration. On May 16 the American ambassador to Britain, Walter Gifford, cabled Acheson that he was becoming "increasingly concerned" about the "belligerent atmosphere" in London. The Foreign Office, he warned, had come to believe that American objections to an invasion "are not very large and can probably be overcome."

"Against this background we fear that Brit, having made implied threat use of force, may eventually be faced with alternatives of either, against their better judgment, making good on this threat and risking unpredictable consequences or backing down and suffering resultant loss prestige and perhaps fatal weakening of their position," Gifford wrote. "It is our estimate that ultimate UK decision whether or not to use force will be in last analysis determined by extent to which US prepared support."

Acheson immediately understood the urgency of this message. He summoned Ambassador Franks and told him that the United States resolutely opposed "the use of force or the threat of the use of force" against Iran, and that Truman himself had "stressed most strongly that no situation should be allowed to develop into an armed conflict between a body of British troops and the Persian forces." His bluntness had the desired effect. Franks immediately sent a message home warning that if Britain went ahead with its invasion plans, Washington's "opposition to the British would probably become even more violent than it is at present."

Truman's position found much support in the American press. The *Wall Street Journal* lamented Britain's reliance on "nineteenth century threats." The *Philadelphia Inquirer* warned that a British invasion of Iran might bring "a quick outbreak of World War III." A popular CBS commentator, Howard K. Smith, asserted that many countries in the Middle East and beyond supported Iran, and that an invasion might "stir all the Southern Asians to a rebellion against the Western foreigner and cause serious trouble for both Britain and the United States."

Foreign Secretary Morrison, who led the war party in London, urged the Americans to change their position. He argued that it would be disastrous for the West if Britain were made to look "feeble and ineffective" at the hands of a man like Mossadegh, "whose fanaticism bordered on the mental." After the World Court issued its "indication," he asked Acheson whether the Americans would support an invasion if Iran refused to climb down. Absolutely not, Acheson replied; a British invasion of Iran under any circumstances would have "disastrous political consequences."

That was enough for Prime Minister Attlee, who had never been enthusiastic about the idea of occupying Iran. On July 19 his cabinet voted to defer the military option, balancing its decision by approving the dispatch of three army battalions to neighboring Iraq. Morrison, however, did not give up. After Mossadegh announced in September that the last Britons would soon be expelled from Abadan, Morrison told the cabinet that the time for invasion had come. Attlee agreed to a show of naval force in the Gulf, but definitively ruled out any more drastic military action.

"An occupation of Abadan Island would not necessarily bring about a change in the Persian Government and might well unite the Persian people against this country, and neither the oil wells nor the refinery could be worked without the assistance of Persian workers," Attlee told the cabinet. "If we attempted to find a solution by force we could not expect to find much support in the United Nations, where the South American governments would follow the lead of the United States and Asian governments would be hostile to us."

Having failed to persuade Attlee to order an invasion, Morrison decided to begin covert action. He turned first to two distinguished scholars who had spent years studying Iran and were sympathetic to the British position there. The first, Ann K. S. Lambton, had been press attaché at the British Embassy in Tehran during World War II and gone on to become one of Britain's leading scholars of Iran. At Morrison's request, she began suggesting "effective lines of propaganda" that the British might use to turn Iranian public opinion against Mossadegh.

Lambton's role was limited to giving advice in London. The other scholar Morrison recruited—at Lambton's suggestion—was a more flamboyant figure, and from him Morrison wanted much more than advice. He was Robin Zaehner, a veteran covert operative who had worked for the Secret Intelligence Service in Iran. Zaehner was fluent in Persian and well acquainted with the leading figures in Iranian politics. A Foreign Office memorandum described him as "a man of great subtlety," but with his squeaky voice and eccentric manner, he was hardly a conventional spy. An American who studied his career portrayed him as a colorful, multifaceted figure:

> Zaehner possessed extraordinary capacity to combine high thought with low living. He relished the lighter side of his duties. He held his own in gossip or discussion, whether about philosophy and religion or about human foibles. He drank heavily. Rather in the tradition of Aldous Huxley, Zaehner also experimented with drugs to increase his sensory perception of eternal verities. . . . To those who wished to learn about Iranian politics he recommended Lewis Carroll's *Through the Looking-Glass*. He tended to tell his superiors what he believed they wanted to hear. His temperament did not draw him to the more sinister side of intelligence operations, nor did he have the discipline for rigorous secrecy. Zaehner was an Oxford *bon vivant* transmogrified into a quasi–Secret Service agent.

In mid-1951 Morrison appointed Zaehner to a post as "acting counselor" at the British Embassy in Tehran. Although technically not an intelligence officer, Zaehner devoted most of his time to meeting with opposition figures and suggesting ways they could help undermine Mossadegh's government. His work greatly encouraged them, and his reports to the Foreign Office also had an important effect. He was the first outsider sent to Iran with the specific

Reza Shah was a harsh tyrant but also a visionary reformer. The British forced him from his throne in 1941. His eldest son, the future Mohammad Reza Shah, stands second from left.

The British built the world's largest oil refinery at Abadan on the Persian Gulf and made huge profits there. Their Anglo-Iranian Oil Company was supposed to be a partnership with Iran, but Iranians were not permitted to audit the books.

Abadan was a colonial outpost, with swimming pools and tennis courts for the British administrators and slum housing for tens of thousands of Iranian workers. Buses, cinemas, and other amenities were reserved for the British.

Prime Minister Mohammad Mossadegh thrilled Iranians when he nationalized the oil company in 1951. Here he is shown in the bed from which he often conducted business.

Mossadegh visited the United States in 1952. President Harry Truman tried to arrange a compromise between Iran and the British.

Henry Grady (above), the American ambassador to Iran, sought to prevent a clash between Mossadegh and the West. So did President Truman's special envoy, W. Averell Harriman (right).

On October 4, 1952, the unthinkable happened: the last Britons sailed away from Abadan. It was a triumph for Iranian nationalism and a humiliating defeat for the British. They set out to reverse it by overthrowing Mossadegh.

Mohammad Reza Shah wanted to guide Iran's future, but Prime Minister Mossadegh believed that monarchs should leave politics to elected leaders. The Shah bitterly resented Mossadegh's efforts to reduce his power.

Prime Minister Winston Churchill believed in covert operations and strongly encouraged the coup. He and Foreign Secretary Anthony Eden failed to win American support while President Truman was in office, but succeeded after Dwight Eisenhower assumed the presidency in 1953.

Soon after Eisenhower approved the coup, the CIA sent one of its most resourceful agents, Kermit Roosevelt, to Iran to carry it out.

The brothers who ran the overt and covert sides of American foreign policy during the Eisenhower administration were determined to overthrow Mossadegh: Secretary of State John Foster Dulles (above) and Director of Central Intelligence Allen Dulles.

The campaign against Mossadegh intensified after an anti-Mossadegh diplomat, Loy Henderson, arrived as American ambassador. Henderson (right) is shown talking to the ill-fated Foreign Minister Hussein Fatemi.

Sir Francis Shepherd, the British ambassador to Iran, worked tirelessly to undermine Mossadegh's government.

Asadollah Rashidian, one of Kermit Roosevelt's key Iranian agents, built support for the coup by bribing politicians, mullahs, newspaper editors, and gang leaders.

General H. Norman Schwarzkopf, father of the Gulf War commander, headed a crack police brigade in Iran during the 1940s and returned on a clandestine mission to help arrange the coup.

Ayatollah Abulqasim Kashani, a powerful fundamentalist cleric, supported Mossadegh at first but then turned against him. Kermit Roosevelt sent him $10,000 the day before the coup.

قبلا بسمه زاهدی نخست وزیر

بنا بست روز تاریخی ۲۲ مردا که قرار ن نخست وزیری مینزان شمالگر

و فختار ازا بید امحبله که وظفه خفار را باحمت نام ملت ایران انجام هیمبه دری

برخوار می مجمد صمری و ن رسسی درا نا کوراز جنگ ل مهب ترین نظت

۱۳۲۲

تومنی بسمری نیه لندم و نسم عرجب ن دکفط قه د ه خود ران اند باد

Princess Ashraf, the Shah's tough-minded twin sister, helped persuade her brother to support the coup. A British agent said he secured her cooperation by gifts of cash and a mink coat.

CIA agents persuaded the Shah to sign a decree dismissing Mossadegh from office and another (above) naming a disaffected officer, General Fazlollah Zahedi, to replace him. The decrees were of dubious legality, but they helped rally support for the coup.

The British and Americans chose General Zahedi (left) as the figurehead leader of their coup. Another key collaborator was Colonel Nematollah Nasiri (right), commander of the Shah's Imperial Guard.

On August 19, 1953, anti-Mossadegh crowds surged through the streets of Tehran. Some military units joined them, and by midnight they had succeeded in overthrowing the government.

© BETTMANN/CORBIS

The Shah, who had fled in panic when the coup seemed to be failing, flew home to reclaim his throne. Soon he began centralizing power in his own hands.

ETALAAT

Mossadegh was arrested, tried by a military tribunal, and found guilty of treason. He spent three years in prison and the rest of his life under house arrest. He died in 1967.

ETALAAT

Mohammad Reza Shah ruled harshly for twenty-five years and was finally overthrown in 1979. Revolutionaries like these carried portraits of Mossadegh, symbolizing their determination to take revenge for the 1953 coup. The new regime in Iran imposed fundamentalist rule, aided anti-Western terror groups, and inspired Islamic radicals in many countries.

assignment of trying to subvert Mossadegh. The progress he made strengthened the hand of those in London who believed that a covert action campaign against Mossadegh might succeed.

As British leaders ordered military steps to intimidate Iran and launched their covert campaign against its government, they also took a series of steps designed to cripple its economy. This might have seemed a logical strategy, since inflicting pain often breaks the will of nations just as it breaks the will of human beings. What the British failed or refused to realize, however, was that Mossadegh and the great majority of Iranians were ready to accept and even embrace much pain in their sacred cause. The Shiite religious tradition blended perfectly with the nationalist passion sweeping through Iran. Together they steeled the will of Iranians.

The British wished to make it impossible for the National Iranian Oil Company to function. The first tactic they used was discreet sabotage at the Abadan refinery. Eric Drake, the general manager at Abadan when it was nationalized, recalled years later that British managers did all they could to assure that machines didn't work and new managers couldn't find out how the place was run. "There was no question of violent resistance," he said, "but it's extraordinary how pieces of the plant would go wrong just when they were supposed to be doing something else."

These steps would not have kept the refinery from running if technicians had been available to run it. The National Iranian Oil Company placed advertisements in several European newspapers and specialized journals announcing that it wished to hire such technicians. British diplomats set out to assure that none would make it to Abadan. They persuaded Sweden, Austria, France, and Switzerland to deny exit visas to interested applicants. In Germany, which was still under Allied occupation, they asked the government to "refuse the grant of passports to German nationals intending to travel to Persia" unless they could prove they were not oil specialists; the Germans were in no position to resist. An American firm publicly offered the Iranian government help "to recruit 2,500 American technicians to run the oil industry," but withdrew the offer after being warned by the State Department that it was "contrary to British interests and embarrassing to the United States." An

American congressman, Owen Harris, introduced a bill authorizing the secretary of the interior to look for qualified experts and help them travel to Iran, but it died after British diplomats protested to the House Foreign Affairs Committee. And in Britain itself, twenty Anglo-Iranian employees who had left Iran but wanted to return were told that under the new sanctions regime, they would not be allowed to convert their salaries into British currency.

This well-coordinated campaign made it all but impossible for Iran to continue producing oil. The British, however, feared that Iran would find a way, either by using Iranian experts or by slipping some foreigners through the blockade. They resolved to assure that if that happened, Iran would find no customers.

Companies in Britain and the United States owned more than two-thirds of the world's oil tankers, but there remained the possibility that tankers from the Soviet Union or elsewhere might begin carrying Iranian oil. To prevent this, the Foreign Office first considered announcing that it would begin to "intercept foreign tankers on the high seas on the grounds that they were carrying stolen oil from Persia." After realizing that such a threat would violate international law, however, it decided on a different tactic. Anglo-Iranian placed advertisements in dozens of newspapers around the world warning that it would "take all such actions as may be necessary" against any country that bought oil from Iran. The company based its threat on the contention that Iranian oil was its lawful property under "the Convention of 29th April 1933." That was misleading language, since conventions are instruments between governments and the 1933 concession agreement was between a government and a company. Officials in several countries recognized that fact and made plans to buy oil that Iran had stockpiled or might produce.

During the summer of 1951, there were still more than three hundred Britons left at Abadan, and one of them, a deputy general manager named Alick Mason, had a way to intercept telegrams sent to the National Iranian Oil Company. In July he intercepted two from American oil companies offering to supply their own tankers if the NIOC would sell them ten million tons of crude over the next year. He informed his superiors in London. They in turn appealed to the State Department, which obligingly persuaded the companies to withdraw their offer. Similar appeals killed incipient deals between the NIOC and companies in Italy and Portugal. The Iranians then tried to arrange barter deals with India and Turkey, but British pressure aborted those deals, too.

As Britain tightened its noose, Iran fell into political turmoil. Bitter debates broke out in the Majlis, including one in which a deputy hurled his briefcase at a cabinet member. Moderates warned that Mossadegh had brought the country to the brink of disaster. Radicals argued with equal passion that he was not confronting the British strongly enough. The press, freer than at any time in Iranian history, was full of denunciations, accusations, and predictions of one form of doom or another. Ambassador Grady warned in interviews with Tehran newspapers that either war with the British or a communist takeover might be imminent.

Those were among Grady's last words as ambassador. His outspoken support for the cause of Iranian nationalism had greatly irritated the British, and, finally, Acheson decided that his "strong personality" had turned him into a liability. He removed Grady in September and replaced him with Loy Henderson, whose worldview was shaped by the East–West confrontation and who soon concluded that Mossadegh was "a madman who would ally himself with the Russians."

As the Americans changed ambassadors in Tehran, the British also adjusted their strategy. Having reluctantly ruled out the option of armed invasion, they decided to take their case to the United Nations Security Council. There they hoped to win approval for a resolution ordering Mossadegh not to expel their oil company from Iran. The debate would also give them a chance to present their case, which they believed was highly persuasive, to the court of world opinion.

Americans warned against this. Henry Grady, by then already a former ambassador, told a London newspaper that the British were foolishly giving Iranians "a great forum to tell the world how their oil company has oppressed the Iranian people, and to show that Western capitalism is tending to control, and possibly destroy, other countries in the underdeveloped part of the world." The State Department worried that the Soviet Union would veto any pro-British resolution, thereby strengthening its image as defender of the world's oppressed. In a note to Herbert Morrison, Acheson warned that forcing a United Nations debate might lead to "an irrevocable freezing of the Iranian situation."

The ever-obtuse Morrison, however, was determined to press ahead. When the American ambassador in London, Walter Gifford, called on him to deliver Acheson's note, he was met with a stern tongue-lashing:

> I had 45 minutes with Morrison this p.m. and found him in a petulant and angry mood. . . . He launched into a tirade about our attitude re Iranian problem. He was unhappy about [American suggestions for a watered-down Security Council resolution], reiterating a number of times "I will not be put in the dock with Mossadegh." . . . He said at one point "We have been the saints and Mossadegh has been the naughty boy." He emphasized he cld not understand US attitude. He expected 100 percent cooperation and was only getting 20 percent. . . . We had persistently inveighed against use of force and then when UK reverted to appeal to [the United Nations] to uphold rule of law, we not only had doubts re wisdom of action, but came up with res which failed to make any distinction between relative guilt and innocence of parties. . . . During all the forgoing conv, Morrison had kept [Acheson's note] folded in front of him. He finally picked it up and read it, shaking his head and muttering "This is defeatist—defeatist."

Morrison was sure that Britain's silver-tongued representative to the United Nations, Sir Gladwyn Jebb, would dominate the debate and run rhetorical rings around his Iranian counterpart. But if he thought that the prospect of confrontation in such august chambers would terrify Iranian leaders, he was quite mistaken. Mossadegh loved it—so much so that he resolved to come to New York and present his case in person.

This was a master stroke. The most eloquent figure Iran had produced in many centuries would now take to the world stage, and he would present not just the case of one small nation against one big company, but that of the wretched of the earth against the rich and powerful. Mossadegh was about to become the preeminent spokesman for the nationalist passion that was surging through the colonial world.

CHAPTER 8

An Immensely Shrewd Old Man

Throngs of admirers jammed the Tehran airport to cheer Mossadegh as he set out on his historic trip to New York. When he landed in Rome, his first stop, his plane was surrounded by news photographers while police officers struggled to control the crush of exuberant Iranian expatriates and other supporters who had waited half the day for a glimpse of him. The same frenzied scene was repeated at his next stop in Amsterdam.

New York, long accustomed to receiving world-famous figures, awaited Mossadegh with much curiosity. He was not just the "symbol of Iran's surging nationalism," as the *New York Times* called him, but a world leader with a great story to tell and a famously theatrical way of telling it. Everyone, with the possible exception of Britain's delegate to the United Nations, was eagerly awaiting his performance. "Whether Mossy is a phony or a genuine tear-jerker," warned the *Daily News,* "he better put everything he's got into his show if he goes on television here."

Mossadegh stepped gingerly from his plane on the afternoon of October 8, 1951. His son and personal physician, Gholam-Hussein, helped him down the steps. He did not speak, but issued a written statement to waiting reporters. It promised that the world would soon hear the story of a "cruel and imperialistic company" that had stolen what belonged to a "needy and naked people" and now sought to use the United Nations to justify its crime.

From the airport Mossadegh was taken to New York Hospital for a medical examination. Doctors pronounced him fit, and he decamped to the Ritz Tower Hotel at the corner of Park Avenue and Fifty-seventh Street. There he spent most of his time preparing the speech he would deliver to the Security Council. This was an era before Castro, before Sukarno, before Nkrumah and Lumumba. The voice of poor countries had seldom been raised in such rarefied chambers. Mossadegh's would be the first that most Westerners had ever heard.

As he waited for his moment, he devoured everything the American press was writing about his forthcoming performance. Typical of these previews was an edition of *Newsweek* that carried the cover line "Mossadegh: Fainting Fanatic." *Newsweek* praised Mossadegh's personal integrity, mentioning that he had turned down both his official limousine and his salary as prime minister; recounted his career as "incorruptible provincial governor, anti-British agitator, enemy of the tough old Shah Reza Khan, red-baiter and founder of the terrorist National Front"; asserted that although many Westerners had at first dismissed him as "feeble, senile, and probably a lunatic," they now saw him as "an immensely shrewd old man with an iron will and a flair for self-dramatization"; and wondered, along with much of the rest of the world, what this "fabulous invalid" would say and do in the days ahead.

"The stage was set for one of the strangest contests in the strange history of the United Nations—the tremulous, crotchety Premier versus Britain's super-suave representative, Sir Gladwyn Jebb," *Newsweek* reported. "And this might be the decisive act in the dramatic, tragic and sometimes ridiculous drama that began when Iran nationalized the Anglo-Iranian Oil Co. five months ago."

The confrontation for which Mossadegh had come to New York began even before he arrived. Gladwyn Jebb, the British delegate, had already given the Security Council a long summation of his government's position. Mossadegh read it carefully. It was a contemptuous dismissal of Iran's position and a ringing declaration that the oil beneath Iran's soil was "clearly the property of the Anglo-Iranian Oil Company."

> The plain fact is that, by a series of insensate actions, the Iranian Government is causing a great enterprise, the proper functioning of which is of immense benefit not only to the United Kingdom and Iran but to the whole free world, to grind to a stop. Unless this is promptly checked, the whole of the free world will be much poorer and weaker, including the deluded Iranian people themselves. . . .
>
> The Iranian Government, for obvious reasons of its own, perpetually represents the Anglo-Iranian Oil Company as a gang of unscrupulous blood-suckers whose one idea is to drain the Iranian nation of any wealth it may possess. . . . These wild accusations are simply not true. . . . Quite apart from its financial contributions to the Iranian economy, the record of the company in Iran has been one which must arouse the greatest admiration from the social point of view and should be taken as a model of the form of development which would bring benefits to the economically less-developed areas of the world. Far from trying to keep down the Iranian people, as has been alleged, the company has strained every effort to improve the standard of living and education of its employees so that they might be able to play a more useful part in the great work which remains to be done in Iran. . . . To ignore entirely these activities and to put forth the company as responsible for oppression, corruption and treachery could be described as base ingratitude if it were not simply ridiculous.

Jebb asked the Security Council to act before October 4, the date by which Mossadegh had vowed to expel the last Britons from Abadan. When he finished, however, the Iranian delegate rose to ask for a ten-day postponement to allow Mossadegh to travel from Tehran to New York. The Council president agreed, and by the time Mossadegh arrived, the situation at Abadan had indeed changed. On October 4 the last British nationals had assembled at the Gymkhana Club, one of their favorite retreats, and were ferried in groups out to the HMS *Mauritius,* which was standing by to take them across the Shatt-al-Arab to Basra. With that step, one of the mightiest commercial enterprises in imperial history closed its doors.

A reporter from the *New York Times* visited the ghostly expanse a few days later. "When seen from a distance across the plain, the fifty-odd steel chimneys of the refinery bear a striking resemblance to the still-standing remains of King Xerxes's Apadana and Hall of a Hundred Columns at Persepolis," he wrote. "But as a traveler draws nearer, the gleaming metal soon identifies the silent towers of idle Abadan as the colossus of the industrial age, not of the fifth century B.C. . . . The cars and buses of the nationalized oil company—all of them British-made—go by. There are people in the streets. But the visitor may scrutinize every passing face in this English town set in southern Iran without finding the features of a single Englishman. Indeed any European is stared at as a curiosity."

Excitement filled the air as the Security Council assembled on October 15 to hear from Mossadegh. Delegates fell silent when he entered the chamber. All gazed at the tall, elegant-looking statesman who had riveted the world's attention since coming to power six months before. Mossadegh seemed completely at ease, and with good reason. He was, after all, a trained lawyer from a distinguished family who had been educated in Europe and honed his persuasive talents in countless trials and parliamentary speeches. More important, he was utterly convinced not only that his case was just but also that Providence had brought him to this moment. He had come to New York to carry out the mission to which he had devoted his life.

A Brazilian diplomat, João Carlos Muniz, was presiding over the Security Council that Monday, and he gaveled it to order punctually at three o'clock. His first act was to invite Mossadegh and Allahyar Saleh, Iran's ambassador to the United Nations, to sit at the table normally reserved for council members. Then he recognized Jebb, who told his fellow delegates that Britain was no longer insisting "purely and simply on the return to the status quo," but only for negotiated relief from "the great damage inflicted not only on it but on the free world as a whole by the actions of the Iranian government." Jebb concluded by turning to face "the representative of Iran, who has come so far, and at such inconvenience to himself, to this meeting." He urged Mossadegh "not to take up an aggressively nationalistic and indeed, I might say, almost isolationist attitude, not to brood unduly on old imagined wrongs, but to concentrate on the broader aspects and to show by his attitude that he too welcomes a constructive solution."

Then it was Mossadegh's turn. He spoke in eloquent French. By way of introduction, he declared that Britain's complaint was baseless and that the Security Council had no jurisdiction over the matter in any case, since Iran was entitled to dispose of its natural resources as it saw fit. But since the United Nations was "the ultimate refuge of weak and oppressed nations," he had decided to appear nevertheless, "after a long journey and in failing health, to express my country's respect for this illustrious institution." His statement was long, detailed, and passionate. Begging the council to indulge him on account of his delicate condition, he said that he would ask Saleh to read most of it. First, however, he spoke himself, giving a concise but highly evocative summary of the case he was laying before the world:

> My countrymen lack the bare necessities of existence. Their standard of living is probably one of the lowest in the world. Our greatest natural asset is oil. This should be the source of work and food for the population of Iran. Its exploitation should properly be our national industry, and the revenue from it should go to improve our conditions of life. As now organized, however, the petroleum industry has contributed practically nothing to the well-being of the people or to the technical progress or industrial development of my country. The evidence for that statement is that after fifty years of exploitation by a foreign company, we still do not have enough Iranian technicians and must call in foreign experts.
>
> Although Iran plays a considerable role in the world's petroleum supply and has produced a total of three hundred fifteen million tons over a period of fifty years, its entire gain, according to accounts of the former company, has been only one hundred ten million pounds sterling. To give you an idea of Iran's profits from this enormous industry, I may say that in 1948, according to accounts of the former Anglo-Iranian Oil Company, its net revenue amounted to sixty-one million pounds; but from those profits Iran received only nine million pounds, although twenty-eight million pounds went into the United Kingdom treasury in income tax alone. . . .
>
> I must add here that the population living in the oil region of southern Iran and around Abadan, where there is the largest oil refinery in the world, is suffering in conditions of absolute misery without even the barest necessities of life. If the exploitation of

our oil industry continues in the future as it has in the past, if we are to tolerate a situation in which the Iranian plays the part of a mere manual worker in the oil fields of Masjid-i-Suleiman, Agha Jari and Kermanshah and in the Abadan refinery, and if foreign exploiters continue to appropriate practically all of the income, then our people will remain forever in a state of poverty and misery. These are the reasons that have prompted the Iranian parliament—the Majlis and the Senate—to vote unanimously in favor of nationalizing the oil industry.

With this, Mossadegh took his seat and handed the text of his statement to Saleh. He began by reading what Mossadegh had singled out as Iran's essential legal argument: "The oil resources of Iran, like its soil, its rivers and mountains, are the property of the people of Iran. They alone have the authority to decide what shall be done with it, by whom and how." Saleh took two hours to read the rest of Mossadegh's statement. It was a history of foreign intervention in Iran, with special attention to the steps Britain had taken "to reduce us to economic servitude."

"The record of British economic exploitation of Iran has been a sorry one," it concluded. "No one should be surprised that its consequence has been the nationalization of our oil industry."

After the reading of Mossadegh's statement was completed, the council voted to meet again the following day to continue its debate. News photographers waiting outside the chamber asked the two adversaries to shake hands for the cameras, and they did. As flashbulbs popped, they had a brief exchange.

"If God wills it, we will be friends again," Jebb told Mossadegh.

"We have always been friends with England," Mossadegh replied. "The former company dragged your country needlessly into this dispute."

The next day, pictures of the two men appeared in newspapers around the world. Mossadegh was the taller, and wore a broad smile. Jebb looked quizzical and bemused.

Tuesday's session began with tributes to Liaquat Ali Khan, the prime minister of Pakistan, who had just been assassinated. Liaquat was a figure much like Mossadegh. He had been a leader of the movement to end British colonialism in India and had worked closely with Pakistan's founding father, Mohammad Ali Jinnah, to build a democratic Muslim republic in what had been India's northern provinces. Following Jinnah's death, he had become what George McGhee, who met him several times, called "the unchallenged leader of his country." Like Mossadegh, he was a visionary statesman, highly educated and erudite. He was committed to secular Islam and sympathetic to Western values but at the same time frustrated by what he saw as crippling vestiges of imperialism that prevented poor countries from achieving true independence. Pakistan never again had a leader of his caliber, just as Iran never had another like Mossadegh.

Liaquat had personified the spirit of the young United Nations, and news of his murder shocked many delegates. They already had much on their minds. Mossadegh's epochal challenge to the British was unfolding at a time of unusual turbulence in the world. The Soviet Union had just conducted its second atomic bomb test, making clear that the threat of annihilation would shape history for generations to come. War was raging in Korea. Kashmir, claimed by both India and Pakistan, was also aflame. A state of emergency was declared in Egypt after an outbreak of anti-British rioting.

An election campaign in Britain was also on the world's agenda that autumn. Winston Churchill was running to reclaim his old job, and in several speeches he denounced Prime Minister Attlee for failing to confront Mossadegh firmly enough. He told a crowd in Liverpool that Attlee had betrayed "solemn undertakings" never to abandon Abadan. "I don't remember a case," he thundered, "when public men have broken their word so abruptly and without even an attempt at explanation." As the campaign progressed, Churchill became so belligerent on the Iran issue that Foreign Secretary Morrison asked him pointedly during one House of Commons debate whether he was urging war. He did not reply, but never denied that he liked the idea of invading Iran.

Despite all that was happening around the world, however, Mossadegh remained the man of the hour. In his sweeping indictment before the Security Council, he found words that stung his adversary and delighted his countless admirers. He began his second day at the microphone by ridiculing the British for trying "to persuade world opinion that the lamb has devoured the wolf."

"The government of the United Kingdom has made abundantly clear that it has no interest in negotiating, and has instead used every illegitimate means of economic, psychological and military pressure that it could lay its hands on to break our will," Mossadegh declared. "Having first concentrated its warships along our coasts and paratroopers at nearby bases, it makes a great parade of its love for peace."

Then it was Jebb's turn. How disappointing it was, he lamented, that Mossadegh's speech had been "so entirely negative, an attitude of mind which I regret to say has characterized the Iranian approach in all our long negotiations hitherto." Mossadegh faced a "distressing situation which has arisen entirely owing to his own folly." Since taking office, he had done nothing but belittle the achievements of the "prudent and far-sighted" Anglo-Iranian Oil Company, urge the appointment of "unqualified Iranians" to technical jobs, and trample on international law by ordering "the expropriation of foreign property." The crisis had grown out of Iran's "persistent refusal to recognize the sanctity of contracts."

On Wednesday, the session's third day, delegates from several countries spoke briefly and then Mossadegh asked to be recognized. He said only that he was "very tired" and handed his text to Mohammad Saleh, sitting beside him. It was a long and impassioned speech on which he had worked for most of the previous twenty-four hours:

> I have not made actual count of the pejorative words used by Sir Gladwyn Jebb in has various statements, but as you leaf through the pages of the record, defamatory word after defamatory word springs to the eye. Our actions are described as "insensate" and our people as "deluded." We have been "precipitate," "arbitrary," and have made life "intolerable." Our legislative process is described as one of "hustling." We are damned as "intransigent" and accused of presenting ultimatums. Our grievances are dismissed as "wild accusations." We are "ridiculous" and exhibit "base ingratitude." We are "intemperate," "exploiters" of our own people, and save our own necks by inflaming our people against foreigners. Our aims are "illusory" and our means of achieving them "suicidal." Our case is presented as one of the lame leading the blind in pursuit of a phantom. . . .
>
> We have long realized that our hopes for developing our country, improving the condition of our people and expanding the opportunities available to them were dependent to a great extent on this extraordinarily important national resource. The

record of the contribution that oil has made to our national prosperity is as pitiable as that of the crumbs which we have been allowed to pick up from the former company's table. . . . I respond readily to the United Kingdom representative's appeal to face the practical facts of the situation, and I am no less eager than he is to negotiate. Wherever the former company may operate in the future, however, it will never again operate in Iran. Neither by trusteeship nor by contract will we turn over to foreigners the right to exploit our oil resources.

The resolution Britain had brought to the Security Council, already diluted at the insistence of the United States, was weakened further by amendments from India and Yugoslavia. Ultimately it become nothing more than a call for goodwill on both sides. Even that was too much for Mossadegh. He insisted that the council had no right to pass any resolution at all. So profound was the impression he had made that most other governments felt they had no choice but to agree. On October 19 the council voted "to postpone the discussion of the question to a certain day or indefinitely." Britain and the United States abstained. It was a humiliating diplomatic defeat for the British.

"The Iranian oil dispute has done something that no other dispute in the history of the United Nations has been able to do," James Reston wrote in the next day's *New York Times*. "It has established the principle of total loss. It has proved what has heretofore been in doubt, namely that it is possible to have an argument in the United Nations in which everybody loses, including the large powers, the small powers, and the United Nations itself."

A solution to the oil dispute was now less likely than ever. Mossadegh remained fiercely determined to press ahead with his nationalization project, and the British remained equally determined to thwart it. President Truman decided to make a last effort at compromise and invited the Iranian leader to Washington.

Mossadegh had already proven himself adept at reaching the American public. He appeared several times on television, and the seeming logic of his case, which he always compared to the struggle for American independence, won him considerable sympathy. His personal quirks—the long, aristocratic face that would suddenly explode into laughter, the way he rested his seemingly weary head on his cane, the grand sweeps of his long arms—added to his appeal. They gave him the endearing aspect of a favorite, perhaps slightly eccentric, uncle or grandfather. Cameras followed him wherever he went in New York.

Before leaving for Washington, Mossadegh addressed Iranian students at Columbia University and told them that if they wanted to help their country, they should concentrate on learning how to run an oil industry. The next morning he set off by train, but instead of traveling directly to Washington, he made a brilliantly conceived stop in Philadelphia. There he visited Independence Hall, which he said symbolized the aspirations that united Americans and Iranians. Hundreds of onlookers cheered as he was photographed beside the Liberty Bell.

Truman had received a confidential profile of Mossadegh that reflected the American view of him. It said that he was "supported by the majority of the population" and described him as "witty," "affable," "honest," and "well informed." This could not have been more different from the British view, in which, according to various diplomatic cables and memoranda, Mossadegh was a "wild," "erratic," "eccentric," "crazy," "gangster-like," "fanatical," "absurd," "dictatorial," "demagogic," "inflammatory," "cunning," "slippery," "completely unscrupulous," and "clearly imbalanced" "wily Oriental" who "looks like a cab horse" and "diffuses a slight reek of opium."

Mossadegh's arrival at Union Station in Washington on October 23, 1951, was unforgettable. He stepped off the train with great difficulty, supported on one side by his cane and on the other by his son's steadying grasp. To all appearances, he was ready to collapse on the spot. Suddenly he saw Secretary of State Acheson, whom he had admired from afar but had never met. His face lit up and he seemed instantly rejuvenated. He dropped his cane, brusquely pushed his son aside, and skipped down the concourse to embrace his host.

The next day, President Truman walked across the street from the White House to meet Mossadegh at Blair House. Once again Mossadegh was the fading invalid who, with his dying breaths, wished to defend his oppressed people against evil. He leaned toward Truman and began feebly, "Mr. President, I am speaking for a very poor country, a country all desert—just sand, a few camels, a few sheep. . . . "

"Yes, and with your oil, just like Texas!" Acheson interjected. Mossadegh loved it. He snapped back in his chair and broke out into one of the laughing fits that were almost as famous as the ones in which he wept.

Truman began by telling Mossadegh that he felt great sympathy for Iran's cause. He was deeply afraid, however, that if the oil crisis spun out of control, Iran might fall into the hands of the Soviets, who were "sitting like a vulture on the fence waiting to pounce." If the Soviets took Iran, he warned, "they would be in a position to wage a world war." Mossadegh said he saw the same danger, but insisted that British intransigence was the factor most likely to throw Iran into chaos.

Recognizing that no compromise would be possible that day, Truman invited Mossadegh to stay in Washington for a while and spend some time with Acheson and George McGhee. To sweeten the invitation, he had arranged for Mossadegh to be installed at Walter Reed Hospital, where he could rest and be given a full battery of tests. To a man who had many ailments and believed he had many more, who felt comfortable in bed and never declined medical attention, this was an irresistible offer. Mossadegh was driven to the hospital that afternoon, and was thrilled to find that the presidential suite had been made ready for him.

Acheson and McGhee visited him the next day to lay out terms of what they believed would be a fair compromise with the British. Their formula, as the *New York Times* described it, was to "assure Iran the owner's control over her oil resource, but provide a so-called 'neutral' company with full authority to operate and manage the vast refineries and distribution facilities, and enable Britain to market the oil." Mossadegh rejected it out of hand.

The same offer had been transmitted to the British, and before they even knew of Mossadegh's reaction, they, too, rejected it. A senior diplomat at the Foreign Office, Sir William Strang, called it "expropriation at the expense of British interests." Chancellor of the Exchequer R. A. Butler said it failed to recognize the essential fact that "our own economic viability was at stake, which was much more important than Persia's."

There were more meetings and discussions, including an

extended debate over how much Iran would charge for its oil, when and if it ever began to flow again. No progress was made. "The general feeling here," James Reston wrote after Mossadegh had been in Washington for a week, "is that the United States intervened in the problem too late and cannot now be expected to find any compromise that will satisfy the United States, Britain and Iran."

Americans were indeed latecomers to the Middle East. The British scorned them as inexperienced and naïve. To a degree they were. They were instinctively repelled by Britain's colonial arrogance, especially in Iran, but did not have enough self-confidence to act decisively on their own.

The American failure to reach a deal with Mossadegh during his visit to the United States was not due to any lack of effort by George McGhee. He visited Mossadegh day after day, first at the hospital and then, after Mossadegh was released with a clean bill of health, at his suite in the Shoreham Hotel. "Despite great efforts I was unable to get him to understand the facts of life about the international oil business," he wrote afterward. "In the end he would always smile and say 'I don't care about that' when I would talk with him about oil prices, discounts or technicians. 'You don't understand,' he would say. 'It is a political problem.'"

In mid-November, after meetings with Mossadegh that lasted a total of seventy hours, McGhee finally gave up. When he came to tell Mossadegh, the old man already knew what was coming. "You've come to send me home," he told McGhee.

"Yes," McGhee replied. "I'm sorry to have to tell you that we can't bridge the gap between you and the British. It's a great disappointment to us, as it must be to you."

Mossadegh accepted the news quietly. He decided that before leaving Washington, he would accept an invitation to address the National Press Club. His speech was a denunciation of Britain, skillfully combined with praise for the United States and an appeal for financial aid. A State Department spokesman said that the appeal would be given "every consideration," but privately Mossadegh was told that a loan was impossible because the British would object too strenuously.

The most telling comment Mossadegh made before leaving Washington on November 18 was to Vernon Walters, who at Averell Harriman's request visited him alone just to be sure that he had not had a last-minute change of heart. "I know what you're here for, and the answer is still no," Mossadegh said when Walters appeared at his door.

"Dr. Mossadegh," Walters replied, "you have been here for a long time. High hopes have been raised that your visit would bring about some fruitful results, and now you are returning to Iran empty-handed."

At this, Mossadegh stared at his friend and asked, "Don't you realize that in returning to Iran empty-handed, I return in a much stronger position than if I returned with an agreement which I would have to sell to my fanatics?"

On his way home, Mossadegh stopped in Egypt. He was given an ecstatic welcome. Egyptians were already in the anti-imperialist frenzy that would produce the Suez crisis a few years later, and whenever Mossadegh appeared in public, they cheered him wildly. Newspapers hailed him as a hero who had "conquered history" and "won freedom and dignity for his country." He stayed for several days, was embraced by King Farouk, and signed a friendship treaty with Prime Minister Nahas Pasha. "A united Iran and Egypt," it pledged, "will together demolish British imperialism."

In Britain, a momentous political change had occurred. While Mossadegh was in the United States, Conservatives led by Winston Churchill had been elected to replace Prime Minister Attlee's Labor government. Like many British leaders of his generation, the seventy-seven-year-old Churchill had great trouble giving up the idea of Britain as an imperial power. As a young soldier in 1898, he had charged the Dervish lines at the decisive Battle of Omdurman that secured Sudan as a British colony. During World War I, he helped conceive the ill-fated Gallipoli campaign in Turkey. Later he directed British efforts to maintain control over Palestine and Mesopotamia and fervently opposed granting independence to India. He saw in Iran what he had seen for decades: a reliable source of oil at bargain prices. Iran was also one of Britain's last great foreign outposts, and Churchill knew that if it were lost, there would be little hope of saving Suez or the others that remained. Holding the line against Third World nationalism was one of his lifelong crusades, and in the sunset of his career he was determined to make a last stand.

Churchill had built his election campaign in part on the charge that Attlee "had scuttled and run from Abadan when a splutter of musketry would have ended the matter." In one of his first acts after taking office, he sent his new foreign secretary, Anthony Eden, to meet Acheson. He directed Eden to press the Iran matter and "be stubborn even if the temperature rises."

The change in Britain's government would prove decisive for Iran. Attlee had done whatever he thought possible on behalf of Anglo-Iranian, stopping only at the use of force. Churchill, who considered Mossadegh "an elderly lunatic bent on wrecking his country and handing it over to the Communists," was willing and even eager to cross that line. The fervor with which Mossadegh was welcomed in Egypt proved to Churchill that he was not only a danger to Britain's oil supply but also an intolerable symbol of anti-British sentiment around the world.

Britain's policy toward Mossadegh toughened immediately. Foreign Secretary Eden told Acheson that the Americans had spent too much time appeasing him, and that inviting him to Washington had been a mistake. From now on, he declared, Britain would be interested only in deposing him.

Among the Americans most devastated by Britain's decision to turn toward force was George McGhee. To him, it was the final blow in a campaign of mutual suicide, "almost the end of the world." His friend Henry Grady had been removed a few weeks earlier as ambassador to Iran, and around the time Mossadegh left Washington, McGhee himself accepted a new post as ambassador to Turkey. Both men had devoted untold amounts of energy to the idea of compromise in Iran, and that idea was now dead.

During that year of 1951, Mossadegh vaulted onto the world stage and came to dominate it. He had become a defining figure whose ideas, for better or worse, were reshaping history. No one was surprised when *Time* magazine chose him—not Harry Truman, Dwight Eisenhower, or Winston Churchill—as its Man of the Year.

Mossadegh looked stately and dignified on the cover of *Time*. The long article inside was full of dismissive insults about this "weeping, fainting leader of a helpless country" who was an "obstinate opportunist" and threw tantrums like "a willful little boy." But it also called him "the Iranian George Washington" and "the most world-renowned man his ancient race had produced for centuries."

Reflecting the ambivalence with which the United States regarded him, *Time* portrayed him as an exasperating and immature figure who nonetheless had a legitimate case to make:

> Once upon a time, in a mountainous land between Baghdad and the Sea of Caviar, there lived a nobleman. This nobleman, after a lifetime of carping at the way the kingdom was run, became Chief Minister of the realm. In a few months he had the whole world hanging on his words and deeds, his jokes, his tears, his tantrums. Behind his grotesque antics lay great issues of peace or war, which would affect many lands far beyond his mountains. . . .
>
> He was Mohammad Mossadegh, Premier of Iran in the year 1951. He was the Man of the Year. He put Scheherazade in the petroleum business and oiled the wheels of chaos. His acid tears dissolved one of the remaining pillars of a great empire. In his plaintive, singsong voice he gabbled a defiant challenge that sprang out of a hatred and envy almost incomprehensible to the West. . . .
>
> The British position in the whole [Middle East] is hopeless. They are hated and distrusted almost everywhere. The old colonial relationship is finished, and no other power can replace Britain. . . . The U.S., which will have to make the West's policy in the Middle East, whether it wants to or not, as yet has no policy there. . . . In its leadership of the non-Communist world, the U.S. has some dire responsibilities to shoulder. One of them is to meet the fundamental moral challenge posed by the strange old wizard who lives in a mountainous land and who is, sad to relate, the Man of 1951.

CHAPTER 9

Block Headed British

On a sunny July day in 1952, eight months after his return from Washington, Prime Minister Mossadegh was driven along an elm-shaded lane to the Saad Abad Palace for a showdown with Mohammad Reza Shah. Iran was no longer big enough for both of them. Behind closed doors at the palace, they faced off in a duel of wits and power. It ended with Mossadegh lying unconscious at the Shah's feet.

This meeting was supposed to be no more than ceremonial. Mossadegh had just been chosen by the Majlis to serve a full two-year term as prime minister, and according to custom, he was presenting the Shah with a list of his cabinet ministers. He took the occasion, however, to make a demand that no Iranian prime minister had ever dared to make. Mossadegh wanted the Shah to recognize the supremacy of the elected government by surrendering control of the war ministry. The Shah was outraged. Without the war ministry he would lose control of the army, the bulwark of his power, and be reduced to the status of a figurehead. Rather than lose his army, he told Mossadegh, he would "pack my suitcase and leave."

Mossadegh, who had mastered the art of political theater before the Shah was born, said not a word. He paused for a few moments to reflect, then rose to walk out. The Shah was struck with fear that the old man would take to the streets and rouse the masses against him. He jumped up, ran to the door, and threw his body across it. Mossadegh insisted that he step aside. Impossible, the Shah replied; their discussion must continue. The standoff lasted for a minute or two. Mossadegh began breathing harder. Then he gasped, took a few steps back, and fainted.

An annex to the 1906 constitution made the Shah supreme commander of the Iranian army but also required him to cooperate with the elected government on political matters. Prime ministers had traditionally interpreted this as allowing the Shah to appoint the minister of war. By breaking with this tradition, Mossadegh pro-voked a crisis. As he lay in bed recovering from his collapse, he decided to resolve it in a way that shocked the country. The next morning, July 17, he resigned from office.

"Under the present circumstances it is impossible to conclude the final phase of the national struggle," he wrote to the Shah. "I cannot continue in office without having responsibility for the Min-istry of War, and since Your Majesty did not concede this, I feel I do not enjoy the confidence of the Sovereign and, therefore, offer my resignation to pave the way for another government which might be able to carry out Your Majesty's wishes."

Did Mossadegh really wish to leave power, or was he just maneuvering for political advantage? At several crucial moments in his career, he had chosen to retire from public life rather than sully himself. He was so mortified by the Anglo-Persian Agreement of 1919 that he applied for residence in Switzerland and told his family he would live the rest of his life in exile. During the long reign of Reza Shah, he remained absolutely aloof from politics. In 1947, after an election-reform bill he had proposed in the Majlis was defeated, he retired to his estate at Ahmad Abad and announced the definitive end of his political life. These episodes reflected a martyr's streak in Mossadegh, perhaps reinforced by Shiite theol-ogy, that disposed him to choose stoic suffering over compromise with iniquity.

By the middle of 1952 Mossadegh was facing many troubles. Britain's boycott of Iranian oil had been devastatingly effective, and he knew that British agents in Tehran were working to subvert his government. For a time he hoped to ride out the crisis with Ameri-can aid, but President Truman, who was under heavy pressure from

London, would not give him any. He sought help from the World Bank, but that effort also failed. Iranians were becoming poorer and unhappier by the day. Mossadegh's political coalition was fraying, and in his new term he could look forward to fighting a swarm of enemies.

It would be naïve, however, to believe that Mossadegh was truly eager to leave the exalted position he had reached in the eyes of Iranians and millions of others around the world. He wanted not to quit but to force Iranians to decide whether they really wanted him as their leader. Resigning was an inspired gamble.

For most of that spring, Mossadegh had been preoccupied with parliamentary elections. He had little to fear from a free vote, since despite the country's problems he was widely admired as a hero. A free vote, however, was not what others were planning. British agents had fanned out across the country, bribing candidates and the regional bosses who controlled them. They hoped to fill the Majlis with deputies who would vote to depose Mossadegh. It would be a coup carried out by seemingly legal means.

Iranian elections took several weeks to complete because of difficulties in transportation and communication. The first results came from big cities, and they were encouraging to Mossadegh. In Tehran all twelve National Front candidates were elected. Results in other parts of the country, where there was no one to monitor the voting, were quite different. These results did not in themselves disturb Mossadegh, whose faith in the popular will was boundless, but he became worried after violence broke out in Abadan and several other parts of the country where elections were being hotly contested. Aides told him that some of the candidates being elected were under the direct control of British agents. He was about to leave for The Hague to defend Iran against another British lawsuit at the World Court and feared that his absence might remove the last checks on his enemies' electoral chicanery. In June, after 80 candidates had been certified as winners of seats in the 136-seat Majlis, his cabinet voted to halt the elections. In a statement he asserted that since "foreign agents" were exploiting the election campaign to destabilize Iran, "the supreme national interests of the country necessitate the suspension of elections pending the return of the Iranian delegation from The Hague."

Mossadegh was legally entitled to take this step as long as the eighty seated members did not veto it, which they did not. He could also claim a measure of moral legitimacy, since he was defending Iran against subversion by outsiders. Nonetheless, the episode cast him in an unflattering light. It allowed his critics to portray him as undemocratic and grasping for personal power.

While Mossadegh dealt with this challenge, he also had to face another that most Iranians considered far more urgent. Their country was spiraling into bankruptcy. Tens of thousands had lost their jobs at the Abadan refinery, and although most understood and passionately supported the idea of nationalization, they naturally hoped that Mossadegh would find a way to put them back to work. The only way he could do that was to sell oil.

During the first half of 1952, tankers from Argentina and Japan managed to make their way into and out of Iranian ports despite Britain's proclaimed embargo. Another brought four thousand tons of Abadan oil to Venice, and after an Italian court rejected Britain's protest, Winston Churchill complained about "what paltry friends and allies the Italians are." Churchill realized that if he did not enforce the embargo more effectively, it would collapse.

In mid-June dock workers at the Persian Gulf port of Bandar Mashur welcomed the tanker *Rose Mary*, which had been chartered by a private Italian oil company that wanted to buy twenty million tons of Iranian crude over the next decade. The company had organized this "experimental voyage" to challenge Britain's embargo. If the *Rose Mary* could make her way safely back to Italy, the embargo would be broken and Iran would be on the road to economic recovery.

As Britain and Iran prepared for confrontation on the high seas, they also clashed at the World Court. The British were seeking an order declaring that the Abadan refinery and surrounding oil fields rightfully belonged to them. Their lawyers argued eloquently, but any hope they had of dominating the proceedings vanished when Mossadegh arrived. A crowd welcomed him at the Peace Palace, cheering wildly and rhythmically chanting his name. Inside, he gave a brief speech asking the judges to consider the moral and political aspects of the case as well as the strictly legal ones. Nationalizing Anglo-Iranian, he said, had been the only possible response to an intolerable situation in which the company had for years treated its Iranian employees "like animals" and manipulated Iranian governments to assure that it could continue plundering the country's most precious natural resource.

After his speech, Mossadegh retired to his hotel and did not appear again in court. Iran's case was presented over the course of three days by a team of Iranian lawyers and an eminent Belgian, Henri Rolin, a professor of international law and former president of the Belgian Senate. Over and over, Rolin returned to his central argument. The Court had no authority in the case, he asserted, because it concerned not two nations but a nation and a private company.

Mossadegh was at his hotel when news came that British warships had intercepted the *Rose Mary* and forced her to port at the British protectorate of Aden. In a court there, British lawyers argued that Anglo-Iranian was the legal owner of all Iranian oil and that therefore the *Rose Mary* was carrying stolen property. The verdict, which to no one's surprise was in Britain's favor, did not come for several months, but news that the Royal Navy was now intercepting tankers carrying Iranian oil was enough to scare off other customers. Mossadegh called a news conference to denounce the seizure, which he called "a vivid example of the way Britain is attempting to strangle us." Many Europeans were sympathetic. "I fear Dr. Mossadegh has managed to leave behind him in The Hague a generally favorable impression," the British ambassador cabled home to London.

Britain's seizure of the *Rose Mary* was a devastating blow to Mossadegh and his government. No oil company would now do business with Iran, so the country's main source of income was gone. Iran had earned $45 million from oil exports in 1950, more than 70 percent of its total export earnings. That sum dropped by half in 1951 and then to almost zero in 1952.

Mossadegh told Iranians that their campaign for national dignity required "deprivation, self-sacrifice and loyalty," and although most agreed, they suffered nonetheless. He eased their pain by promoting the export of products other than oil, especially textiles and foodstuffs, and by negotiating barter agreements with several countries. These and other steps kept Iran from collapsing, but they were no substitute for the income that oil exports would have earned.

The divisive election, the tightening British oil embargo, and the World Court case all weighed on Mossadegh's mind as he returned home from The Hague at the end of June. Two weeks later, he had his fainting fit in the Shah's salon and, the next day, resigned his office. His resignation was a godsend for his British enemies and for the Shah. They had hoped to manipulate the Majlis into blocking his reelection. Now he had done them the unimaginable favor of leaving on his own accord.

British officials had chosen the man they wished to succeed Mossadegh. He was the wily seventy-two-year-old politician Ahmad Qavam, who had served as prime minister in the mid-1940s. The British scholar/agent Robin Zaehner reported from his post in Tehran that "it was Qavam's desire to work closely with the British and to preserve their legitimate interests in Persia. . . . [He] greatly preferred that British influence should be exercised in Persia rather than that of the Americans (who were foolish and without experience) or that of the Russians, who were Persia's enemies."

At first the Shah was reluctant to support Qavam. His experience with Mossadegh had soured him on strong prime ministers, and he wanted one who was weak and pliable. Qavam was neither. The British, however, insisted on him. In the hours after Mossadegh submitted his resignation on July 17, the Shah mused inconclusively about how to proceed. That night a group of forty pro-British Majlis members met and nominated Qavam. Twenty-seven others gathered nearby to declare their undying loyalty to Mossadegh, the only figure capable of ruling Iran "at this momentous time in our history."

In the end the Shah succumbed to British pressure, as he was wont to do, and accepted Qavam. Foolishly believing that he had won a firm mandate, Qavam immediately began issuing harsh proclamations declaring that the day of retribution had come. He denounced Mossadegh for failing to resolve the oil crisis and for launching "a widespread campaign against a foreign state." Iran, he declared, was about to change. "This helmsman is on a different course," he declared in his first statement as prime minister. Anyone who objected to his new policies would be arrested and delivered into "the heartless and pitiless hands of the law."

Many Iranians did not realize that Mossadegh was really out of power until they heard Qavam deliver this proclamation over the radio. It triggered an explosion of protest. Crowds poured onto the streets of Tehran and other cities, chanting, "Ya Marg Ya

Mossadegh!" (Death or Mossadegh!). Qavam ordered the police to attack and suppress them, but many officers refused. Some joined the protesters and were joyfully embraced.

This spontaneous outburst was, above all, an expression of support for Mossadegh's decision to confront the Anglo-Iranian Oil Company. Many Iranians, however, were also drawn to him because of his commitment to social reform. Mossadegh had freed peasants from forced labor on their landlords' estates, ordered factory owners to pay benefits to sick and injured workers, established a system of unemployment compensation, and taken 20 percent of the money landlords received in rent and placed it in a fund to pay for development projects like pest control, rural housing, and public baths. He supported women's rights, defended religious freedom, and allowed courts and universities to function freely. Above all, he was known even by his enemies as scrupulously honest and impervious to the corruption that pervaded Iranian politics. The prospect of losing him so suddenly, and of having him replaced by a regime evidently sponsored from abroad, was more than his aroused people would accept.

On July 21 National Front leaders called for a general strike to show the nation's opposition to Qavam and support for Mossadegh, "the only popular choice to lead the national struggle." Within hours, much of the country was paralyzed. Ayatollah Kashani, who had learned that Qavam planned to arrest him, issued a *fatwa* ordering soldiers to join the rebellion, which he called a "holy war against the imperialists." Tudeh militants, still angry at Qavam for engineering the withdrawal of Soviet troops from Azerbaijan in 1947, eagerly joined the fray with cries of "Down With the Shah! We Want a People's Republic!"

Qavam and the Shah were shocked by this rebellion and responded by calling out elite military units. Soldiers opened fire on protesters in several parts of Tehran. Dozens fell dead. Young military officers, appalled by the carnage, began talking of mutiny. The Shah had completely lost control of the situation. His only choice was to ask for Qavam's resignation. Qavam submitted it at four o'clock that afternoon. Upon receiving it, the Shah sent for Mossadegh.

Their meeting was unexpectedly cordial. The Shah said he was now prepared to accept Mossadegh as prime minister and give him control of the war ministry. He asked if Mossadegh still wished to maintain the monarchy. Mossadegh assured him that he did, presuming of course that kings would accept the supremacy of elected leaders.

"You could go down in history as an immensely popular monarch if you cooperated with democratic and nationalist forces," he told the Shah.

The next day the Majlis voted overwhelmingly to reelect Mossadegh as prime minister. Qavam's term had lasted just four days. His fall on "Bloody Monday" was a huge, almost unimaginable victory for Iranian nationalists. It was an even greater personal triumph for Mossadegh. Without having given a single speech or even stirred from his home, he had been returned to power by a grateful nation.

The next day brought another piece of electrifying news. The World Court had turned down Britain's appeal, refusing to be drawn into the oil dispute. In London, the *Daily Express* carried the banner headline "Mossadegh's Victory Day." It was that and much, much more.

Mossadegh's support was now so broad and fervent that he could probably have dismissed the Shah, proclaimed the end of the Pahlavi dynasty, and established a republic with himself as president if he had wished. Instead he sent the Shah a peace offering. It was a copy of the Koran with a handwritten inscription: "Consider me an enemy of the Koran if I take any action against the constitution, or if I accept the presidency in case others nullify the constitution and change the form of our country's government."

For the British, this turn of events was a most disappointing setback. In the course of a single week they had gone from vague plotting to spectacular victory to utter defeat. With all that was at stake, however, they were hardly ready to give up. Instead they began carefully reviewing what they had done wrong. They concluded that they had made several mistakes. British intelligence officers had left too much of the planning and execution to Iranians. They had placed their faith in a civilian, Qavam, rather than in a military officer. Perhaps most important, they had acted alone, without American help. Next time—they were determined that there would be a next time—they would not repeat these errors.

□ □ □

The next round of British plotting was shaped by a series of insightful cables that George Middleton, the British chargé d'affaires in Tehran, wrote in the days following the July uprising. Middleton considered the uprising to have been "a turning point in Persian history" because it marked the emergence of a new political force, the mob. Britain's plan to replace Mossadegh had failed because a mob intervened. Next time, he wrote, the British must have the mob on their side.

Middleton also observed that during the uprising, a fair number of army officers had shown themselves less than loyal to Mossadegh. Under the right circumstances, they might join a future rebellion, but they would have to be rallied to the cause by an officer they trusted and admired. Middleton had an idea who that officer might be. He suggested Mossadegh's former interior minister, General Fazlollah Zahedi.

This was a fine choice. Zahedi was far from an ideal candidate—the *New York Times* described him as "a boulevardier with a penchant for gambling and beautiful women"—but was better than anyone else available. He had spent most of his life in uniform and was personally acquainted with almost every Iranian officer.

At the age of twenty-three, as a company commander, Zahedi had led troops into battle against rebel tribesmen in the northern provinces. Two years later Reza Shah promoted him to the rank of brigadier general. Impressed with his loyalty and his firm hand, the Shah made him governor of Khuzistan, the province where the Abadan refinery was located, in 1926; chief of the Tehran police in 1932; and commander of the important Isfahan garrison in 1941.

Zahedi shared Reza Shah's view of what Iran needed. Both men were soldiers at heart, strong, harsh, and ambitious. When World War II broke out, both sought to help the Germans. After the British deposed Reza Shah and forced him into exile, they focused on Zahedi. They identified him as a profiteer who was making huge sums from grain hoarding, but would have left him to his devices had it not been for his close connections to Nazi agents. When they discovered that he was organizing a tribal uprising to coincide with a possible German thrust into Iran, they decided to act.

In September 1942 senior officers of the Secret Intelligence Service summoned the legendary agent Fitzroy MacLean, whose exploits had taken him to clandestine battlegrounds from Tripoli to Tashkent, to a meeting in London. They told him that they wanted Zahedi gone. "How it was to be done they left me to work out by myself," MacLean wrote afterward. "Only two conditions were made: I was to take him alive and I was to do it without creating a disturbance."

The simplest approach would be to kidnap Zahedi from his home, but when MacLean arrived in Isfahan, he discovered that the home was too well guarded. His next idea was to snatch the general from his car, but that also proved impractical because military security was too tight. MacLean decided that he would have to find a ruse by which he could be introduced into Zahedi's presence.

His plan, which he laid out in a cipher telegram to London, was to masquerade as a Baghdad-based brigadier in the British army; send a message telling Zahedi that he was passing through Isfahan and wanted to pay his respects; arrive with one or two "resourceful characters"; and then, when he was alone with the general, pull a pistol and force him into their waiting car. Nearby, a platoon of infantrymen would be waiting "to lend a hand in case anything went wrong." MacLean's superiors granted him everything he asked, including permission to kill Zahedi if that became necessary, but on one point they would not yield. No one under any circumstances could be allowed to pretend he was a British brigadier. A real one would be supplied if necessary.

MacLean traveled to Qom, 150 miles north of Isfahan, where the local British commander had been instructed to give him whatever he needed. He needed a platoon of soldiers and rounded one up without difficulty after letting it be known that he was recruiting for a commando mission. At a ruined fort in the nearby desert, he and his men rehearsed for several days. Then, on the day before the planned abduction, he set out for Isfahan. With him was a genuine brigadier, supplied by the British consulate in Qom, "a distinguished officer whose well-developed sense of humor caused him to enter completely into the spirit of the somewhat equivocal role that had been allotted to him."

The arrangement to meet General Zahedi went perfectly. MacLean arrived in a car flying a large Union Jack. The guard at the gate was deep in conversation with a British agent who was part of MacLean's team and looked up only briefly as he passed. Two nondescript trucks, their cargo space covered with tarpaulins, were parked nearby. Inside were the soldiers MacLean had spent the last week training. They waited while he entered the brigade head-quarters:

> When, a couple of minutes later, General Zahedi, a dapper figure in a tight-fitting gray uniform and highly polished boots, entered the room, he found himself looking down the barrel of my Colt automatic. There was no advantage in prolonging a scene which might easily have become embarrassing. Without further ado, I invited the general to put his hands up and informed him that I had instructions to arrest him and that, if he made any noise or attempt at resistance, he would be shot. Then I took away his pistol and hustled him through the window into the car which was waiting outside with the engine running.... Soon we reached the point in the desert where we had spent the night, and here I handed over my captive to an officer and six men who were standing by to take him by car to the nearest landing-ground, where an airplane was waiting to fly him to Palestine. ... In the general's bedroom I found a collection of automatic weapons of German manufacture, a good deal of silk underwear, some opium, [and] an illustrated register of the prostitutes of Isfahan.

Zahedi spent the rest of the war in a British internment camp. After his release, he resumed his career as if nothing had happened, serving as military commander in Fars province and then returning to his old job as police chief in Tehran. Mohammed Reza Shah named him to the Senate in 1950 and the next year persuaded Mossadegh to choose him as interior minister. Mossadegh dis-missed him a few months later, after he ordered the massacre of rioters who were protesting Averell Harriman's visit. Although Zahedi was no longer in the army, he was the president of the Retired Officers Association, which was made up mostly of men whom Mossadegh had cashiered and who were anxious for revenge. This constituency, coupled with his own boldness and well-known ruthlessness, led the British to choose him as the figurehead leader of their coup. They were willing to forget the unpleasantness of the past, and so was he.

The combination that George Middleton recommended in his cables—a mob plus Zahedi—became the core of the plot against

Mossadegh, and it never changed. Before serious planning could begin, however, the British had to win American cooperation. Prime Minister Churchill, who in the words of one of his foreign spies "enjoyed dramatic operations and had no high regard for timid diplomatists," spent the second half of 1952 trying to enlist President Truman.

In August Mossadegh invited an American oil executive named Alton Jones to visit Iran. Truman thought this was a fine idea and gave it his blessing, but when Churchill learned of it, he was mightily upset. He protested that any friendly overtures from the United States would undermine his campaign to isolate Mossadegh. Britain was supporting the Americans in Korea, he reminded Truman, and had a right to expect "Anglo-American unity" on Iran.

Nothing substantial came out of the Jones mission, but that did not shake Truman or his senior advisers from their desire to seek compromise with Mossadegh. They had concluded, in Acheson's words, "that the British were so obstructive and determined on a rule-or-ruin policy in Iran that we must strike out on an independent policy or run the risk of having Iran disappear behind the Iron Curtain." Truman urged Churchill to accept the fact of nationalization, which he said "seems to have become as sacred in Iran's eyes as [the] Koran." To continue resisting it, he warned, could provoke upheaval that would send Iran "down the Communist drain" and be "a disaster to the free world."

Churchill replied by proposing that he and Truman "send a joint telegram personal and confidential to Mossadegh." He wrote a draft. It was couched in friendly language but offered only a rehash of old British proposals. Truman would not sign. Doggedly Churchill pressed his argument that Britain and the United States must "gallop together" against Mossadegh. "I do not myself see," he told Truman, "why two good men asking only what is right and just should not gang up against a third who is doing wrong."

Finally Truman agreed to sign a watered-down version of Churchill's letter. It asked Mossadegh to do two things he had sworn never to do: allow the return of Anglo-Iranian to its old position in Iran and accept arbitration by the World Court based on the company's position before it was nationalized. If he complied, Britain would lift its economic embargo and the United States would give Iran $10 million in aid.

A few days after receiving the letter, Mossedegh read it scornfully to the Majlis. It was an affront, he said, because it failed to recognize that the "former company" had been finally and irrevocably nationalized. As for the aid offer, it "smacked of charity," which Iran did not want. To rising applause he declared that Britain "for centuries has been used to plundering poor nations," and that Iran would no longer accept its "oppressive terms." He concluded with a telling moral observation: "Abiding by law and respecting the rights of the weak not only would not diminish, but would greatly enhance the position and prestige of the strong."

Mossadegh then asked for and won Majlis support for a counterproposal. Iran would accept mediation by the World Court, but on two conditions. First, the Court would have to decide the case according to either Iranian law or "any law in any country nationalizing its industries in similar circumstances." Second, if the British were going to demand compensation, Iran must be allowed to make a counterclaim for its lost revenues.

These terms were reasonable enough to worry Churchill. Over the next few weeks he sent a series of cables to Truman urging him not to succumb to the temptation to negotiate. "We cannot I am sure go further at this critical time in our struggle," he insisted in one of them. "Mossadegh will come to reasonable terms on being confronted with a continued Truman-Churchill accord."

As these cables were flashing across the Atlantic, Churchill's foreign secretary, Anthony Eden, was hearing good news from his embassy in Tehran. General Zahedi had proven highly responsive to British overtures. He was ready to join a coup against Mossadegh, naturally with himself as the designated successor. Encouraged by this development, Eden sent Mossadegh a cold note rejecting his terms.

Unlike some of the other outsiders who shaped the Western intervention in Iran, Eden was familiar with the region. At Oxford he had studied Persian, which he considered "the Italian of the East." He read the epic *Shahnameh*, early Persian poetry, and inscriptions written by Darius. After graduating, he joined the Foreign Office. He was an undersecretary when Britain negotiated the 1933 accord that outraged Mossadegh and other Iranian nationalists. Later he made several extended visits to Iran. They did not leave him with a high opinion of the natives.

Eden, like Churchill, was a fervent defender of the colonial system. His contempt for the political and intellectual capacity of people in poor countries, which he did not hide, startled some foreigners. One of them was Dean Acheson, who was taken aback by Eden's view of Iranians. "They were rug dealers and that's all they were," Acheson lamented about Eden's attitude. "You should never give in, and they would always come around and make a deal if you stayed firm."

Eden's dismissive note confirmed Mossadegh's belief that Britain would never offer him anything but hostility. His belief turned to certainty when he learned of General Zahedi's meetings with British agents. Zahedi had also begun meeting with Ayatollah Kashani, who had been elected speaker of the Majlis and increasingly saw Mossadegh as a political rival. Tehran was alive with rumors that a coup was imminent. There was only one way for Mossadegh to rid himself of the British agents who were plotting it. On October 16 he announced that Iran was breaking diplomatic relations with Britain.

By the end of that month all British diplomats, and with them all British intelligence agents, were gone from Iran. It was a heavy and fateful blow. With it, Mossadegh dashed Britain's hopes of organizing a coup. If there was to be one, the Americans would have to stage it.

Having expelled the British before they could strike against him, Mossadegh and his allies moved to arrest General Zahedi and place him on trial for treason. They were stymied at first because, as a senator, Zahedi enjoyed parliamentary immunity. The Senate's two-year term had recently expired, however, and although senators had voted to remain in office for another four years, their action was plainly illegal. On October 23 the Majlis declared the Senate dissolved. The moment this act became law, Zahedi was subject to arrest. To avoid it, he went into hiding.

Britain now had no intelligence agents in Iran, Zahedi was out of circulation, and the Truman administration remained implacably against the idea of intervention. Plans for a coup were at a standstill. That was fine with Truman, who believed that the British were at least as much to blame for the "awful situation" as was Mossadegh. "We tried," he lamented in a handwritten letter to Henry Grady, his former ambassador in Tehran, "to get the block headed British to have their oil company make a fair deal with Iran. No, no, they could not do that. They knew all about how to handle it—we didn't according to them."

British leaders might have despaired at this point, but they saw a bright glimmer of hope on the horizon. A presidential election was forthcoming in the United States, and Truman was not running for reelection. The Republican candidate to replace him, Dwight Eisenhower, was running on a vigorously anticommunist platform. Eisenhower's rhetoric greatly encouraged Churchill and Eden. The moment he was elected, they called off their effort to influence Truman and shifted their focus to the incoming team.

Election day found Kermit Roosevelt in Tehran. His job running CIA operations in the Middle East gave him professional interests there and he visited from time to time, but this was no routine stop. The abrupt departure of British intelligence officers from Iran was a major event in Roosevelt's world. The British had spent decades building a covert network there, and now it was leaderless. This was an extraordinary opportunity for the United States. Roosevelt was determined to exploit it as best he could.

Born in Buenos Aires, where his father had business interests, brought up near grandfather Theodore's estate on Long Island, and educated at Harvard, Roosevelt was the prototype of the gentleman spy. He was in his twenties when World War II broke out, a junior faculty member in the Harvard history department. Eager for adventure, he joined the Office of Strategic Services, which was so clandestine that even many of the people who knew it existed did not know what its initials stood for; they called it Oh So Secret or, because its ranks were filled with well-connected Ivy Leaguers, Oh So Social. What Roosevelt did as an OSS agent is unknown, although he apparently spent time in Egypt and Italy. Not even his family ever found out. "That was spook talk," his wife said years later. "He didn't talk spooks to me."

Photos of Roosevelt taken around the time he went to Iran show him wiry and boyishly handsome, with dark-rimmed glasses and a winning smile. His family knew him as a bumbler who could barely change a light bulb, but at work he conveyed a very different impression. Associates described him as supremely self-confident without being overbearing. One writer later called him "insouciant coolness personified." During his reconnaissance mission in

November 1952, he did not meet any Iranians whom he knew to be British agents, but he was perceptive enough to sense that there were plenty of them around.

On his way home, Roosevelt stopped in London. He had friends in the upper ranks of the Secret Intelligence Service and had been musing with them for more than a year about ways of dealing with Mossadegh. Now, for the first time, these musings began to seem realistic. His friends told him that they were more determined than ever to carry out a coup and that both Eden and Churchill were pushing them, the latter "with special vehemence." Roosevelt was most intrigued:

> What they had in mind was nothing less than the overthrow of Mossadegh. Furthermore, they saw no point in wasting time by delay. They wanted to start immediately. I had to explain that the project would require considerable clearance from my government and that I was not entirely sure what the results would be. As I told my British colleagues, we had, I felt sure, no chance to win approval from the outgoing administration of Truman and Acheson. The new Republicans, however, might be quite different.

CHAPTER 10

Pull Up Your Socks
and Get Going

Excitement surged through the corridors of power in London when news came that Dwight Eisenhower had been elected president of the United States. British leaders had spent many frustrating months trying to persuade Harry Truman to join their campaign against the Iranian government. His steadfast refusals deeply discouraged them, but now the climate in Washington was radically changed. What had come to seem impossible was suddenly very possible indeed.

Over the years, Britain had assembled a formidable network of clandestine agents in Iran. Under the direction of "Monty" Woodhouse, the chief of the British intelligence station in Tehran during the early 1950s, these agents became proficient at everything from bribing politicians to organizing riots. Woodhouse and all other British spies, however, had to leave Iran when Prime Minister Mossadegh shut the embassy from which they worked. They left behind a fine band of subversives.

The principal figures in this underground network were the three extraordinary Rashidian brothers. Their father had made a fortune in shipping, banking, and real estate, and he bequeathed to them not just his wealth but his boundless admiration for all things

British. Beginning in the early 1950s the Secret Intelligence Service paid them £10,000 each month, the equivalent of $28,000, a staggering sum by Iranian standards, to suborn Iranians in what the CIA called "such fields as the armed forces, the Majlis (Iranian parliament), religious leaders, the press, street gangs, politicians and other influential figures."

"Seyfollah, the eldest and a musician and philosopher, was the brains of the triumvirate and a superb conversationalist and host," one historian wrote about the brothers. "He was a student of history and liked to quote Machiavelli. Asadollah was the organizer, political activist and confidante of the Shah, while Qodratollah was the businessman and entrepreneur."

Directors of the Secret Intelligence Service were pained to think that such outstanding agents were going to waste in Iran when there was such urgent business to be done there. Eisenhower's election gave them hope that the Americans would pick up where they had been forced to leave off. Kermit Roosevelt encouraged them further during his visit to London. So eager were they to resume their plotting that they could not even wait for Eisenhower to take office. In mid-November of 1952, less than two weeks after the election, they sent Woodhouse to Washington.

Woodhouse met with his CIA counterparts and with men who would take important posts in the Eisenhower administration. Since he had no love for the Anglo-Iranian Oil Company—he considered its directors "stupid, boring, pigheaded and tiresome"—and since he knew that American officials didn't care much about its troubles anyway, he shaped his appeal around the rhetoric of anti-communism:

> I argued that even if a settlement of the oil dispute could be negotiated with Mossadegh, which was doubtful, he was still incapable of resisting a coup by the Tudeh party, if it were backed by Soviet support. Therefore he must be removed. I had with me a draft plan for the purpose. . . .
>
> Two separate components were dovetailed into the plan, because we had two distinct kinds of resources: an urban organization run by the [Rashidian] brothers, and a number of tribal leaders to the south. We intended to activate both simultaneously. The urban organization included senior officers of the army and

police, deputies and senators, mullahs, merchants, newspaper editors and elder statesmen, as well as mob leaders. These forces, directed by the brothers, were to seize control of Tehran, preferably with the support of the Shah but if necessary without it, to arrest Mossadegh and his ministers. At the same time, tribal leaders were to make a show of force in the direction of major cities in the south. . . .

I had obtained the Foreign Office's agreement to a list of fifteen politicians, any one of whom would be acceptable to us as prime minister if he were equally acceptable to the Americans. The list was in three categories, crudely labeled "Old Gang," "New Gang," and "Intermediate." The third category included General Fazlollah Zahedi, who soon emerged in discussion as the figure most likely to be acceptable to both British and American policymakers. I had been in touch with him before we were expelled from Tehran, and it was clear that the Americans were also in touch with him since we had left. He was an ironic choice, for during World War II he had been regarded as a German agent. An operation to kidnap him and put him out of circulation had then been organized by Fitzroy MacLean. Now we were all turning to him as the potential savior of Iran.

Over the course of his meetings in Washington, Woodhouse detected "steadily increasing interest" in his proposal for what the British called "Operation Boot." Frank Wisner, a New York lawyer who had become the CIA's director of operations, was strongly positive. So was Wisner's newly named boss, Allen Dulles. State Department officials were markedly less enthusiastic, but John Foster Dulles would overrule their reluctance as soon as he was sworn in as secretary of state.

By the time Woodhouse flew home, the incoming administration had committed itself, albeit informally, to a covert operation aimed at removing Mossadegh. It had also accepted Britain's nominees to play the two key roles: General Zahedi as Iran's designated savior and Kermit Roosevelt as the CIA field commander who would place him in office. A plan would be ready soon after Eisenhower took office. John Foster Dulles and Allen Dulles would win his approval and then do the deed.

The Dulles brothers, whose work was vital to the success of Operation Ajax, were unique in American history. Never before or since have siblings run the overt and covert sides of United States foreign policy simultaneously. During their terms as secretary of state and director of central intelligence, they worked in near-perfect harmony to achieve their common goals. Among the first and most urgent was Mossadegh's overthrow.

Foster and Allie, as the brothers were known, were born into privilege. Their grandfather, John Watson Foster, was secretary of state when they were children, and he often allowed them to meet his guests and eavesdrop on their meetings. During the era of McKinley and Theodore Roosevelt, they spent many formative hours in Washington salons and acquired an easy familiarity with the ways of power. Allie, who from childhood displayed what his biographer called "an insatiable curiosity about the people around him," took secret notes on what he heard.

Both brothers attended Princeton and did well, with Foster, the elder by five years, graduating first in his class. Although they were always close, they had quite different personalities. Allie was affable and easygoing. He enjoyed tennis, wine, and elegant parties, and at one point had a mistress who was undergoing analysis by Carl Gustav Jung. Foster was stern and gruff, known for opening and closing meetings with grunts instead of expressions of welcome or thanks. It was said that even his friends didn't like him much.

By the time the brothers had both graduated from Princeton, one of their uncles, Robert Lansing, was Woodrow Wilson's secretary of state. Partly as a result of his influence, they both pursued interests in world affairs. Allie joined the State Department when World War I broke out. He was sent to Bern, which as the capital of neutral Switzerland was a center of émigré life, and then to Berlin and Istanbul, also hotbeds of intrigue. At each post he plunged eagerly into intelligence work. He proved himself highly adept at recruiting informers, debriefing travelers, observing military movements, and assessing the strengths and weaknesses of foreign governments.

While Allie was learning the espionage business, Foster launched his legal career in New York. After he graduated from law school, his grandfather arranged an interview for him at the legendary firm of Sullivan & Cromwell. He was hired as a junior clerk and soon found himself working with one of the most quietly influential groups of men in the world. Sullivan & Cromwell was no ordinary law firm but a center of international business and finance. Its lawyers were brokers among kings, presidents, and plutocrats, and its clients included many of the world's most important banks and business cartels. Foster dealt directly with many of them, including J. P. Morgan & Company, the International Nickel Company, and the Cuban Sugar Cane Corporation. He distinguished himself as a maker of high-level deals and an expert in international finance. When the firm's managing partner died in 1926, Foster was given the job. One of his first decisions was to recruit his brother.

Allen Dulles was fresh out of law school and had not even been admitted to the bar, but his unusual skills and wide range of contacts made him a great asset to Sullivan & Cromwell, which advertised itself as having "unusual and diversified means of obtaining information." In effect he was an intelligence officer for hire. He enjoyed his work but longed for more excitement. When World War II broke out, he, like Kermit Roosevelt, joined the OSS. He was posted in Europe, where he studied the Nazi intelligence system and worked to penetrate and undermine it.

Foster spent the war years at home, making speeches and publishing articles warning of the threat that Soviet expansionism posed to "the accumulated civilization of these centuries." He became a leading figure in Republican politics. In 1948 he served as the foreign policy adviser to the Republican presidential candidate, Governor Thomas Dewey of New York. Many assumed that he would become secretary of state when Dewey won, but after Dewey's surprising loss to Truman he had to return to his law practice and bide his time. Allen, who rejoined the firm after the war, had dreamed of becoming Dewey's ambassador to France, but that plan, too, was spoiled by the election result.

The Dulles brothers developed a special interest in Iran. Foster always mentioned Iran when he spoke or wrote about countries he believed might soon fall to communism. Allen visited Tehran in 1949 on behalf of a Sullivan & Cromwell client, an engineering firm looking for construction contracts. His trip gave him a chance to observe both the twenty-nine-year-old Shah, whom his wife called "the gloomy prince," and the fiery opposition leader, Mohammad Mossadegh. Later that year, when the Shah visited New York, Allen arranged a "small private dinner" for him and one hundred members of the Council on Foreign Relations.

In 1947 the wartime OSS was transformed into the Central Intelligence Agency. Allen Dulles had many friends in the new agency, and at their request, he wrote a series of secret reports urging it to launch a worldwide program of "covert psychological warfare, clandestine political activity, sabotage and guerrilla activity." Soon after Truman chose General Walter Bedell Smith as the director of central intelligence, Smith brought Dulles into the agency, first as a consultant and then as deputy director.

Allen Dulles was one of the country's most ambitious intelligence experts. John Foster Dulles had become widely known as a world-class international lawyer who moved easily in elite Republican circles. Both reached the pinnacle of power when Eisenhower took office.

"Beedle" Smith stayed with them, moving from the CIA to become undersecretary of state. Smith had been Eisenhower's chief of staff during the war and remained one of his most trusted friends. In his new position, he was ideally placed to assure that the CIA, the State Department, and the White House would work seamlessly on sensitive projects like the coup against Mossadegh.

On a cold day shortly before Eisenhower's inauguration, Smith summoned Kermit Roosevelt for a gruff conversation about Iran. Smith had supported the idea of a coup during the Truman administration, but his superiors overruled him. Now he was eager to proceed. It had been two months since Woodhouse's visit to Washington, and Smith was losing patience.

"When are those ——ing British coming to talk to us?" Smith demanded. "And when is our goddamn operation going to get underway?" Roosevelt assured him that everyone was ready, but it would be unseemly to move before Eisenhower was inaugurated.

"Pull up your socks and get going," Smith told him. "You won't have any trouble in London. They'll jump at anything we propose. And I'm sure you can come up with something sensible enough for Foster to OK. Ike will agree."

Eisenhower was inaugurated on January 20, 1953. Days later, the American ambassador in Tehran, Loy Henderson, began contacting Iranians he thought might be interested in working to overthrow Mossadegh. Like his new bosses in Washington, Henderson had given up hope for a compromise. In one cable to Washington, he described Mossadegh as "lacking in stability," "clearly dominated by emotions and prejudices," and "not quite sane." In another, he asserted that the National Front was composed of "the street rabble, the extreme left . . . extreme Iranian nationalists, some but not all of the more fanatical religious leaders, [and] intellectual leftists, including many who had been educated abroad and did not realize that Iran was not ready for democracy." He and George Middleton, his British counterpart, took the extraordinary step of composing a joint message to their home offices expressing their shared conclusion that the longer Mossadegh remained in power, the likelier it was that Iran would fall to communism.

Through an emissary, Henderson even opened a channel to General Zahedi, who, he told Dulles in a cable, was "not ideal" but had "more chance of piloting Iran through the turbulent days following Mossadegh's resignation than any other candidate now on the horizon." Zahedi had assured Henderson that if he reached power, he would "take a strong stand toward the Communists." He added, however, that it would be "impossible for Iranians to remove the present government by their own efforts."

Henderson sent a cable to Washington endorsing this view. It was received with great enthusiasm, so much so that Beedle Smith gave it to Eisenhower with a cover note calling it "very accurate." Smith also sent a reply to Henderson telling him that the United States had decided it could "no longer approve of the Mossadegh government and would prefer a successor government." He sent copies of his cable to CIA headquarters in Washington and to the CIA station in Iran. It amounted to a formal, though secret, declaration of war on Mossadegh.

Only one important figure in the Eisenhower administration still hoped for compromise with Mossadegh: President Eisenhower himself. Two weeks before his inauguration, he met with Churchill in New York and did not seem at all interested when Churchill mentioned Iran. In fact, he complained that Britain's efforts to involve the United States in its Iranian troubles had done nothing but "get Mossadegh to accuse us of being a partner in browbeating a weak nation."

Churchill was wise enough not to press his case at that moment. He knew that planning for a coup was already well underway, and that the Dulles brothers were on his side. In February he dispatched "C," the chief of British intelligence, Sir John Sinclair, to Washington to convey the intensity of his interest.

While Sinclair was in Washington, Iranian tribal leaders who were on the British payroll, working with General Zahedi, launched a short-lived uprising in the southern provinces. Mossadegh suspected the Shah was involved and suggested that he consider leaving Iran until passions cooled. By all accounts including his own, the Shah was more than willing to go. Minister of Court Hussein Ala described him as being in an "almost hysterical state" and on the brink of a "complete nervous breakdown and irrational action."

Mossadegh's foreign-sponsored enemies, however, cleverly turned news of the Shah's planned trip to their advantage. In sermons, street-corner speeches, and newspaper articles, they charged that Mossadegh was forcing the Shah to leave against his will and that his next step would certainly be to abolish the monarchy. They organized a mob to converge on Mossadegh's house on the night of February 28, and as the crowd swelled in size, a jeep carrying an army colonel and one of the most colorful gang leaders in Tehran, Shaban "The Brainless" Jafari, smashed through the front gate. Mossadegh, in his pajamas, was forced to flee over his back garden wall. A British diplomat cabled home that the mob "was certainly organized by Kashani, and was not a spontaneous expression of a loyalty deep-seated or significant enough to stiffen the Shah."

By the next afternoon Tehran was quiet again, partly because the Shah had announced that he was canceling his travel plans. The sudden appearance of a paid mob and its willingness to attack the prime minister, however, contributed to an atmosphere of growing instability. It also gave coup planners more ammunition for their campaign to persuade Eisenhower that Iran was sliding dangerously toward chaos.

Neither Eisenhower nor anyone in his inner circle ever wrote an account of how he came to support the idea of a coup. Evidence suggests, however, that he did so during March, two months after his inauguration. The Dulles brothers seized on the violence that erupted in Tehran on February 28. Even Ambassador Henderson acknowledged that the protest had been organized rather than genuine, but evidently no one told that to Eisenhower. Instead, Allen Dulles sent him an intelligence estimate warning that "the

Iran situation has been slowly disintegrating" and "a Communist takeover is becoming more and more of a possibility."

It was not an easy sell. At a meeting of the National Security Council on March 4, Eisenhower wondered aloud why it wasn't possible "to get some of the people in these down-trodden countries to like us instead of hating us." Secretary of State Dulles did not reply directly, but he delivered a sobering analysis of the situation in Iran. His words, as reported by the official note-taker, suggested that the United States could no longer stand by without acting:

> The probable consequences of the events of the last few days, concluded Mr. Dulles, would be a dictatorship in Iran under Mossadegh. As long as the latter lives there was little danger, but if he were to be assassinated or removed from power, a political vacuum would occur in Iran and the Communists might easily take over. The consequences of such a takeover were then outlined in all their seriousness by Mr. Dulles. Not only would the free world be deprived of the enormous assets represented by Iranian oil production and reserves, but the Russians would secure these assets and thus henceforth be free of any anxiety about their petroleum situation. Worse still, Mr. Dulles pointed out, if Iran succumbed to the Communists there was little doubt that in short order the other areas of the Middle East, with some sixty percent of the world's oil reserves, would fall into Communist control.

Later that week, Foreign Secretary Eden visited Washington. At several of his top-level meetings, Eden broached the subject of Iran and the proposed coup. He found everyone except Eisenhower sympathetic. Alton Jones, the oil executive who had traveled to Iran the year before, was a personal friend of Eisenhower's, and Eisenhower told Eden that he wanted to send Jones back "to make the best arrangement he could to get the oil flowing again." He said he considered Mossadegh "the only hope for the West in Iran," precisely the view Truman had held.

"I would like to give the guy ten million bucks," Eisenhower told the surprised Eden.

Eden tried gently to change Eisenhower's mind, telling him at one point that "we would be better occupied looking for alternatives to Mossadegh, rather than trying to buy him off." In the best diplomatic tradition, however, he left the real work to the intelligence officers he had brought with him. While he spoke softly at the White House, they were honing their plot with comrades at the CIA and the State Department.

The Dulles brothers had developed an excellent sense of how to bring their boss around to their way of thinking. On March 7 John Foster Dulles and Eden issued a joint communiqué saying they had agreed on a new offer that would allow Iran to "retain control of its own oil industry and of its own oil policies." That sounded fine to Eisenhower, but it did not honestly reflect the offer itself, which, like every other one the British had made over the past two years, was based on the premise that they would return to run the Iranian oil industry. Mossadegh rejected it and told Ambassador Henderson that he was disappointed that the Eisenhower administration had "allowed the United Kingdom to formulate United States policies concerning Iran." He made several counterproposals, even offering at one point to submit to mediation by Switzerland or Germany, but the British and their new friends in Washington ignored them.

While Eden was in Washington, the Rashidian brothers were doing their best to stir up trouble in Iran. Partly through their efforts, prominent figures who had been part of Mossadegh's coalition began to turn against him. Ayatollah Kashani, the most outspoken defector, damned Mossadegh with the vitriol he had once reserved for the British. He began using thugs to intimidate his rivals and even pushed a bill through the Majlis pardoning Khalil Tahmasibi, the convicted assassin of Prime Minister Razmara. Other former Mossadegh allies who broke with him to pursue their own agendas included Muzzaffar Baqai, head of the worker-based Toilers party, and Hussein Makki, who had helped lead the takeover of the Abadan refinery and was at one point considered Mossadegh's heir apparent. Robin Zaehner wrote in a report to London that the successful effort to pull Kashani, Baqai, and Makki away from the National Front was "created and directed by the brothers Rashidian."

These defections greatly weakened the National Front and left Mossadegh isolated and vulnerable. They also immeasurably strengthened the Dulles brothers in their effort to persuade President Eisenhower that the time had come for the United States to act. At a National Security Council meeting on March 11, Secretary of State Dulles asserted that Americans must become "senior partners with the British in this area." Eisenhower expressed no disagreement.

"The President said that he had very real doubts whether, even if we tried unilaterally, we could make a successful deal with Mossadegh," the note-taker at that meeting reported. "He felt that it might not be worth the paper it was written on, and the example might have grave effects on United States oil concessions in other parts of the world."

Eisenhower had come to the conclusion that Iran was collapsing, and that the collapse could not be prevented as long as Mossadegh was in power. He stopped inquiring about the prospects for compromise. Those around him took his change in tone as a sign that he would not resist the idea of a coup. On March 18 Frank Wisner sent a message to his British counterparts saying that the CIA was now prepared to discuss the details of a plot against Mossadegh. Two weeks later, Allen Dulles approved the dispatch of $1 million to the CIA station in Tehran, for use "in any way that would bring about the fall of Mossadegh."

These developments greatly encouraged the British. During April, the Foreign Office formally embraced Operation Ajax. Then, in what amounted to explicit recognition that command was passing from their hands to the Americans, British agents sent word to the Rashidian brothers that they should now work with the CIA.

Iranians connected to the Rashidian network decided that they could push Iran further toward chaos by kidnapping high government officials. Their preferred targets, Foreign Minister Fatemi and General Riahi, the newly appointed chief of staff, traveled with too many bodyguards, so they settled on the Tehran police chief, General Mahmoud Afshartus. Some of the plotters had personal ties to Afshartus, and one invited the chief to his home on April 19. There he was seized, blindfolded, and spirited to a cave outside of town. Police officers identified the kidnappers almost immediately, but as the officers closed in, one of Afshartus's captors shot and killed him.

This murder had the desired effect. It shocked the country and also eliminated a popular officer who might have been a formidable obstacle to the success of the forthcoming coup. General Zahedi, who had resurfaced after treason charges against him were dropped, was implicated in the killing. He took refuge in the Majlis, under Ayatollah Kashani's protection.

Unaware of how decisively the Americans had turned against him, Mossadegh next decided to appeal directly to Eisenhower. In a letter dated May 28 he said that Iranians were "suffering financial hardships and struggling with political intrigues carried on by the former oil company and the British government." They would be deeply grateful for "prompt and effective aid" from the United States, or for American support for a stalled $25-million loan that Mossadegh was seeking from the Export-Import Bank, or at least for permission to sell oil to American companies. Eisenhower took a month to reply. When he did, it was to suggest that Mossadegh could best repair Iran's economy by resolving his dispute with the British:

> The failure of Iran and the United Kingdom to reach an agreement with regard to compensation has handicapped the Government of the United States in its efforts to help Iran. There is a strong feeling in the United States, even among American citizens most sympathetic to Iran and friendly to the Iranian people, that it would not be fair to the American taxpayers for the United States Government to extend any considerable amount of economic aid to Iran so long as Iran could have access to funds derived from the sale of its oil. . . . I note the concern reflected in your letter at the present dangerous situation in Iran, and sincerely hope that before it is too late, the Government of Iran will take such steps as are in its power to prevent a further deterioration in that situation.

This letter told Mossadegh what Eisenhower's intimates already knew: that the new administration had reversed American policy toward Iran. No longer would there be efforts to make the best of the situation, as under Truman, and no longer would there be criticism of the British for favoring a coup. In fact, by the time Eisenhower sent his reply to Mossadegh, both men knew what was afoot.

Eisenhower had already given tacit approval to the coup plot, but because of its momentous scope, tacit approval was not enough. On June 14 Allen Dulles went to the White House to brief him. Sensing the president's desire not to know too much, Dulles gave him only what Kermit Roosevelt called "the most 'broad brush' outline of what was proposed." That was all Eisenhower needed, and he gave his blessing. Around the same time Churchill gave his own secret—and much more enthusiastic—approval.

Planning for the plot was already quite advanced by the time Eisenhower and Churchill formally endorsed it. Two veteran intelligence officers, one American and one British, had met in Cyprus to draw up a detailed blueprint. Both were old Iran hands. The CIA man was Donald Wilber, who had worked for years as an archaeologist and an architect in the Middle East, served in Iran during World War II as an OSS agent, and then divided his time between advanced studies at Princeton and work as a consultant to the CIA specializing in psychological warfare. In 1952 Wilber had spent six months running the CIA's "political action" office in Tehran, an assignment that gave him a firsthand view of political and military factions favoring and opposing Mossadegh. His British counterpart, Norman Darbyshire, had served extended tours of duty in Iran and worked closely with Robin Zaehner. When the British intelligence station in Tehran was forced to close, it was moved to Cyprus and Darbyshire was named to head it.

These two agents, now working for governments that shared the same goal in Iran, struck up a close working relationship, as a CIA history of the coup—written by Wilber himself—later reported:

> It soon became apparent that Dr. Wilber and Mr. Darbyshire held quite similar views of Iranian personalities and had made very similar estimates of the factors involved in the Iranian political scene. There was no friction or marked difference of opinion during the discussions. It also quickly became apparent that the SIS was perfectly content to follow whatever lead was taken by the Agency. It seemed obvious to Wilber that the British were very pleased at having obtained the active cooperation of the Agency and were determined to do nothing which might jeopardize US participation. At the same time there was faint envy expressed over the fact that the Agency was better equipped in the way of funds, personnel and facilities than was SIS.

Wilber and Darbyshire agreed that although General Zahedi had his weaknesses, he was the only Iranian with enough "vigor and courage" to rally opposition forces. Their plan to place him in power, which would be altered several times before the blow was struck, was carefully considered and straightforward:

  ☐   Through a variety of means, covert agents would manipulate public opinion and turn as many Iranians as possible against Mossadegh. This effort, for which $150,000 was budgeted, would "create, extend and enhance public hostility and distrust and fear of Mossadegh and his government." It would portray Mossadegh as corrupt, pro-communist, hostile to Islam, and bent on destroying the morale and readiness of the armed forces.

☐   While Iranian agents spread these lies, thugs would be paid to launch "staged attacks" on religious leaders and make it appear that they were ordered by Mossadegh or his supporters.

☐   Meanwhile, General Zahedi would persuade and bribe as many of his fellow officers as possible to stand ready for whatever military action was necessary to carry out the coup. He was to be given $60,000, later increased to $135,000, to "win additional friends" and "influence key people."

☐   A similar effort, for which $11,000 per week was budgeted, would be launched to suborn members of the Majlis.

☐   On the morning of "coup day," thousands of paid demonstrators would stage a massive antigovernment rally. The well-prepared Majlis would respond with a "quasi-legal" vote to dismiss Mossadegh. If he resisted, army units under Zahedi's control would arrest him and his key supporters, and then seize military command posts, police stations, telephone and telegraph offices, radio stations, and the national bank.

Working closely with comrades in Washington and Tehran, with whom they were in constant contact over a Cyprus-based radio network, Wilber and Darbyshire finished this blueprint at the end of May. On June 3 Ambassador Henderson arrived in Washington to be briefed on its contents. He stayed to attend a crucial meeting on June 25, at which plans for the coup were laid out in detail.

President Eisenhower did not wish to hear details of covert operations and so did not attend this meeting. His closest foreign policy advisers, however, were all there. The meeting was held in John Foster Dulles's office at the State Department. When the plotters had assembled, Dulles picked up the report Wilber and Darbyshire had written and said, "So this is how we get rid of that madman Mossadegh!"

Kermit Roosevelt explained how he proposed to carry out the

coup, and when he was finished, Dulles asked the others what they thought. Allen Dulles and Beedle Smith endorsed the plan without reservation. So did Secretary of Defense Charles Wilson. Two senior State Department officials—Henry Byroade, the assistant secretary for Middle East affairs, and Robert Bowie, the director of the policy planning staff—went along with slightly less enthusiasm, certainly realizing that they would not remain in their jobs long if they dissented. When it was Henderson's turn to speak, he said he had no love for "this kind of business," but that in this case "we have no choice."

"That's that, then," Secretary of State Dulles said with an uncharacteristic grin. "Let's get going."

With this unanimous vote, the United States gave its final go-ahead for Operation Ajax, or Operation Boot, as the British continued to call it. The governments in London and Washington were finally united in their enthusiasm. One looked forward to recovering its oil concession. The other saw a chance to deliver a devastating blow against communism.

There was dissent from this new unity. Some of it came from career diplomats like Charles Bohlen, a former ambassador to the Soviet Union, who subjected one British diplomat in Washington to what the diplomat called "an emotional tirade" against the planned coup. Several CIA officers also opposed the idea. One of them was Roger Goiran, the chief of the CIA station in Tehran.

Goiran had built a formidable intelligence network, known by the code name Bedamn, that was engaged in propaganda activities aimed at blackening the image of the Soviet Union in Iran. It also stood ready to launch a nationwide campaign of subversion and sabotage in case of a communist coup. The Bedamn network consisted of more than one hundred agents and had an annual budget of $1 million—quite considerable, in light of the fact that the CIA's total worldwide budget for covert operations was just $82 million. Now Goiran was being asked to use his network in a coup against Mossadegh. He believed that this would be a great mistake and warned that if the coup was carried out, Iranians would forever view the United States as a supporter of what he called "Anglo-French colonialism." His opposition was so resolute that Allen Dulles had to remove him from his post.

While Allen Dulles marshaled resources for Operation Ajax,

John Foster Dulles became its most enthusiastic cheerleader. He followed the preparations with delight and also great impatience. At one point he became alarmed when Iran was discussed at a high-level meeting but no mention was made of the planned coup. The next morning he telephoned his brother at the CIA to ask anxiously whether something had gone wrong. According to a memo of their conversation: "The Secy called and said in your talk about Iran yesterday at the meeting you did not mention the other matter, is it off? AWD said he doesn't talk about it, it was cleared directly with the President, and is still active. . . . AWD said it is moving along reasonably well."

Thus reassured that the plot was afoot, Secretary of State Dulles confined his public statements to generalized laments about the course of events in Iran. His comment at a news conference in July might have been read as a warning couched in highly diplomatic language. "Recent developments in Iran, especially the growing activity of the illegal Communist party, which appears to be tolerated by the Iranian government, have caused us concern," he said. "These developments make it more difficult for the United States to give assistance to Iran so long as the government tolerates this sort of activity."

By the time Kermit Roosevelt entered Iran on July 19, the country was aflame. Mossadegh's supporters in the Majlis had voted to remove Ayatollah Kashani from his position as speaker, and the resulting clash led more than half the deputies to resign. Demonstrations demanding dissolution of the Majlis shook Tehran. Mossadegh announced that he would hold a referendum on the question and pledged to resign if voters did not vote to oust the existing Majlis. The referendum, hurriedly convened at the beginning of August, was a disastrous parody of democracy. There were separate ballot boxes for yes and no votes, and the announced result was over 99 percent in favor of throwing out the Majlis. The transparent unfairness of this referendum was more grist for the anti-Mossadegh mill.

Mid-August found Roosevelt and his team of Iranian agents in place and ready to strike. They had pushed Iran to the brink of chaos. Newspapers and religious leaders were screaming for Mossadegh's head. Protests and riots organized by the CIA had turned the streets into battlegrounds. Antigovernment propaganda, in Donald Wilber's words, "poured off the Agency's presses and was rushed by air to Tehran." Mossadegh was isolated and weaker than ever. Against this background, Roosevelt had every reason to be confident when he sent Colonel Nasiri into action on August 15. He had laid his plans so carefully that when he awoke the next day to find that his coup had failed, he decided to try again.

CHAPTER 11

I Knew It!
They Love Me!

A sharp knock on the door of an apartment in one of Tehran's northern suburbs brought two audacious co-conspirators together for the first time. One was the most wanted man in Iran. The other would have been even more wanted if the police knew he existed.

Kermit Roosevelt had much to worry about as he knocked. The night before, he and his men had failed in an attempt to overthrow Prime Minister Mossadegh. His superiors at the CIA in Washington were urging him to flee. Roosevelt, however, had resolved to risk a second attempt.

Extra police officers were on the street that Sunday morning, August 16, 1953. Sirens wailed as security agents swooped down on conspirators implicated in the abortive coup. Roosevelt drove carefully, stopped at red lights, and arrived at General Zahedi's apartment without incident.

By this hour Zahedi had hoped to be prime minister. Instead, he was a hunted fugitive. If he had any hope of success now or even of saving his skin, it lay with Roosevelt. Zahedi knew who must be knocking and opened the door himself.

Roosevelt skipped the pleasantries. He had come to ask just one question: Was Zahedi prepared to try again? Without hesitation, Zahedi said that he was. That was the answer Roosevelt needed.

Both men then agreed that it was too dangerous for Zahedi to remain where he was. Roosevelt had arranged to hide him at the villa of a fellow agent, three blocks from the American embassy. They walked down the apartment stairs and slipped into Roosevelt's car. The putative leader of Iran lay on the floor in back, covered with a blanket, as he was driven to his new hideout.

After stashing Zahedi, Roosevelt drove back to what he had begun calling his "battle station" at the embassy compound. There he met two American diplomats who had been assigned to monitor the plot. Both told him frankly that they thought the game was up. The handful of officials in Washington who knew about Operation Ajax were also ready to surrender. Beedle Smith, the undersecretary of state who had been one of the coup's most fervent promoters, sent a gloomy note to President Eisenhower saying that the United States would now "probably have to snuggle up to Mossadegh."

Roosevelt, however, still had considerable assets. One was General Zahedi, who had many friends in the officer corps and was willing to do whatever necessary to reach power. Equally formidable was a far-flung network of Iranian agents and subagents. This network had been assembled at great cost and had shown its ability to spread inflammatory rumors, place provocative articles in newspapers, manipulate politicians, influence mullahs, and produce hired crowds on short notice. It had not yet been fully tested.

Roosevelt also had the two treasured *firmans,* decrees that the Shah had signed dismissing Prime Minister Mossadegh and naming Zahedi to replace him. They gave the planned coup an air of legitimacy. Few Iranians would stop to debate whether the Shah had the legal right to issue such decrees. For them, respecting royal power was an ancient tradition. The *firmans* gave the plotters of Operation Ajax a way to wrap themselves in that tradition.

At their hurried meeting that morning, General Zahedi had urged Roosevelt to make copies of the *firman* naming Zahedi prime minister and to distribute them throughout the city, especially in the tough southern neighborhoods where mobs were recruited. This was a brilliant idea, and Roosevelt immediately embraced it. By midday he had commandeered one of the few copying machines to be found in Tehran. He not only sent copies of the *firman* out with every agent he could find but also arranged for facsimiles to appear on the front pages of the next day's newspapers. Later he dispatched trusted couriers, including two Iranian officers armed with false identity papers, to carry copies to military commanders in outlying cities.

To assure that the *firman* reached as wide an audience as possible, Roosevelt sent a message to the two American news correspondents in Tehran, who represented the Associated Press and the *New York Times*. It was an invitation to a secret meeting with General Zahedi. Both eagerly accepted, and a car was dispatched to pick them up. When they got to the safe house, however, they were brought not to Zahedi but to his sharp-minded son Ardeshir. He presented them with copies of the *firman* and, in perfect English, delivered an impassioned speech about its importance.

Even given the circumstances, it was a very odd meeting. The man on whose behalf it was called never appeared. Security was provided by the host's young wife, who sat in a rocking chair close to Ardeshir Zahedi with a pistol under her knitting. Most curious to the reporters, however, was a large and unfamiliar machine that was clattering loudly nearby.

"Lo and behold, there was a huge copying machine," Kennett Love of the *New York Times* recalled later. "Now this was 1953, and a copying machine is about the size of two refrigerators. But at that time neither I nor most American journalists or most American people would have been able to tell you what the initials CIA stood for."

By Sunday afternoon Roosevelt had conceived his new plan. On Monday and Tuesday his agents would spread across Tehran to bribe politicians, mullahs, and anyone else who might be able to turn out crowds at a crucial moment. During those same two days he would send mobs into the street to commit mayhem in Mossadegh's name. Then on Wednesday he would pull his mobs off the street, use military and police units to storm government buildings, and strike the final blow by capturing Mossadegh.

To accomplish all this, Roosevelt relied on a handful of proven Iranian agents. Most important were the three Rashidian brothers. Roosevelt had known them for several years, had arranged for them to be flown to CIA headquarters in Washington for what he called "thorough tests of their veracity," and had developed great admiration for their tradecraft. Besides the Rashidians, who were originally British assets, Roosevelt also used several Iranians who had been trained by the CIA. The two best, Ali Jalili and Farouk Keyvani, began working for the CIA in early 1951 as organizers of the propaganda and sabotage network known as Bedamn. They had organized riots and carried out other clandestine tasks so successfully that the CIA came to consider them "vitally important principal agents of the Tehran station." Like the Rashidians, they had been brought to Washington, debriefed at length by Kermit Roosevelt and other CIA operatives, given code names (sometimes "Nossey" and "Cafron," other times "Nerren" and "Cilley"), and chosen as key operatives in the plot against Mossadegh. They and the Rashidians, however, never met. Roosevelt kept the identities of his main Iranian operatives secret even from each other.

As Roosevelt prepared his second attempt against Mossadegh, he ordered these and other agents to begin circulating a false version of the first one. The story they were to give out was that Mossadegh had tried to seize the Shah's throne but was thwarted by patriotic officers. Corrupt newspaper editors gave this lie front-page coverage. Only a few reported the truth, which was that Mossadegh had been the coup's intended victim, not its instigator.

Mossadegh and his aides, however, paid little attention to the newspapers. They believed that the Shah had been behind Saturday's rebellion. If that was true, then his flight into exile meant that there would be no more attempts at what Foreign Minister Fatemi called "royal robbery of the rights of the people." They never imagined that the plotters who launched the Saturday coup would soon try again.

When a reporter asked Fatemi how his government would deal with captured plotters, he replied offhandedly that officials were "considering what to do" but had "not yet reached the stage of decisions." Other cabinet ministers, including Mossadegh himself, also let their guard down. They withdrew loyal troops from the streets and spent crucial hours asking one another questions raised by the Shah's flight into exile. Had he abdicated? Must a regency council be appointed? Was there to be a new dynasty? Should the monarchy be abolished?

While government officials airily debated their country's long-term future, Kermit Roosevelt was hard at work trying to shape its next few days. He knew he would need military units to help carry out his coup and asked the military attaché at the American embassy, General Robert McClure, to find some. McClure, who was well acquainted with Iranian officers, decided to start at the top, with the chief of staff, General Riahi.

He could not have had high hopes, because Riahi was known for his loyalty. Even if Riahi would not switch sides and join the plotters, however, McClure hoped that at least he would remain neutral. His first gambit was to suggest that Riahi leave town. Perhaps, he ventured, the two of them could head out to the countryside for a few days of fishing. Riahi coldly declined. Then McClure, who was not known for subtlety, abruptly changed his tone. He told Riahi that his military mission was accredited to the Shah, and therefore he would always recognize the Shah's legitimacy. Iranian commanders, he added bluntly, should do the same. Riahi became indignant and showed him the door.

Later that Sunday, McClure had a second failure. Roosevelt sent him by plane to Isfahan, with instructions to try to enlist the garrison commander there, but once again McClure's imperious style worked against him. He waved a copy of the *firman* and brusquely told the commander that he must send troops to fight Mossadegh. The commander replied that he took orders only from Iranians, not Americans. Two rebuffs in the space of a few hours cost McClure his temper. As he left the Isfahan garrison, he turned back to the commander and angrily vowed, "I will kick Mossadegh out of office!"

By the time McClure's plane landed back in Tehran, he had calmed down and decided what to do next. Accompanied by a couple of aides, he set out on a tour of small military outposts in the capital itself. At each post he offered the commander money and a promise of promotion if the coup succeeded. This time he had better luck. Several officers accepted his emoluments, including two who commanded infantry regiments and one who commanded a tank battalion. They promised to be ready when called.

Roosevelt now had military units standing by to crush street disorders. His next task was to arrange the disorders. For this, he called on his energetic and well-connected agents Jalili and Keyvani. First, he told them, he wanted "black" crowds that would rampage through the streets shouting their allegiance to communism and Mossadegh. They were to break windows, beat innocent bystanders, shoot at mosques, and generally arouse the outrage of citizens. Then there had to be "patriotic" mobs that would suppress these rowdies, preferably with the help of friendly police officers.

Jalili and Keyvani were worried. They had provided services like this before, but what Roosevelt was now proposing would be by far their biggest operation. It could also place them in great danger, especially if the operation failed. At one point they went so far as to suggest that they would like to pull out of the plot altogether. Roosevelt persuaded them to stay by offering them a simple choice. If they stayed, they would receive $50,000 for their rowdies and themselves. If not, he would kill them. They decided to take the cash. Roosevelt handed it to them on the spot.

That Sunday had begun in abject defeat. By the time evening fell, Roosevelt could feel his confidence returning. Before retiring for the night, he sent a cable to Washington saying that there might still be a "slight remaining chance for success."

No one in Washington shared Roosevelt's optimism. Soon after he awoke on Monday morning, he was handed a cable from headquarters urging him to leave Iran as soon as possible. It was the second time in thirty-six hours that his superiors had advised him to flee. This time he obliged by preparing an escape plan—it involved him, Zahedi, and a handful of others fleeing on a plane owned by the American air attaché—but thought no more of it.

At midmorning news from the street began to trickle in. It was all good. Gangs of thugs pretending pro-Mossadegh sympathies were making their way from the slums of Tehran's south side toward the center of town. Some true nationalists and communists innocently joined them. By the time they reached Parliament Square, which was dominated by a towering equestrian statue of Reza Shah, they numbered in the tens of thousands. How many were true militants and how many provocateurs is uncertain, but there were plenty of both.

Cheers went up when several men began climbing up to the monument. One carried a heavy chain coiled around his neck. He wrapped one end of it around the bronze horse's neck and tossed the other end down to the ground, where it was hooked to the bumper of what Kennett Love called "a sort of military-looking command car." Then the men began sawing and chiseling away at the horse's feet. Finally, with a great crash, the statue fell to the ground. It was another victory in Roosevelt's campaign to polarize Iran.

"This was the best thing we could have hoped for," he wrote later. "The more they shouted against the Shah, the more the army and the people recognized them as the enemy. If *they* hated the Shah, the army and people hated them. And the more they ravaged the city, the more they angered the great bulk of its inhabitants. Nothing could have dramatized the guts of the conflict more effectively or more rapidly. On Sunday there had been some rioting and pillaging, but Monday put the frosting on the cake."

Mossadegh had naively ordered police officers not to interfere with people's right to demonstrate, so the mob was able to rampage more or less at will. This was a great boon to Roosevelt, since any riots at all, even ones that he did not control, served to persuade Iranians that their country was sinking into chaos and needed a rescuer. Still, Roosevelt worried that Mossadegh might change his mind and order the police to crack down. The police might even prove bold enough to fight against rebellious soldiers when the coup reached its climax. Roosevelt cast about for a way to blunt their power.

He found his instrument that afternoon, when Ambassador Loy Henderson unexpectedly turned up. After attending the meeting in Washington at which the coup was given final approval, Henderson had thought it wise not to return to his post until Mossadegh was overthrown. He traveled to a resort in the Austrian Alps and waited for news. On August 14, unable to sit still so far away from the action, he flew to Beirut. When he heard radio reports that the coup had failed, he commandeered a Navy plane from the local American embassy and flew to Tehran. Upon arriving at the embassy, he went straight to Roosevelt, who briefed him on the state of affairs.

Roosevelt confessed with considerable understatement that he had "run into some small complications." Henderson asked if there was anything he could do to help. After a moment of reflection, Roosevelt came up with an outlandish idea. He would make Henderson his tool in an attempt to unnerve Mossadegh.

Roosevelt knew that Mossadegh was a deeply compassionate man who could be moved to tears by the plight of a single widow or orphan. Not a conspirator by nature, Mossadegh had an almost childlike faith in the sincerity of most other people. He was also a very decent, even chivalrous man who appreciated form, ceremony, and diplomacy. Despite the troubles of recent months, he had a soft spot for Americans. If Roosevelt could find a way to exploit these traits in his adversary's character, he might throw "the old bugger" off balance or force him to make a false move. It was a classic challenge of psychological warfare, and it would produce the most surreal encounter of Operation Ajax.

"What in heaven's name do I do?" Henderson asked when Roosevelt proposed sending him to Mossadegh.

"My suggestion," Roosevelt replied, "would be to complain about the way Americans here are being harassed. Anonymous telephone calls saying, 'Yankee go home!' or calling them obscene names. Even if a child picks up the phone, the caller just shouts dirty words at him."

Henderson agreed to do as Roosevelt wished. He added that if Mossadegh asked him about American support for subversion in Iran, he would "make it quite plain that we have no intention of interfering in the internal affairs of a friendly country." Roosevelt considered this a noble sentiment but said nothing.

Monday evening was "a most active and trying time for the station," according to the CIA's postmortem. Roosevelt spent four hours in an intensive planning session with his key operatives, among them the Rashidian brothers, General Zahedi and his son Ardeshir, and General Hedayatollah Guilanshah, a former air force commander who had committed himself to the plot. All were smuggled into and out of the embassy compound under blankets or in car trunks.

Roosevelt was now acting entirely on his own. There had been no backup plan in case the first coup failed, so he simply improvised as he went along. He was in constant motion and had neither the time nor the desire to clear his decisions with superiors. Even if he had wanted to do so, communications technology was cumbersome and unreliable. So during those crucial days, no one in Washington or London had any idea what he was doing.

From the beginning, Roosevelt had realized that the fate of Mossadegh's government would ultimately be decided on the streets. His Iranian agents were able to produce crowds almost instantly. He devised a plan to use both pro- and antigovernment riots, but in the end the nature of the mob's demands was almost irrelevant. A mob crying for Mossadegh's ouster was, of course, ideal, but one that supported him was also helpful because it would help polarize opinion and perhaps even provoke royalist soldiers into repressive reaction. All that really mattered was that Tehran be in turmoil.

The riots that shook Tehran on Monday intensified on Tuesday. Thousands of demonstrators, unwittingly under CIA control, surged through the streets, looting shops, destroying pictures of the Shah, and ransacking the offices of royalist groups. Exuberant nationalists and communists joined in the mayhem. The police were still under orders from Mossadegh not to interfere. That allowed rioters to do their job, which was to give the impression that Iran was sliding toward anarchy. Roosevelt caught glimpses of them during his furtive trips around the city and said that they "scared the hell out of me."

The crucial event of that day, however, took place not on the streets but behind closed doors. At midafternoon Ambassador Henderson came to call on Mossadegh. The old man was at a distinct disadvantage. He had no idea that clandestine agents based at the American embassy were working day and night to overthrow his government. And since he did not imagine that there existed such a person as Kermit Roosevelt, he could not guess that Roosevelt was using Ambassador Henderson to lay a trap for him. Still, he knew that outside powers had been involved in Saturday's failed coup. He should have been on guard.

Mossadegh received the ambassador in formal attire, signaling the importance of their meeting. He was distinctly cool, with what Henderson called "smoldering resentment" palpable behind his courtesy. The United States had taken the official position that the Shah was still Iran's leader, and Mossadegh protested this American support for "a man who is now no more than a rebel." Henderson replied that although the Shah had indeed fled, the Prophet Mohammad had also fled from Mecca in his time, and from that moment his influence had only grown. This comment surprised Mossadegh, and he paused to consider it. Henderson decided that it was time to deliver the speech Roosevelt had devised for him. He spoke sternly, his voice rising to a crescendo of staged indignation.

"I must tell you that my fellow citizens are being harassed most unpleasantly," he began. "Not only do they get threatening phone calls, often answered by their children, who are then subjected to rude words children should not even hear; not only are they insulted in the streets when going peacefully about their business. In addition to all the verbal aggression they are exposed to, their automobiles are damaged whenever they are left exposed. Parts are stolen, headlights are smashed, tires are deflated, and if the cars are left unlocked, their upholstery is cut to pieces. Unless this kind of harassment is stopped, Your Excellency, I am going to ask my government to recall all dependents and also all men whose presence here is not required in our own national interest."

Mossadegh might well have laughed at this mendacious monologue. Americans had organized the upheaval in Iran, but Henderson was portraying them as its victims. As proof, he offered highly exaggerated accounts of supposed outrages. But amazingly, Mossadegh seemed genuinely pained by these fanciful stories and alarmed at the prospect of Americans leaving Iran. Henderson reported that he was "visibly shaken" and quickly "became confused, almost apologetic."

Roosevelt had perfectly analyzed his adversary's psyche. Mossadegh, steeped in a culture of courtliness and hospitality, found it shocking that guests in Iran were being mistreated. That shock overwhelmed his good judgment, and with Henderson still in the room, he picked up a telephone and called his police chief. Trouble in the streets had become intolerable, he said, and it was time for the police to put an end to it.

With this order, Mossadegh sent the police out to attack a mob that included many of his own most fervent supporters. Then, to assure that his partisans would not return to the streets the next day, he issued a decree banning all public demonstrations. He even telephoned leaders of pro-government parties and ordered them to keep their people at home. He disarmed himself. It was his "fatal mistake," according to an account published in *Time* magazine a week later.

Over the next couple of hours, Mossadegh made several other missteps. Determined to show how serious he was about cracking down on street protests, he mobilized soldiers commanded by General Mohammad Daftary, an officer known for his zeal in repressing civil strife. But Daftary, who had been Tehran's police chief under the assassinated Prime Minister Razmara several years before, was also an outspoken royalist and close to Zahedi. There was every reason to suspect that if ordered into action, he would lead his men directly to the side of the conspirators. That is precisely what he did. The next day they fought not to defend but to depose the government.

Soon after Mossadegh issued his fateful order, the crackdown began. "Policemen and soldiers swung into action last night against rioting Tudeh (Communist) partisans and Nationalist extremists," Kennett Love reported in the *New York Times*. "The troops appeared to be in a frenzy as they smashed into rioters with clubs, rifles and night sticks, and hurled tear gas bombs."

Among those who had no idea of the turning tide in Tehran was His Imperial Majesty, Mohammad Reza Shah. After arriving in Baghdad, he had insisted that he was not involved in an attempted coup but had dismissed Mossadegh for "gross violations of the constitution." Like almost everyone else involved in the plot, he assumed that Saturday's failure meant the end of Operation Ajax. On Tuesday morning he and Empress Soraya boarded a British Overseas Airways Corporation jet and flew to Rome. "Both looked worn, gloomy and anxious as they left the aircraft," the *London Times* reported.

The Shah seemed resigned to a long absence from Iran. When an American reporter asked him if he expected ever to return, he replied, "Probably, but not in the immediate future." A British correspondent predicted that he would "probably join the small colony of exiled monarchs already in Rome."

As the Shah was checking into the Excelsior Hotel in Rome, however, Roosevelt was working hard to bring him home. The next day would be the climactic one. If everything went as planned, by midday the streets would be full of boisterous pro-Shah demonstrators. Citizens would see them as decent people fed up with the chaos of recent days, and a sympathetic constabulary would not interfere.

With the help of his invaluable Iranian agents, Roosevelt had organized a most extraordinary mob. Along with street thugs and other unsavories, it included many members of Tehran's traditional athletic societies. These athletes prided themselves not just on their strength but on acquired skills like juggling and acrobatics. On festive occasions they would join parades or give shows. These were not wealthy men. Some earned their livings with enterprises like protection rackets at the vegetable market. They expected the leaders of their societies to help sustain them. When the CIA came looking for rioters, they were ready and eager.

"In Iran you can get a crowd that's fearsome," John Waller, the head of the CIA's Iran desk, mused afterward. "Or you can get a friendly crowd. Or you can get something in between. Or one can turn into the other."

Roosevelt had already assured himself of support from the police force, which had fallen largely under General Daftary's sway, and from several military units. Now he also had the makings of a fine mob. The indispensable Assadollah Rashidian, however, was worried that the mob would not be big enough. He urged Roosevelt to strengthen his hand by making a last-minute deal with Muslim religious leaders, many of whom had large followings and could produce crowds on short notice. The most important of them, Ayatollah Kashani, had already turned against Mossadegh and would certainly be sympathetic. To encourage him, Rashidian suggested a quick application of cash. Roosevelt agreed. Early Wednesday morning he sent $10,000 to Ahmad Aramash, a confidant of Kashani's, with instructions that it be passed along to the holy man.

Wednesday was August 19, the 28th of Mordad by the Iranian calendar. On this day Roosevelt hoped to change the course of a nation's history. After he packed up the $10,000 for Kashani and sent his couriers on their way, though, he found himself with little to do. The time had come for others to act. Roosevelt could only wait and watch.

The news that his agents brought during the morning hours was all encouraging. People by the thousands were gathering at mosques and public squares. In their vanguard, giving the whole event a carnival air, were the outlandish athletes. Some waved barbells over their heads. Others juggled heavy pins. Many bared their barrel chests and wore little more than extravagant mustaches and loincloths. More than a few carried knives or homemade clubs. It was as exotic a tribe as ever marched to overthrow a government:

> They started with the Zurkaneh giants, weight lifters who developed their physiques through an ancient set of Iranian exercises which included lifting progressively heavier weights. The Zurkanehs had built up tremendous shoulders and huge biceps. Shuffling down the street together, they were a frightening spectacle. Two hundred or so of these weightlifters began the day by marching through the bazaar, shouting "Long Live the Shah!" and dancing and twirling like dervishes. Along the edges of the crowd, men were passing out ten-rial notes. . . . The mob swelled; the chant "Long Live the Shah!" was deafening. As the throng passed the offices of a pro-Mossadegh newspaper, men smashed the windows and sacked the place.

No one tried to stop the insurgents as they marched toward the city center. Police officers at first encouraged them and then, as the afternoon wore on, began leading them. There was no counterdemonstration. Mossadegh's supporters, respecting his wish and the message of the previous night's beatings, had stayed home.

The only other group that could have mobilized to defend the government was Tudeh, but its leaders spent the day in meetings, unable to decide whether to act. Mossadegh did not trust them anyway and did not want their help. One Tudeh leader had called him the day before and volunteered Tudeh shock troops if Mossadegh would arm them. "If ever I agree to arm a political party," he swore in reply, "may God sever my right arm!"

Mossadegh's hostility was not, however, the real reason Tudeh leaders did not call out their street fighters on that crucial day. Like most of the world's communist parties, Tudeh was controlled by the Soviet Union, and in times of crisis it followed orders from Moscow. On this day, however, no orders came. Stalin had died a few months earlier and the Kremlin was in turmoil. Soviet intelligence officers who would normally be concentrating on Iran were preoccupied with the more urgent challenge of staying alive. Whether any of them even considered trying to defend Mossadegh is among the remaining mysteries of Operation Ajax. Scholars have sought access to records in Moscow that might resolve it, but their requests have been denied.

As the morning wore on, crowds surging out of Tehran's southern slums filled the air with chants of "Death to Mossadegh!" and "Long live the Shah!" Hundreds of soldiers joined in, some of them in trucks or atop tanks. So did tribesmen from outside the city, mobilized by chiefs who had been paid by Kermit Roosevelt's agents. Groups of rioters attacked and burned eight government buildings and the offices of three pro-government newspapers, including one, *Bahktar-e-Emruz,* that was owned by Foreign Minister Fatemi. Others attacked the foreign ministry, the general staff headquarters, and the central police station. They raked all three buildings with gunfire and were met with withering volleys in return. Men fell by the dozen.

Roosevelt's agents kept bringing him good news. Late in the morning, one of them reported that the "huge mob" had occupied every one of the city's main squares. Another told him that the garrison commander in Kermanshah, four hundred miles to the west, had joined the cause and was leading his men toward the capital. A squad led by Ali Jalili captured the military police headquarters and freed plotters who had been arrested after Saturday's coup attempt. Among them was Colonel Nasiri, who immediately began marshaling his Imperial Guard to help the insurgents.

Some of the tens of thousands of people who took over the streets that day had always opposed Mossadegh for one reason or another. Others were former supporters who had turned against him during the political conflict of recent months. Many were what the *New York Times* called "bazaar thugs and bully-boys" who had no political convictions at all and marched because they had been paid a good day's wage to do so.

"That mob that came into north Tehran and was decisive in the overthrow was a mercenary mob," asserted Richard Cottam, who was on the Operation Ajax staff in Washington. "It had no ideology, and that mob was paid with American dollars."

Mobs, however, need leadership to be effective, and while gang leaders like Shaban the Brainless were big and strong, they were by no means clever. Most of the leaders who emerged over the course of that Wednesday were midranking military officers. Like their civilian counterparts, they were a mixture of the committed and the suborned. A goodly number had been persuaded to join the coup by the authority of the *firman* naming Zahedi as prime minister. If the Shah had spoken, they reasoned, the army was bound to obey.

These soldiers lent the uprising an air of legality. They also brought considerable firepower, including tanks and artillery, and they led the attacks on many government buildings. Without their moral authority and combat skills, the coup might well have failed.

Everything seemed to be going according to plan when, just before midday, the door to Roosevelt's command post burst open. He looked up, in hope of seeing another agent with reports from the front line, but instead saw his radio operator, distraught and on the verge of tears. In his hand he held an urgent message from Beedle Smith in Washington. Smith had sent it twenty-four hours earlier, but there had been a delay passing it through the relay station in Cyprus. It was another order, in stronger language than the two previous ones, for Roosevelt to flee immediately.

This message could not have arrived at a more absurdly inappropriate moment. Roosevelt, who could sense that victory was at hand, broke out laughing when he read it. "Never mind, chum," he told the confused radio man. "Buried underground as you are, you have no way of knowing. But the tide has turned! Things are going our way! Right will triumph! All for the best, in the best of all possible worlds!"

Roosevelt sent the radio man back to his burrow with a reply for General Smith. It said: "Yours of 18 August received. Happy to report R. N. Ziegler [Zahedi] safely installed and KGSAVOY [the Shah] will be returning to Tehran in triumph shortly. Love and kisses from all the team."

That was, of course, premature, but it reflected the supreme confidence that Roosevelt now felt. By his own account, he was "grinning from ear to ear." He had not eaten a proper meal in days and suddenly he felt hungry. An acquaintance of his who was a counselor to Ambassador Henderson maintained a home in the embassy compound, and he strolled over for lunch and a drink.

Outside, Tehran was in upheaval. Cheers and rhythmic chants echoed through the air, punctuated by the sound of gunfire and exploding mortar shells. Squads of soldiers and police surged past the embassy gate every few minutes. Yet Roosevelt's host and his wife were paragons of discretion, asking not a single question about what was happening.

A radio was on. Although the announcer was reading nothing

more interesting than grain prices, Roosevelt listened carefully. He had sent one of his Iranian teams to storm the station. If things went well, the programming would soon change.

As the three Americans ate in silence, the radio announcer started speaking ever more slowly, as if he were falling asleep. After a time, he stopped altogether. Obviously something unusual was happening at the station. Roosevelt smiled knowingly at his baffled luncheon partners. There were several minutes of dead air, followed by the sounds of men arguing. "It doesn't matter who reads it, the important thing is that it be read!" one finally shouted with an air of authority. Then, in loudly emotional tones, he began shouting what Roosevelt called "well-intended lies, or pre-truths."

"The government of Mossadegh has been defeated!" the man cried. "The new prime minister, Fazlollah Zahedi, is now in office. And His Imperial Majesty is on his way home!"

Roosevelt did not recognize the voice—an army officer had beaten his agent to the microphone—but the message was just as he had wished: "The government of Mossadegh was a government of rebellion, and it has fallen." Roosevelt rose from the table, thanked his hosts for their hospitality, and withdrew.

It was shortly after two o'clock as Roosevelt made his way back to the command post. His comrades, who had also been listening to Radio Tehran, were in ecstasy. When Roosevelt appeared, they looked up, and for a silent moment all shared the delicious realization that the day was theirs. A moment later they were dancing around the narrow room. Roosevelt remembered them "literally bubbling over with joy."

What should they do next? One agent, surmising that the mob was now at its peak of enthusiasm, suggested that it was time to produce Zahedi. Roosevelt said no, it was still too soon.

"There is nothing to be gained by rushing," he said. "Let's wait till the crowd gets to Mossadegh's house. That should be a good moment for our hero to make his appearance."

Military units led by anti-Mossadegh officers had already begun converging on the house. Inside, loyal soldiers built fortifications and prepared for battle. They were armed with rifles, machine guns, and Sherman tanks mounted with 75-millimeter cannons. Late in the afternoon the assault began. Defenders beat back wave after wave, leaving the sidewalks littered with bodies. Then, after an hour of one-sided combat, the assailants gave a great cheer. Friendly army units had arrived with tanks of their own. A close-quarters artillery duel soon broke out. Operation Ajax was approaching its climax.

Once Roosevelt learned that the assault had begun, he decided to fetch General Zahedi from the hideout where he had been closeted for two days. Before leaving, he summoned General Guilanshah, who, like Zahedi, was at a CIA safe house impatiently awaiting instructions. Roosevelt asked the general to find a tank and bring it to Zahedi's hideout. He scribbled the address on a scrap of paper and then drove there himself.

When Roosevelt arrived, Zahedi was sitting in a basement room wearing only underwear. He was thrilled to hear that his moment had finally come. As he was buttoning the tunic of his dress uniform, there was a rumble outside. General Guilanshah had arrived with two tanks and a cheering throng.

In later years, perhaps inevitably given his grandfather's fame as a swashbuckler, a story took hold that Roosevelt had ridden triumphantly atop the lead tank as it crashed through the streets of Tehran toward Mossadegh's house. In fact, Roosevelt realized as soon as he heard the crowd accompanying General Guilanshah that he should not even be seen in Zahedi's presence. As the door to the basement burst open, he jumped into a small cavity behind the furnace. From there, he watched the jubilant crowd embrace Zahedi, lift him high, and carry him out.

After the column departed, Roosevelt crept out of his hiding place, walked back to his car, and drove through the tumultuous streets toward the embassy. There he and his aides toasted impending victory. "Actually, to all intents and purposes it was no longer impending but won," he wrote afterward. "Our colonel from the west [Kermanshah] would not reach Tehran until evening, but the rumor of his movement had given us all we needed. The actual arrival of his troops simply added more enthusiasm to a town already drunk with victory."

The tank on which Zahedi was riding turned first toward Radio Tehran. There, surrounded by delirious admirers, he made his way toward the upstairs studio. It had been decided that martial music should be played before Zahedi spoke to the nation, and one of Roosevelt's agents had brought along a likely-looking record from the embassy library. As Zahedi approached, a technician played the first song. To everyone's embarrassment, it turned out to be "The Star-Spangled Banner."

Another, more anonymous tune was quickly chosen and played. Zahedi then stepped to the microphone. He declared himself "the lawful prime minister by the Shah's order" and promised that his new regime would do everything good: build roads, provide free health care, raise wages, and guarantee both freedom and security. About oil he said nothing at all.

Military and police units loyal to Zahedi were taking control of Tehran. One seized the telegraph office and sent messages across the country declaring that Mossadegh had been deposed. Another found and captured General Riahi, the army chief of staff. Several joined the battle outside Mossadegh's home.

At this moment, completely unaware of these events, the dejected Mohammad Reza Shah was dining at his Rome hotel, accompanied by his wife and two aides. Suddenly, a handful of news correspondents burst into the dining room, pushed their way to the Shah's table, and thrust wire service reports from Tehran into his hands. At first he was incredulous. "Can it be true?" he blurted. The color drained from his face. His hands began shaking violently. Finally he jumped to his feet.

"I knew it!" he cried out. "I knew it! They love me!"

Empress Soraya, less moved, rose and placed her hand on her husband's arm to steady him. "How exciting," she murmured.

After the shock passed, the Shah regained his composure. He turned to the correspondents and told them, "This is not an insurrection. Now we have a legal government. General Zahedi is premier. I appointed him." After a pause he added, "Ninety-nine percent of the population is for me. I knew it all the time."

Still in something of a daze, the young monarch made his way to the hotel lounge, where a throng of reporters and curious tourists was gathering. His first desire, he told them, was to return home. "It is a cause of grief to me that I did not play an important part in my people's and my army's struggle for freedom and, on the contrary, was away and safe," he said. "But if I left my country, it was solely because of my anxiety to avoid bloodshed."

Although the coup was now on the brink of success, Mossadegh still resisted. As fighting raged around his house, he sat with remarkable calm in his bedroom. Bodyguards had covered most of the window with a steel plate, so he could hear but not see what was happening outside. When his personal aide, Ali Reza Saheb, urged him to flee, he shook his head and replied, "If it's going to happen, if it's going to be a coup d'etat, I think it is better that I stay in this room and I die in this room."

The attackers outside felt momentum on their side. They had heard Zahedi proclaim his victory over the radio, and they knew that a friendly column of soldiers from Kermanshah was approaching. As ammunition supplies inside the house began to dwindle, they tightened their circle.

Loyal military officers might have rushed to defend Mossadegh if they had known what was happening. They did not, largely because General Riahi, who would have called them into action, was under arrest. Before being arrested, however, Riahi managed to call his deputy, General Ataollah Kiani, who commanded the Ishrat Abad barracks in what was then an outlying Tehran neighborhood. Kiani immediately ordered an infantry battalion and a tank battalion to assemble and follow him toward the city center. Before he had gone far, he ran into a rebel column commanded by General Daftary. Of the two men, Daftary was by far the more sophisticated and persuasive.

"We are colleagues and brothers, all faithful to the Shah," he told Kiani. "We should not fire at each other."

After a few more minutes of honeyed words, Kiani was won over. The two generals and their aides embraced in what Iranians call a "kissing party." Kiani's men, who might have saved Mossadegh, returned to their barracks.

Fighting at Mossadegh's house raged for two hours. After the firing from inside stopped, a platoon of soldiers stormed in. They found the house empty. Mossadegh had escaped at the last moment, pushed over a back garden wall by fleeing aides. Officers poked around the house for an hour or so, packed the best pieces of Mossadegh's furniture onto waiting trucks, and drove off. They had chased the old man away, and even though they did not have him, they knew they had done well.

As the victorious soldiers melted into the night, rioters who had cheered them on swarmed into the house to loot and destroy. Some set fires. Others pulled doors, windows, and appliances onto the sidewalk and began selling them, haggling over prices as flames lit up the night behind them. Mossadegh's refrigerator went for the equivalent of thirty-six dollars.

Back at the embassy compound, the handful of covert agents who had planned the coup were, in Roosevelt's words, "full of jubilation, celebration, and occasional totally unpredictable whacks on the back as one or the other of us was suddenly overcome with enthusiasm." Diplomats on the embassy staff looked on curiously. They asked nothing and Roosevelt told them nothing.

Around the time that Mossadegh's house was being set afire, a car pulled up at the gate of the American embassy. The driver honked wildly, and Roosevelt hurried out to see who it might be. It was Ardeshir Zahedi. He jumped from the car, and the two men hugged each other fervently.

"You must come now to my father, to pay your respects to the new prime minister!" Ardeshir said.

"Let's have a brief word with Ambassador Henderson before we go," Roosevelt replied. "I think he deserves to be told officially, and you are the proper person to do it."

Arm in arm, the two co-conspirators half-danced their way along a path that led to the ambassador's residence. Henderson was sitting beside his swimming pool. He had put a bottle of champagne on ice, and when his visitors arrived, he popped the cork. They told him the glorious news, including the fact that the new prime minister had named two of Roosevelt's Iranian agents as cabinet ministers. First they drank to the new government, then to the Shah, then to Eisenhower and Churchill, and finally to one another. When the bottle was empty, Ardeshir said that it was time for him to take Roosevelt to meet the country's new leader. He took his leave from Henderson with a warm embrace.

General Zahedi had established temporary headquarters at the Officers Club near the center of town. The mood there was ecstatic, and when Roosevelt arrived, he was swamped by well-wishers. He didn't recognize most of them, but many seemed to know him. Everyone, even people he had never seen, wanted to hug him and kiss both his cheeks. Zahedi finally rescued him and called for order. He made a brief speech and then called on Roosevelt.

Wild cheers erupted as Roosevelt stepped forward. A few people in the club knew that he had organized the coup, and others no doubt suspected it. This, however, was no time for gloating.

Roosevelt spoke only a few disingenuous sentences, with Ardeshir translating.

"Friends, Persians, countrymen, lend me your ears!" he began, and the din subsided. "I thank you for your warmth, your exuberance, your kindness. One thing must be clearly understood by all of us. That is that you owe me, the United States, the British, *nothing at all.* We will not, cannot, should not ask anything from you—except, if you would like to give them, brief thanks. Those I will accept on behalf of myself, my country and our ally most gratefully."

There was another round of hugging and kissing, and then, as quickly as he could, Roosevelt withdrew. For days he had been working without a break, the fate of a nation in his hands. Now exhaustion began to overwhelm him. He commandeered a car and driver, made his way back to the embassy compound, walked through the darkness to the home where he had been given lunch, and knocked on the door. Minutes later he was sound asleep.

About three hundred people died in Wednesday's fighting, half of them in the final battle at Mossadegh's house. Some of the civilian victims were found with 500-rial notes still in their pockets. Roosevelt's men had distributed the notes that morning to dozens of their subagents.

The next day, newspapers around the world reported Mossadegh's fall. Most of their accounts were as perceptive as could have been expected, given the fact that the true story was a closely guarded secret and would remain so for decades.

"The sudden reversal was nothing more than a mutiny by the lower ranks against pro-Mossadegh officers," Kennett Love wrote in the *New York Times.* "Wednesday morning at about nine, a group of weightlifters, tumblers and wrestlers armed with iron bars and knives began marching toward the center of the city shouting pro-Shah slogans. That was all the troops needed. Ordered to break up the demonstration, they turned their weapons against their officers. Spontaneously the mobs shifted from Mossadegh's to the Shah's bandwagon."

Don Schwind of the Associated Press, who like Love had been on the streets watching the coup unfold, filed a chronology of the day's events. He reported that the coup "started rolling" at nine o'clock in the morning, as "mobs armed with sticks and stones," together with soldiers and police officers, began marching toward the city center. "By 7:00 P.M. local time, the last nest of resistance in the capital, Mossadegh's home and the compound surrounding it, was in the hands of Zahedi's forces," he concluded. "The first Zahedi men to break into Mossadegh's room found only the body of his personal bodyguard. Mossadegh and his cabinet colleagues are still missing."

For Roosevelt and his co-conspirators, this was, as the CIA post-mortem put it, "a day that should never have ended, for it carried with it such a sense of excitement, of satisfaction, and of jubilation that it is doubtful any other can come up to it." Festivities at the Officers Club continued through much of the night. Zahedi, realiz-ing instinctively that he must take quick and decisive steps to con-solidate his new power, slipped out for a quick tour of police stations, accompanied by Hamid Reza, the crown prince, who sym-bolized Zahedi's ties to the royal family. The tour convinced him that police commanders were loyal to his new regime. Thus assured, he returned to the Officers Club and slept for a few hours.

Immediately after rising on Thursday, Zahedi summoned General Nader Batmanqelich, a veteran officer who had provided valuable military help the night before in exchange for a promise that he would be named chief of staff if the coup succeeded. When Batmanqelich arrived, Zahedi quickly swore him in and then gave him his first orders. He was to suppress all demonstrations, close all borders, and purge pro-Mossadegh officers from the army and the police.

There was much more for Zahedi to do in his first hours as prime minister. First he convened a quick meeting of his newly named cabinet. Then he drafted an order replacing several gover-nors suspected of pro-Mossadegh sympathies. He ordered the release of many prisoners, including twenty who had been charged in the murder of the police chief Mahmoud Afshartus earlier that year. His only trip outside the Officers Club was to Radio Tehran, where he broadcast a brief speech giving Mossadegh twenty-four hours to surrender.

It was a quick role reversal. Just four days before, Zahedi had been the fugitive and Mossadegh the prime minister who demanded, in a broadcast over the same radio station, that he turn himself in within twenty-four hours. Mossadegh had offered a reward of 100,000 rials, the equivalent of $1,200, for information about Zahedi's whereabouts. Now Zahedi offered the same sum for information about Mossadegh.

At midmorning the new prime minister dispatched a telegram to Mohammad Reza Shah, telling him that Iranians were "counting the minutes" until his arrival. The Shah's departure from Rome, however, had hit some minor snags. Empress Soraya had not borne up well under the pressure of recent months, and at the last moment it was decided that she should stay in Rome for treatment of "nervous strain." Then someone pointed out that although the British had placed a chartered airliner at the Shah's disposal, his already battered nationalist credentials might be further weakened if he returned to Tehran in a plane with British markings. It was decided that he should wait for another one.

Mossadegh could not have hidden for long even if he wanted to, so Zahedi was not surprised when he telephoned the Officers Club at six o'clock that evening to arrange his surrender. Zahedi asked him where he was hiding, which turned out to be a private home downtown, and sent General Batmanqelich to pick him up. As a precaution against an assassination attempt by Mossadegh's ene-mies—or a rescue attempt by his friends—Zahedi ordered tanks onto the street and machine-gunners onto rooftops along the route.

An hour later the car carrying Mossadegh pulled into the court-yard of the Officers Club. The prisoner, haggard and dressed in pajamas, leaned heavily on a yellow Malacca cane as he emerged. Guards saluted him, and he saluted them back. Inside, he was helped to an elevator and taken to Zahedi's office on the third floor.

"Peace be with you," Mossadegh told the man who had defeated him.

"And also with you," Zahedi replied.

The two men spent twenty minutes behind closed doors. From all indications they spoke without rancor. When they emerged, Zahedi ordered that Mossadegh and the three aides who had sur-rendered with him be brought to comfortable suites upstairs. He then directed Tehran Radio to stop calling them insulting names and to refer to them instead as "their excellencies."

The Shah was less generous. As Mossadegh was surrendering in Tehran, he was touching down in Baghdad aboard a Dutch airliner that had been chartered at a reported cost of $12,000. Eight Iraqi air force fighters escorted his plane to the airport, and as he stepped off, a military band played the Iranian national anthem. When reporters asked him what he had planned for the deposed prime minister, he turned serious.

"The crimes of Mossadegh are the most serious a person can be responsible for," the Shah said solemnly. "Mossadegh is an evil man who wanted only one thing out of life: power at all costs. To accomplish this end he was willing to sacrifice the Iranian people, and he almost succeeded. Thank God my people finally understood him."

What a difference six days had made! On Sunday the Shah had passed through Baghdad as a ragged exile. Now he was on his way home as a triumphant monarch. The Beechcraft in which he had fled was still on the tarmac. He flew it home himself.

The Shah's plane touched down in Tehran at seventeen minutes after eleven o'clock on that Saturday morning and taxied to a stop in front of a stiff formation of soldiers from the Imperial Guard. He emerged resplendent in an air force uniform that had been flown to him in Baghdad for the occasion. Prime Minister Zahedi was the first to pay his respects, falling to his knees and pressing his lips to the monarch's proffered hand. Hundreds of other admirers had turned out, and when Zahedi stepped back, they surged forward. Several of them, including Colonel Nasiri, General Batmanqelich, Ayatollah Kashani, Shaban the Brainless, and Ambassador Loy Henderson, had given crucial help to Operation Ajax. The Shah greeted each of them and then turned to survey the delirious crowd. "His eyes were moist," one correspondent reported, "and his mouth was set in an effort to control his emotions."

In a radio address that evening, the Shah promised to "repair the damage done to the country." He left no doubt that he blamed Mossadegh for most of it. "I nurse no grudge in my heart, and extend clemency," he said. "But when it comes to violations of the constitution which we are under oath to preserve—an oath that was forgotten by some—and to dissolution of the Majlis, disintegration of the army and the dissipation of treasury funds, the law must be carried out, as desired by the people."

Prime Minister Zahedi, who was with the Shah as he spoke, embraced this tough line. Reporters asked him why Mossadegh, now accused of such high crimes, was being held in relative luxury at the Officers Club. "That bad man has been treated too well so far," he replied. "Tomorrow I will send him to the city jail."

Zahedi was emboldened not just by his victory but by concrete, though secret, expressions of support from the United States. The CIA had decided in advance to give his new government $5 million immediately after he took power, and it was provided as planned. There was also an extra million for Zahedi himself.

With the new regime now firmly in control, it was time for Kermit Roosevelt to leave Iran as quietly as he had arrived four weeks earlier. Before departing, however, he wished to see the Shah one last time. Discretion dictated that their meeting should be as secret as their previous ones, since Roosevelt's presence in Tehran, not to mention the nature of his activities, was still unknown to all but a very few Iranians. He sent word that he would like to stick to the midnight schedule of past weeks and suggested Sunday evening.

That final meeting was unlike any of their previous ones. The car that brought Roosevelt through the gates of the Saad Abad Palace was officially marked as property of the United States. Roosevelt sat tall inside instead of lying under a blanket. Royal guards who had looked away when he arrived for past visits saluted him crisply.

A courtier met Roosevelt, escorted him up the palace's twenty-nine wide steps, and brought him to the Shah's lavishly appointed sitting room. The monarch motioned him to be seated. Vodka was served, and each man took a glass. The Shah raised his and told Roosevelt, "I owe my throne to God, my people, my army—and to you!" They drank quietly, savoring their triumph.

"It is good to see you here, rather than in an anonymous car on the street outside," the Shah told Roosevelt after that first toast.

"It *is* good, Your Majesty."

"The new prime minister, who is now your good friend, as you know, will be coming shortly. Is there anything you would like to discuss before he arrives?"

"Well, sir," Roosevelt ventured after a moment's hesitation, "I wonder if you have had a chance to make up your mind on what you will do with Mossadegh, Riahi and the others who plotted against you?"

"I have thought much about that. Mossadegh as you know surrendered himself just before my return. He will be sentenced, if the court follows my suggestion, to three years of house arrest in his village. After that he will be free to move about in, but not outside, that village. Riahi will spend three years in jail and will then be released to do as he pleases—*if* what he pleases is not objectionable. A few others will get similar punishment. There is one exception. Hussein Fatemi cannot be found yet, but he will be. He was the most vituperative of them all. He urged on the Tudeh gangs that pulled down statues of me and my father. When we find him, he will be executed."

Roosevelt said nothing in reply. A few moments later Prime Minister Zahedi was escorted in. He bowed to the Shah and smiled broadly at Roosevelt, who repeated that the new regime owed nothing to the United States since "the outcome is full repayment."

"We understand," Zahedi answered. "We thank you and will always be grateful."

The three people in that palace room were among the few who had any idea how Operation Ajax was engineered. They took a silent moment to share their satisfaction. "We were all smiles now," Roosevelt wrote afterward. "Warmth and friendship filled the room."

After a few minutes, the Shah rose to escort Roosevelt back to his car. On the way out he reached into his jacket, pulled out a gold cigarette case, and presented it to his guest "as a souvenir of our recent adventure." Then, unexpectedly, a barrel-chested military officer appeared. It was Colonel Nasiri, who had played key roles in both the failed coup on Saturday and the successful one four days later.

"I have made only one promotion," the Shah said. "I present you now to *General* Nasiri."

It was after one o'clock in the morning when Roosevelt returned to the embassy compound. Ambassador Henderson was waiting for him. Henderson had arranged for Roosevelt's departure later that morning, aboard the naval attaché's plane to Bahrain.

Roosevelt barely slept. Soon after dawn he was driven to a remote hangar at the Tehran airport. Several of the men with whom he had carried out the coup were there to send him off. "I stumbled onto the plane," he wrote later, "with tears in my eyes."

CHAPTER 12

Purring Like a Giant Cat

A few days after Mossadegh surrendered to the new regime, a platoon of soldiers appeared at his suite in the Officers Club. The new prime minister, Fazlollah Zahedi, had ordered him transferred to a military prison. There he remained for ten weeks while an indictment was drawn up. When it was ready, Mossadegh was brought before a military tribunal and charged with treason for having resisted the Shah's dismissal order and for "inciting the people to armed insurrection." He defended himself vigorously, asserting that the *firman* had been delivered as part of a midnight coup d'etat and was in any case illegal, since Iranian prime ministers could not be dismissed without a no-confidence vote in the Majlis.

"My only crime," Mossadegh told his judges, "is that I nationalized the Iranian oil industry and removed from this land the network of colonialism and the political and economic influence of the greatest empire on earth."

The guilty verdict was a foregone conclusion. Along with it came the sentence: three years in prison, followed by house arrest for life. Mossadegh served the full prison term and upon his release in the summer of 1956 was brought to his home in Ahmad Abad.

One morning soon after his arrival, the new secret police, called Savak, organized a crude maneuver to impress upon him the terms of his incarceration. A gang of thugs turned up in front of his home, and they began shouting violent anti-Mossadegh slogans. At their head was none other than the gang leader Shaban the Brainless, who had become one of the regime's favorite enforcers. For a time the mob seemed ready to storm the house. It retreated after one of Mossadegh's grandsons fired several rifle shots into the air from inside. Several minutes later two Savak officers arrived and asked to see the prisoner. They carried a letter for him to sign. It was a request that Savak agents be assigned to protect him. Mossadegh, who understood the realities of power, signed it without protest. Within an hour Savak agents took up posts outside and inside the walled complex where he lived. Their standing orders, which did not change for the rest of Mossadegh's life, were to allow no one other than relatives and a few close friends to visit him.

In the weeks following the coup, most of Mossadegh's cabinet ministers and prominent supporters were arrested. Some were later released without charge. Others served prison terms after being convicted of various offenses. Six hundred military officers loyal to Mossadegh were also arrested, and about sixty of them were shot. So were several student leaders at Tehran University. Tudeh and the National Front were banned, and their most prominent supporters were either imprisoned or killed.

Hussein Fatemi, who had been Mossadegh's foreign minister, was the most prominent figure singled out for exemplary punishment. Fatemi was a zealous antimonarchist, and during the turbulent days of August 1953 he had attacked the Shah, whom he called "the Baghdad fugitive," with special venom. Iran had fallen into its misery, Fatemi asserted at one point, because "for the last ten years a dirty, hateful and shameful royal court has been the servant of the British embassy." In one speech he addressed the absent monarch: "O traitor Shah, you shameless person, you have completed the criminal history of the Pahlavi regime! The people want revenge. They want to drag you from behind your desk to the gallows." Now that the tables were turned, the Shah had his chance, and he did not miss it. Just as he had promised Kermit Roosevelt, he arranged for Fatemi to be summarily tried, convicted of treason, and executed.

Fatemi had once compared the Shah to a snake "who bites

mortally when the opportunity presents itself." In the end he was among those who suffered the deadly bite. Because of his fate, and also because he was the only member of Mossadegh's inner circle who was a descendant of the Prophet Mohammad, his memory is honored in Iran today. One of the main boulevards in Tehran is Dr. Hussein Fatemi Avenue.

In the years after Mossadegh fell from power, Mohammad Reza Shah made him a nonperson about whom it was considered unseemly to speak. Little could be published about him, and nothing at all that was positive. In 1962, having consolidated his increasingly repressive regime, the Shah allowed the National Front to emerge from its illegality and hold a rally, on the condition that each speaker mention Mossadegh's name just once. One hundred thousand people turned out. They knew the stipulation the Shah had placed on speakers, and when each mentioned Mossadegh the allotted one time, they let out a thunderous cheer. That was the last time the Shah allowed the National Front to gather in public.

Mossadegh's wife died in 1965, and although she had stayed in Tehran during the years he was at Ahmad Abad, they remained very close and her death severely affected him. In a letter to a friend he wrote that he was "deeply in pain from this tragedy . . . and now I pray God to take me soon, too, and relieve me of this pathetic existence." Several months later he developed an ailment that was diagnosed as throat cancer. Mohammad Reza Shah sent him a message suggesting that he seek treatment abroad, but Mossadegh refused and chose an Iranian medical team instead. He traveled to Tehran with a police escort and spent several months there under medical treatment. Doctors succeeded in removing his tumor but then subjected him to heavy doses of cobalt. That may have done more harm than good. His health continued to decline. On March 5, 1967, at the age of eighty-five, he died. No public funeral or other expression of mourning was permitted.

The Anglo-Iranian Oil Company, which later changed its name to British Petroleum, tried to return to its old position in Iran, but public opinion was so opposed that the new government could not permit it. Besides, the logic of power dictated that since the United States had done the dirty work of overthrowing Mossadegh, American companies should share the spoils. Ultimately, an international consortium was organized to assume the rich concession.

Anglo-Iranian held 40 percent of the shares, five American companies together held another 40, and the remainder was distributed to Royal Dutch/Shell and Compagnie Française de Pétroles. The non-British companies paid Anglo-Iranian $1 billion for their 60 percent of the concession. Although the consortium was run by foreigners, it retained the name Mossadegh gave it—National Iranian Oil Company—to preserve the façade of nationalization. It agreed to share its profits with Iran on a fifty-fifty basis but not to open its books to Iranian auditors or to allow Iranians onto its board of directors.

In the years that followed, Mohammad Reza Shah became increasingly isolated and dictatorial. He crushed dissent by whatever means necessary and spent huge amounts of money on weaponry—$10 billion in the United States alone between 1972 and 1976. He had that amount of free cash because of the sharp increase in oil prices during those years. The $4 billion that Iran received from the consortium in 1973 reached $19 billion just two years later.

On the rare occasions when he mentioned Mossadegh, the Shah was contemptuous of his "infantile xenophobia" and "strident nationalism." He told one friend: "The worst years of my reign, indeed of my entire life, came when Mossadegh was prime minister. The bastard was out for blood, and every morning I awoke with the sensation that today might be my last on the throne."

When Iranians' anger began boiling over in the late 1970s, the Shah found that since he had crushed all legitimate political parties and other opposition groups, there was no one with whom he could negotiate a compromise. In desperation, he named a prime minister, Shapour Bakhtiar, who had been deputy minister of labor in Mossadegh's government. The Shah must have felt history's breath on his neck when Bakhtiar visited Mossadegh's grave in Ahmad Abad immediately after taking office, made a speech there pledging fidelity to "Mossadegh's ideals", named a government made up largely of National Front sympathizers, and placed a photo of Mossadegh behind him whenever he addressed the press. At that point, however, doom was so close that the Shah had no choice but to accept such effrontery.

Ayatollah Ruhollah Khomeini, who as a young mullah had strongly opposed Mossadegh, emerged in the late 1970s as Mohammad Reza Shah's most potent enemy. The Shah had sent him into exile in 1964, but from Turkey, Iraq, and finally Paris, he continued preaching his fundamentalist message. When Bakhtiar became prime minister, Khomeini scorned and denounced him. "Why do you talk of the Shah, Mossadegh, money?" he demanded in one radio speech. "These have already passed. Islam is all that remains."

In one of the most stunning political collapses of the twentieth century, the Shah was forced to flee his homeland in January 1979. This time the CIA was not able to return him to his throne. The next year he died in Egypt, reviled by almost everyone. Ayatollah Khomeini replaced him as the arbiter of Iran's destiny.

Men associated with Mossadegh and his ideals dominated Khomeini's first government. The prime minister was Mehdi Bazargan, whom Mossadegh had dispatched to Abadan in 1951 to run the refinery there after the British departed. Ibrahim Yazdi, the head of a small political party dedicated to preserving Mossadegh's legacy, became deputy prime minister and then foreign minister. In the first postrevolutionary election, Khomeini permitted another Mossadegh admirer, Abolhassan Bani-Sadr, to run for and win the presidency.

For a brief period after the revolution, it seemed that from the grave, Mossadegh was returning to power. The high school in Ahmad Abad was named after him. So was the main street in Tehran, which had formerly been Pahlavi Avenue. A commemorative stamp was issued in his honor. On March 5, 1979, the twelfth anniversary of his death, an enormous crowd flooded into Ahmad Abad. It was one of the largest gatherings in modern Iranian history. People had to park their cars miles away and walk the rest of the distance. President Bani-Sadr led the tributes and announced plans to move Mossadegh's body to a mausoleum in Tehran. The family demurred, wisely suspecting that if political tides changed, the mausoleum might be desecrated.

These tributes to Mossadegh were in part an effort by Iranians to give him the homage they had not been permitted to give while the Shah was in power. They were also intended as a message to Ayatollah Khomeini and his mullahs. By celebrating Mossadegh, Iranians were expressing their wish for a regime like his: nationalist, democratic, and based on the rule of law. It soon became clear that Khomeini had not the slightest intention of establishing such a

regime. He had broadened his mass appeal by embracing supporters of the National Front, but as soon as he consolidated power, he
pushed them out. Before long, he began arresting them. Among
those who had to flee the country to save their lives was Hedayat
Matine-Daftary, the only one of Mossadegh's grandchildren who
had been bold enough to venture into politics.

The window that had been opened for Mossadegh's admirers was now closed. Tehran's main street was renamed again, this
time in honor of the Twelfth Imam. Mossadegh's secularism was as
abhorrent to the new regime as his democratic vision had been to
the old one. The mullahs, like Mohammad Reza Shah before them,
came to realize that allowing Iranians to honor Mossadegh would
inevitably lead to calls for a government based on his principles.
That they could not tolerate, and so they did all they could to suppress his memory.

The men who organized and carried out the 1953 coup soon scattered. General Zahedi, the prime minister who replaced Mossadegh,
pleased the Shah with his repressive campaign against nationalists
and leftists. Before long, however, the two men had a falling out.
Zahedi, like Mossadegh, was a strong figure who believed that
prime ministers should be free to run their own governments.
The ambitious Shah could not abide that. Just two years after the
coup, he forced Zahedi from office and later sent him abroad as
ambassador to the United Nations office in Geneva. He died there
in 1963.

Zahedi's son Ardeshir, whose quick wits and perfect English
made him a valuable asset to the coup plotters, went on to a long
and successful career. Although he was still in his midtwenties
when his father became prime minister, he quickly emerged as a
highly influential figure, serving simultaneously as his father's closest adviser and as a chamberlain to the Shah. His influence did not
diminish after his father's fall, and in 1957 he married the Shah's
eldest daughter, Princess Shahnaz. Wary of his growing power,
the Shah sent him off to golden exile as ambassador to Great Britain, where those who knew of his role in the coup embraced him.
Later he returned to Tehran for a term as foreign minister and
then became the ambassador to the United States. In that post he

defended the Shah to the bitter end. After the Islamic Revolution of 1979, he moved to a villa in Switzerland. He never admitted his role in the coup and even published a rambling article asserting that the CIA was not involved either.

"Mossadegh's fall was not due to any dirty tricks the CIA might have played," he wrote. "My father never had any meetings with CIA agents."

Asadollah Rashidian, whose subversive network of journalists, politicians, mullahs, and gang leaders was crucial to the success of Operation Ajax, prospered in the years that followed. He and his brothers remained in Tehran, and his business ventures flourished under the Shah's patronage. His home became a salon at which politicians and other influential figures spent many evenings discussing the nation's future. Several times the Shah used him as a secret emissary to foreign governments. In the mid-1960s, however, the Shah became uncomfortable with the presence in Tehran of such a sophisticated and well-connected figure, especially one who knew so many secrets. Rashidian sensed this and moved to his beloved England to live out his remaining years in comfort.

Not everyone who helped stage the coup was lucky enough to live into retirement. One to whom the Shah was especially ungrateful was General Nasiri, the officer who led the first, unsuccessful coup against Mossadegh and who also played an important role in the one that succeeded. For years after Mossadegh's defeat, Nasiri served faithfully as commander of the Imperial Guard. He did the Shah's bidding so willingly and discreetly that in 1965 he was placed in charge of the brutally repressive Savak. In that post he did the Shah's dirtiest work without complaint for more than a decade. Enemies of the Shah accused him of horrific crimes. When they began their final drive to power in the late 1970s, the Shah sought to placate them by removing Nasiri from office. Later, claiming to be shocked at reports that Savak had employed torturers, the Shah threw his old friend into prison. Soon after the 1979 revolution, mullahs dispatched Nasiri to a firing squad. Tehran newspapers published photos of his bloody corpse.

Mossadegh's loyal chief of staff, General Riahi, spent a year in prison after the coup and then returned to his original profession, engineering. After the 1979 revolution, he became minister of defense. He served for a few months, until the tide of radicalism overwhelmed Mehdi Bazargan's government, and then returned to private life until his death several years later in Tehran.

The Shah gave Shaban the Brainless, the most famous leader of the mob that rampaged through Tehran during the fateful days of August 1953, a yellow Cadillac convertible. He became a familiar figure on the streets of Tehran, driving slowly around town with a pistol on each hip, ready to jump out and attack anyone who seemed pro-Mossadegh or anti-Shah. Savak agents called on him from time to time when they wanted someone beaten or otherwise intimidated. After the Islamic Revolution, Shaban moved to Los Angeles and published a memoir denying that he had done much of what Iranians had seen him do.

Princess Ashraf, the Shah's strong-willed twin sister, became something of an international celebrity in the years after her brother was returned to his throne. For a time she served as chairman of the United Nations Human Rights Commission, where she defended his regime against what she called "unsubstantiated allegations of widespread tortures and killings by Savak." By her own account, her life was unhappy, marked by three failed marriages and the shock of her son's murder in Paris after the Islamic Revolution, evidently at the hands of killers dispatched from Tehran. After the revolution, comforted by her share of the billions of dollars her family had spirited out of Iran over the years, she took up residence in New York. In a memoir she admitted that there had been such a thing as Operation Ajax and even put its cost at $1 million, but denied what other participants reported about her role.

Monty Woodhouse, the British agent whose clandestine mission to Washington in January 1952 laid the groundwork for what was then called Operation Boot, returned after its success and had a friendly chat with Allen Dulles. "That was a nice little egg you laid when you were here last time," Dulles told him. Woodhouse was later elevated to the peerage as Lord Terrington. He became a Conservative member of Parliament and the chief editor of Penguin Books. His great passion in later life was the history of Greece and Byzantium, about which he wrote extensively. He also wrote a memoir in which he spoke frankly about both his role in the Iran coup and the coup's aftermath.

"It is easy to see Operation Boot as the first step towards the Iranian catastrophe of 1979," Woodhouse conceded. "What we did not foresee was that the Shah would gather new strength and use it so tyrannically, nor that the US government and the Foreign Office would fail so abjectly to keep him on a reasonable course. At the time we were simply relieved that a threat to British interests had been removed."

Herbert Morrison, the British foreign secretary whose belligerence helped set his country on a collision course with Iran, retired from politics in 1959 at the age of seventy-one and was named to a life peerage. In his later years he seemed scarcely to remember the passion with which he had denounced Mossadegh and defended the Anglo-Iranian Oil Company. His autobiography includes detailed accounts of his role creating the National Fire Service and passing the Road Traffic Act of 1930, but he devoted less than a page to Iran. He asserted that he had favored "sharp and forceful action" against Mossadegh, but that Prime Minister Attlee refused to approve an invasion because it "would take a lot of time and might therefore be a failure."

Attlee wrote in his memoir that choosing Morrison as foreign secretary was "the worst appointment I ever made." He never regretted his decision not to go to war in Iran. "Such action would no doubt have been taken in former times, but would, in the modern world, have outraged opinion at home and abroad," he wrote. "In my view, the day is past when commercial undertakings from industrialized countries, having obtained some concession, can carry on their business without regard to the feelings of the people of the country in which they are operating. . . . The Anglo-Iranian Oil Company showed a lack of sensitivity in not realizing this."

Winston Churchill's biographers have paid almost no attention to his central role in the coup against Mossadegh. Most books about him do not even mention it. Churchill once said privately that he considered the coup to have been "the finest operation since the end of the war," but he never considered it more than an obscure footnote to his career.

The chief hero or villain of the piece, Kermit Roosevelt, went on to an oddly undistinguished career. On his way home from Tehran after the coup, he stopped in London and gave Churchill a private briefing. "Young man," Churchill told him when he finished, "if I had been but a few years younger, I would have loved nothing better than to have served under your command in this great venture."

A few days later Roosevelt repeated his briefing at the White House for President Eisenhower, John Foster Dulles, Allen Dulles, and a small group of other senior officials. Soon afterward, at a secret ceremony, Eisenhower awarded him the National Security Medal.

Roosevelt concluded his White House briefing by warning that the CIA should not take his success in Iran to mean that it could now overthrow governments at will. The Dulles brothers, however, took it to mean exactly that. They were already plotting to strike against the left-leaning regime in Guatemala and asked Roosevelt to lead their coup. He declined. In 1958 he left the CIA. After spending six years with Gulf Oil, he struck out on a series of moderately successful consulting and lobbying ventures. He died in 2000, still considering August 1953 to have been the highlight of his life. Until his dying day, he believed fervently that the coup he had engineered was right and necessary.

Was it? There can, of course, be no final answer to this crucial question. A host of factors influence the course of history, and drawing conclusions about causes and effects is always dangerous. Nonetheless, few would deny that the 1953 coup in Iran set off a series of unintended consequences. Its most direct result was to give Mohammad Reza Shah the chance to become dictator. He received enormous amounts of aid from the United States—more than $1 billion in the decade following the coup—but his oppressive rule turned Iranians against him. In 1979 their anger exploded in a shattering revolution led by Islamic fundamentalists.

Soon after the Shah was overthrown, President Jimmy Carter allowed him to enter the United States. That sent Iranian radicals into a frenzy of rage. With the blessing of their new leaders, they stormed the American embassy in Tehran and held fifty-two American diplomats hostage for more than fourteen months. Westerners, and especially Americans, found this crime not only barbaric but inexplicable. That was because almost none of them had any idea of the responsibility the United States bore for imposing the royalist regime that Iranians came to hate so passionately. The hostage-takers remembered that when the Shah fled into exile in 1953, CIA agents working at the American embassy had returned him to his throne. Iranians feared that history was about to repeat itself.

"In the back of everybody's mind hung the suspicion that, with the admission of the Shah to the United States, the countdown for another coup d'etat had begun," one of the hostage-takers explained years later. "Such was to be our fate again, we were convinced, and it would be irreversible. We now had to reverse the irreversible."

The hostage episode changed the course of American political history and poisoned relations between Iran and the United States. It led the United States to support Iraq in its long and horrific war with Iran, in the process consolidating the Iraqi dictatorship of Saddam Hussein. Within Iran, it strengthened the most militant elements in the revolutionary coalition. One of Ayatollah Khomeini's closest advisers, Ayatollah Ali Khamenei, who later succeeded him as the country's supreme leader, justified the regime's radicalism by declaring, "We are not liberals like Allende and Mossadegh, whom the CIA can snuff out."

Fundamentalist clerics who consolidated power in Iran during the early 1980s not only imposed a form of religious fascism at home but turned their country into a center for the propagation of terror abroad. Their support for the hostage-takers who seized American diplomats in Tehran was only the beginning of their fierce anti-Western campaign. Soon afterward, they began financing and arming Hamas, Hezbollah, and other Middle Eastern factions known for their involvement in political kidnapping and assassination. They sent agents around the world to kill scores of Iranian dissidents and other perceived enemies, among them former prime minister Shapour Bakhtiar. American investigators implicated them in both the 1983 suicide bombing that killed 214 American marines in Beirut and the 1996 attack that killed another 19 marines in Saudi Arabia. Prosecutors in Argentina asserted that they ordered one of the most heinous anti-Semitic crimes of the post-Holocaust era, the 1994 bombing of the Jewish community center in Buenos Aires, which took ninety-three lives.

With their devotion to radical Islam and their eagerness to embrace even the most horrific kinds of violence, Iran's revolutionary leaders became heroes to fanatics in many countries. Among those who were inspired by their example were Afghans who founded the Taliban, led it to power in Kabul, and gave Osama bin-Laden the base from which he launched devastating terror attacks. It is not far-fetched to draw a line from Operation Ajax through the

Shah's repressive regime and the Islamic Revolution to the fireballs that engulfed the World Trade Center in New York.

The world has paid a heavy price for the lack of democracy in most of the Middle East. Operation Ajax taught tyrants and aspiring tyrants there that the world's most powerful governments were willing to tolerate limitless oppression as long as oppressive regimes were friendly to the West and to Western oil companies. That helped tilt the political balance in a vast region away from freedom and toward dictatorship.

As a postrevolutionary generation came of age in Iran, Iranian intellectuals began assessing the long-term effects of the 1953 coup. Several published thoughtful essays that raised intriguing questions. One appeared in an American foreign-policy journal:

> It is a reasonable argument that but for the coup, Iran would be a mature democracy. So traumatic was the coup's legacy that when the Shah finally departed in 1979, many Iranians feared a repetition of 1953, which was one of the motivations for the student seizure of the U.S. embassy. The hostage crisis, in turn, precipitated the Iraqi invasion of Iran, while the [Islamic] revolution itself played a part in the Soviet decision to invade Afghanistan. A lot of history, in short, flowed from a single week in Tehran. . . .
>
> The 1953 coup and its consequences [were] the starting point for the political alignments in today's Middle East and inner Asia. With hindsight, can anybody say the Islamic Revolution of 1979 was inevitable? Or did it only become so once the aspirations of the Iranian people were temporarily expunged in 1953?

From the vantage point of history, it is easy to see the catastrophic effects of Operation Ajax. They will continue to plague the world for many years. But what would have been the effect of *not* launching the coup? President Truman insisted until his last day in office that the United States must not intervene in Iran. What if President Eisenhower had also held this view?

Those who defend the coup argue that the Soviet Union was waiting for a chance to strike against Iran. They say that a preemptive coup was necessary because rolling back a Soviet takeover would have been very difficult and perhaps impossible. In their view, the gamble that the Soviets would not act, or that their action could be reversed, was too risky.

"It was a question of much bigger policy than Iran," John Waller, one of the last surviving veterans of Operation Ajax, asserted decades later. "It was about what the Soviets had done and what we knew about their future plans. It's interesting to see what Russia put on its priority list, what it wanted. Iran was very high on it. If anybody wasn't worried about the Soviet menace, I don't know what they could have been believing in. It was a real thing."

Sam Falle, who as a young British diplomat accompanied Monty Woodhouse on his mission to Washington and was later posted in Tehran, held to the same conclusion. In his memoir he wrote that the coup "was of course immoral" because it constituted interference in the internal affairs of a foreign country. But he added, "1952 was a very dangerous time. The Cold War was hot in Korea. The Soviet Union had tried to take all Berlin in 1948. Stalin was still alive. On no account could the Western powers risk a Soviet takeover of Iran, which would almost certainly have led to World War III."

History casts some doubt on these fears. Stalin had tried during the late 1940s to subvert Iran through a combination of military and political means, and for a time his soldiers actually controlled a large swath of northern Iran. Diplomatic pressure from Washington and Tehran forced him to withdraw. This suggests that the Soviets might have been reluctant to try again.

After Stalin's death in early 1953, a regime emerged in the Kremlin that adopted a less aggressive foreign policy. It was not clear at the time, however, that this would be the case. A reckless brute like Beria might have come to power rather than the relatively moderate Khrushchev, and he might have been ready to launch even the most provocative expansionist adventures. This was a danger the CIA believed it could not ignore.

Another open question is the strength of the pro-Soviet Tudeh party during the early 1950s. The Dulles brothers claimed that Tudeh had assembled a vast network that was ready to seize power as soon as Mossadegh fell or was pushed from office. Scholars who have studied Tudeh and its allied organizations doubt this. Tudeh was divided between intellectuals who opposed Mossadegh because they saw him as an obstacle to communism and a mass base made up largely of people who admired him. It had cells in the army and civil service, but they may not have been as large or influential as they were made to seem. Long after the coup, a scholar interviewed the American diplomat who specialized in monitoring Tudeh during the early 1950s, along with two CIA agents who were posted with him at the United States embassy in Tehran. They admitted "that the Tudeh was really not very powerful, and that higher-level U.S. officials routinely exaggerated its strength and Mossadegh's reliance on it."

The crucial question of whether the American coup was necessary to prevent the Soviets from staging a coup of their own cannot be conclusively answered. No one will ever know how the Soviets might have acted or how successful they would have been. The coup certainly had disastrous aftereffects. What might have been the effects of not carrying it out must remain forever in the realm of speculation.

How did Iran reach the tragic crossroads of August 1953? The main responsibility lies with the obtuse neocolonialism that guided the Anglo-Iranian Oil Company and with the British government's willingness to accept it. If the company had shown even a modicum of good sense, it could have reached a compromise with the Iranian authorities. If it had cooperated with Prime Minister Razmara, who wanted the British to remain in Iran, Mossadegh might never even have come to power. But the men who ran the company, and the government officials who coddled them, were frozen in their imperial mindset and contemptuous of Iranians and their aspirations. Dean Acheson had it exactly right when he wrote: "Never had so few lost so much so stupidly and so fast."

Acheson also, however, laid blame on Mossadegh himself, whom he described as "inspired by a fanatical hatred of the British and a desire to expel them and all their works from the country regardless of the cost." Certainly, Mossadegh was almost as resistant to compromise as were the British. At several points he might have declared victory and made a deal. In the summer of 1952, for example, he was an unassailable national hero. He had been returned to power by a spontaneous mass uprising and had won a great victory over the British at the World Court. President Truman was on his side. A more pragmatic leader might have seized on this moment, but Mossadegh was not a pragmatist. He was a visionary, a utopian, a millenarian. The single-mindedness with which he pursued his campaign against Anglo-Iranian made it impossible for him to compromise when he could and should have.

Another great failure in Mossadegh's judgment was his inability or refusal to understand how the world looked to Western leaders. They were in a state of near-panic about the spread of communist power. Mossadegh believed that his conflict with Anglo-Iranian had nothing to do with the global confrontation between East and West. This was highly unrealistic. The men who made decisions in Washington and Moscow viewed everything that happened in the world as part of the war they were waging for control of the world's destiny. It was foolish of Mossadegh to believe that he could separate Iran's grievance, justified though it was, from this all-encompassing conflict.

Mossadegh was also naïve in his assessment of the communists who controlled Tudeh and were working assiduously to penetrate Iran's government, army, and civil society. He detested autocracy and believed that all Iranians should be allowed to say and do what they wished. The fact that communists had taken advantage of democratic systems in Eastern Europe to seize power and destroy democracy seemed not to affect him. His refusal to crack down on communist movements in Iran put him on Washington's death list. This may have been unjust, but it was the harsh reality of the age. By failing to recognize it, Mossadegh strengthened his enemies.

Never during his twenty-six months in power did Mossadegh attempt to forge the National Front into a cohesive political movement. It remained a loose coalition without central leadership or an organized political base. In the Majlis election of 1952 Mossadegh made no effort to assemble a slate of candidates committed to its program. This made it highly vulnerable to outsiders who sought to break it apart, and prevented it from developing a following that might have been mobilized to defend the government at crucial moments.

Despite his historic misjudgments, however, Mossadegh can hardly be considered to have been a failure as prime minister. His achievements were profound and even earth-shattering. He set his people off on what would be a long and difficult voyage toward democracy and self-sufficiency, forever altering not only their history but the way they viewed themselves and the world around

them. He dealt a devastating blow to the imperial system and hastened its final collapse. He inspired people around the world who
believe that nations can and must struggle for the right to govern
themselves in freedom. He towers over Iranian history, Middle
Eastern history, and the history of anticolonialism. No account of
the twentieth century is complete without a chapter about him.

Mossadegh and the Anglo-Iranian Oil Company brought disaster on themselves by refusing repeated efforts at compromise. Their
final crack-up, however, would not have happened if British and
American voters had not cooperated. They did so quite unwittingly. Iran was a visible but not overwhelming issue in the political
campaign that brought the aging Winston Churchill back to power
in London. It was hardly an issue at all in Dwight Eisenhower's
campaign, although fear of a worldwide communist advance certainly shaped the perceptions of many voters. The outcome of both
elections was determined as much by a simple desire for change as
by anything else. In faraway Iran these outcomes shaped the course
of all future history. If Churchill and Eisenhower had not won,
there would have been no Operation Ajax.

The election in the United States was especially significant
because it brought John Foster Dulles and Allen Dulles to power.
They were driven men, intensely focused on the worldwide communist threat. Their decision to make Iran the first battleground
of their crusade may or may not have been wise, but they deserve
to be judged harshly for the way they made it. Even before taking their oaths of office, both brothers had convinced themselves
beyond all doubt that Mossadegh must go. They never even considered the possibility that a coup might be a bad idea or that it might
have negative consequences. History might view their action more
favorably if it had been the result of serious, open-minded reflection and debate. Instead, it sprang from petulant impatience, from
a burning desire to do something, anything, that would seem like
a victory over communism. Ideology, not reason, drove the Dulles
brothers. Iran was the place they chose to start showing the world
that the United States was no longer part of what Vice President
Richard Nixon called "Dean Acheson's college of cowardly Communist containment."

There was no substantial difference in the way Truman and
Eisenhower assessed the communist threat. Both believed that

Moscow was directing a relentless campaign of subversion aimed at world domination, that Iran was one of this campaign's likeliest targets, and that the United States had no higher national priority than to resist and defeat it. They differed profoundly, however, in their views of how to shape America's resistance. Truman accepted and even welcomed the rise of nationalism in the developing world. He believed that by placing itself alongside nationalist movements, the United States could show the world that it was the truest friend of Asia, Africa, and Latin America. The idea of overthrowing foreign governments was abhorrent to him, in part because he recognized that the long-term consequences were entirely unpredictable and might well be catastrophic.

Truman spent many hours thinking and talking about Iran, but Eisenhower was far less engaged. He allowed the Dulles brothers to shape his administration's policy toward the restive Third World. They were anxious for quick and visible successes in their anticommunist crusade and saw covert action as a way to achieve them. Preemptive coups, actions against threats that had not yet materialized, seemed to them not only wise but imperative. They did not worry about the future consequences of such coups because they believed that if the United States did not sponsor them, its own future would be endangered.

The success of Operation Ajax had an immediate and far-reaching effect in Washington. Overnight, the CIA became a central part of the American foreign policy apparatus, and covert action came to be regarded as a cheap and effective way to shape the course of world events. Kermit Roosevelt could sense this view taking hold even before he had finished delivering his White House briefing on September 4, 1953.

"One of my audience seemed almost alarmingly enthusiastic," he wrote afterward. "John Foster Dulles was leaning back in his chair. Despite his posture, he was anything but sleepy. His eyes were gleaming; he seemed to be purring like a giant cat. Clearly he was not only enjoying what he was hearing, but my instincts told me that he was planning as well."

Dulles was indeed planning. The next year he and his brother organized the CIA's second coup d'etat, which led to the fall of President Jacobo Arbenz of Guatemala and set off a sequence of events in that country that led to civil war and hundreds of thousands of violent deaths. Later the CIA set out to kill or depose foreign leaders from Cuba and Chile to the Congo and Vietnam. Each of these operations had profound effects that reverberate to this day. Some produced immense misery and suffering and turned whole regions of the world bitterly against the United States.

The final question to be answered is why Operation Ajax succeeded. The answer has a great deal to do with luck and happenstance. Had key participants made different decisions at any one of a half-dozen different points, the coup would have failed.

Kermit Roosevelt might have decided to give up and go home after the failed attempt of August 15. More plausibly, Mossadegh and his advisers might have dealt more sternly with the plotters. "Mossadegh should have reacted immediately and had them all shot," Shapour Bakhtiar said in an interview years later. That would almost certainly have saved the day, but it was not Mossadegh's nature.

The coup might also have failed if Mossadegh had been quicker to order his police to crack down on the hostile crowds that Roosevelt and his agents sent into the streets; if, when Mossadegh finally did order a crackdown, he had chosen a loyal officer rather than the outspokenly conservative General Daftary to carry it out; if Daftary had not intercepted and managed to turn back the loyalist column headed by General Kiani that was on its way to defend the government; if the loyal chief of staff, General Riahi, had managed to escape capture and mobilize more loyal units; if Mossadegh had called his supporters onto the streets instead of ordering them to stay home in the twenty-four hours before the final blow was struck; or if communists from the well-organized Tudeh party had decided to swing into action on Mossadegh's behalf.

Undoubtedly, there would have been no coup in August 1953 if it had not been for the CIA. The CIA devised Operation Ajax, paid a large sum to carry it out—estimates of the final cost range from $100,000 to $20 million, depending on which expenses are counted—and assigned one of its most imaginative agents to direct it. Yet Kermit Roosevelt and his comrades could not have succeeded without help from Iranians. Two groups provided invaluable help. First were the Rashidian brothers and other covert agents who had spent years building the subversive network that Roosevelt found waiting for him when he arrived. Second were the military officers who provided decisive firepower on the climactic day.

Iran was falling toward chaos during Mossadegh's last weeks. British and American agents had worked relentlessly to split the National Front and the rest of Iranian society, and their efforts proved how vulnerable an undeveloped society can be to a sustained campaign of bribery and destabilization. Yet Mossadegh himself helped bring Iran to the dead end it reached in mid-1953. It may be an exaggeration to assert, as some have done, that at some level he actually wished to be overthrown. Nonetheless, he had run out of options. Many Iranians sensed this and were ready for a new beginning.

Foreign intelligence agents set the stage for the coup and unleashed the forces that carried it out. At a certain point, however, the operation took on a momentum of its own. The great mob that surged through the streets of Tehran on August 18 was partly mercenary and partly a genuine expression of people's loss of faith in Mossadegh. The CIA laid the groundwork for that day's events but even in its own postmortem admitted: "To what extent the resulting activity stemmed from the specific efforts of all our agents will never be known."

Iranians understood very soon after the coup that foreigners had played a central role in organizing it. In the United States, however, that realization was very slow in coming. Only when anti-American hatred exploded in Iran after the Islamic Revolution of 1979 did Americans even realize that their country was unloved there. Slowly, they were able to discover the reason why.

Just four months after Mossadegh's overthrow, Richard Nixon traveled to Iran and pronounced himself much impressed with both Prime Minister Zahedi and Mohammad Reza Shah. President Eisenhower was more circumspect. He did not visit Iran until 1959 and stayed for just six hours. The Shah gave him a festive welcome and presented him with a silver peacock inlaid with sapphires and rubies. In private, however, the two leaders had a disagreement that foreshadowed trouble to come. Eisenhower warned the Shah that military strength alone could not make any country secure, and urged him to pay attention to his people's "basic aspirations."

The Shah replied that security in the Middle East could be achieved "only by building Iran's military strength."

Eisenhower never admitted the American role in Operation Ajax. In his memoir, he recalled receiving a briefing about it but said it was written, rather than oral, and described Roosevelt as "an American in Iran, unidentified to me." He was a bit more candid in his diary. There he wrote: "The things we did were 'covert.'" He admitted, as he did not in his memoir, that Roosevelt had given him a personal briefing about the coup. "I listened to his detailed report," he wrote, "and it seemed more like a dime novel than historical facts."

Forty-seven years after the coup, the United States officially acknowledged its involvement. President Bill Clinton, who had embarked on what proved to be an unsuccessful effort to improve American relations with Iran, approved a carefully worded statement that could be read as an apology. Secretary of State Madeleine Albright delivered it during a speech in Washington.

"In 1953 the United States played a significant role in orchestrating the overthrow of Iran's popular prime minister, Mohammad Mossadegh," she said. "The Eisenhower administration believed its actions were justified for strategic reasons. But the coup was clearly a setback for Iran's political development. And it is easy to see now why many Iranians continue to resent this intervention by America in their internal affairs."

A handful of American historians have devoted themselves to studying the 1953 coup and its effects. They agree, to different degrees and with different emphases, that the coup defined all of subsequent Iranian history and reshaped the world in ways that are only now becoming clear. Here are some of their observations:

> *James A. Bill:* American policy in Iran during the early 1950s succeeded in ensuring that there would be no Communist takeover in the country at the time, and that Iranian oil reserves would be available to the Western world at advantageous terms for two decades afterwards. It also deeply alienated Iranian patriots of all social classes and weakened the moderate, liberal nationalists represented by organizations like the National Front. This paved the way for the incubation of extremism, both of the left and of

the right. This extremism became unalterably anti-American. . . . The fall of Mossadegh marked the end of a century of friendship between the two countries, and began a new era of U. S. intervention and growing hostility against the United States among the weakened forces of Iranian nationalism.

Richard W. Cottam: The decision to overturn Mossadegh was a truly historic one. Iran was at the point of change at which the percentage of the population entering the political process, or disposed to do so, was increasing in geometric progression. These awakening individuals would look to leaders whom they recognized and trusted for the norms, values and institutions they could support. Had Mossadegh, the National Front and the religious leaders who interpreted the Koran more liberally remained in control of the Iranian government, they could have served as the socializing agents for this awakening mass. Instead, they were replaced by a royal dictatorship that stood aloof from the people. . . . U. S. policy did change Iran's history in fundamental ways. It helped oust a nationalist elite which had looked to the United States as its ideological ally and its one reliable external supporter. In helping eliminate a government that symbolized Iran's search for national integrity and dignity, it helped deny the successor regime nationalist legitimacy.

Mark J. Gasiorowski: In retrospect, the United States–sponsored coup d'etat in Iran of August 19, 1953, has emerged as a critical event in postwar world history. . . . Had the coup not occurred, Iran's future would undoubtedly have been vastly different. Similarly, the U. S. role in the coup and in the subsequent consolidation of the Shah's dictatorship were decisive for the future of U. S. relations with Iran. U. S. complicity in these events figured prominently in the terrorist attacks on American citizens and installations that occurred in Iran in the early 1970s, in the anti-American character of the 1978–79 revolution, and in the many anti-American incidents that emanated from Iran after the revolution, including, most notably, the embassy hostage crisis. Latter-day supporters of the coup frequently argue that it purchased twenty-five years of stability in Iran under a pro-American regime. As the dire consequences of the revolution for U. S. interests continue to unfold, one can wonder whether this has been worth the long-term cost.

James F. Goode: Mossadegh was no saint, as even his advisors recognized. He could be stubborn and narrow-minded. Yet he was the most popular leader in modern times, at least prior to the [Islamic] revolution. . . . If Mossadegh was a prisoner of the past—opposed to dictatorial rule, supportive of constitutional government, hating foreign influence—the Americans were no less prisoners of the Cold War mindset that would not tolerate neutralism in the struggle against godless Communism.

Mary Ann Heiss: In the long term it may well be true that the inability of the British and the United States to deal with Mossadegh, whose policies seem moderate in hindsight, cleared the path not so much for the Shah and his agents over the next several decades but for the far more radical, dangerous and anti-Western regimes that would follow after 1979. . . . U. S. involvement in the [1953] coup and the 1954 consortium agreement convinced the Iranian people that the United States cared little for their interests, that it was more concerned with propping up British imperialism than with assisting their national self-determination and independence. These convictions led Iranian nationalists to dub the United States the Great Satan and to blame it for all their nation's ills during the next twenty-five years. . . . By subverting Iranian nationalism, the oil dispute of the 1950s laid the seeds for the Islamic Revolution that would come twenty-five years later and that would usher in even more anti-Western regimes in Tehran than Mossadegh's. As a result, its consequences continue even now to cast a shadow over the Persian Gulf and beyond.

Nikki R. Keddie: The 1953 coup, which culminated a year later in an oil agreement leaving effective control of oil production and marketing and fifty percent of the profits in the hands of the world oil cartel companies, had an understandably traumatic effect on Iranian public opinion, which has continued down to the present. . . . Feelings against the United States government became far stronger when it became known that the United States was heavily involved in the 1953 overthrow of Mossadegh. American support over twenty-five years for the Shah's dictatorship and nearly all its ways added to this anti-American feeling. Hence, in both the British and American cases, however exaggerated and paranoid some charges by Iranians may be, suspiciousness and hostility have their roots in real and important occurrences; chiefly, participation in the overthrow of popular revolutionary movements and support of unpopular governments.

William Roger Louis: Nations, like individuals, cannot be manipulated without a sense on the part of the aggrieved that old scores must eventually be settled. . . . In the short term, the intervention of 1953 appeared to be effective. Over the longer term, the older advice not to interfere would seem to be the better part of political wisdom.

These views come close to a consensus. They eerily vindicate those who opposed the use of force against Mossadegh. President Truman predicted that mishandling the Iran crisis would produce "a disaster to the free world." Henry Grady, his ambassador in Tehran, warned that a coup would be "utter folly" and would push Iran into "a status of disintegration with all that implies." Anyone reading those words in the quarter-century after 1953 would have thought them wildly mistaken. Later history, however, redeems them and the men who spoke them. The results of Operation Ajax were just as dire as they predicted, although the backlash—or "blowback," as intelligence agents call it—took longer to materialize than anyone expected.

A fair case can be made that Iran was not ready for democracy in 1953. It might well have fallen into disarray if the United States had not intervened, although if American and British intelligence officers had not meddled so shamelessly in its domestic politics, it might also have returned to relative calm. It is difficult to imagine, however, an outcome that would have produced as much pain and horror over the next half-century as that produced by Operation Ajax. Only a Soviet takeover followed by war between the superpowers would have been worse.

The coup bought the United States and the West a reliable Iran for twenty-five years. That was an undoubted triumph. But in view of what came later, and of the culture of covert action that seized hold of the American body politic in the coup's wake, the triumph seems much tarnished. From the seething streets of Tehran and other Islamic capitals to the scenes of terror attacks around the world, Operation Ajax has left a haunting and terrible legacy.

Epilogue

My Iranian tour guide looked tired but happy when we met in the faded lobby of the Laleh Hotel in Tehran. A conspiratorial grin spread across his face. "I have worked a miracle for you," he told me triumphantly. "We are going to Ahmad Abad!"

I had come to Iran looking for traces of Mohammad Mossadegh. The trip had not been easy to arrange. When I met with an Iranian diplomat in New York to apply for a visa, he told me that my project sounded intriguing, but that it would have to be fully reviewed by the Islamic authorities in Tehran. Over the next few months I called him almost every day, but there was never any hint of progress. Finally I concluded that this path was leading nowhere. I wanted to be in Iran for the forty-ninth anniversary of the 1953 coup, and he admitted that there seemed little prospect of that.

"Maybe I should apply for a tourist visa," I suggested.

"You could try," he replied.

His tone sounded less than encouraging, but I took him at his word. I found a travel agent who specializes in sending people to exotic countries. Two weeks later, with her help, I had a visa in hand.

On the long Turkish Airlines flight across the Atlantic and then

216

on to Tehran, I wondered what awaited me. My first hint that I was not entirely welcome came when I checked into the Laleh, which is one of the city's largest hotels. Less than a year had passed since the 9/11 terror attacks in New York, and the desk clerk gave me the key to Room 911. To my protests, he could only shrug and reply that this was the room to which I had been assigned.

A few hours later the telephone rang. I had asked an Iranian friend to try to find people who might have known Mossadegh or been loyal to the National Front, and she now insisted that I come to see her immediately. When I arrived, she told me that a government official had called her with a stern warning. She was not to telephone anyone on my behalf and should also tell me that if I met with anyone at all, I would be summarily deported. What, then, about our plans to travel to Ahmad Abad on the anniversary of the August 19 coup?

"I can't go with you," she said. "They don't want me to do any work for you at all."

The anniversary was still a few days away. Tehran offers little in the way of diversion, and on my visa application I had expressed a desire to return to Isfahan, which I had visited on an earlier trip. I spent several days there and found the spectacular tiled palaces and mosques as dazzling as I had the first time. On my flight back to Tehran I sat next to a middle-aged businessman who, like everyone I met in Iran, detested the Islamic regime and thought well of Americans. Naturally I asked him about my favorite subject.

"You're too young to remember Mossadegh," I ventured, "but you must have heard about him. What did you hear? What did you learn?"

He paused for a moment to reflect. To speak of Mossadegh is not forbidden in Iran, nor would Iranians obey any such prohibition. But for five decades, excepting only a brief couple of years after the Islamic Revolution of 1979, he has been cast as a dubious figure at best, more likely a traitor.

"I don't know that much about him," my new acquaintance told me. "I know he nationalized our oil industry. But the main thing about Mossadegh is that he represents freedom. In his time there was free speech, there were free elections, people could do what they wanted. He reminds us that there was a time in Iran when we had democracy. That's why our government is afraid of him."

When I arrived back at the Laleh, I was assigned once again to Room 911. My guide—American tourists in Iran must travel with a guide—was not happy to learn that I wished to visit Mossadegh's home at Ahmad Abad. I had planned simply to hire a taxi and go there, but the guide told me that was quite impossible. This struck me as odd, since Ahmad Abad is a farm village far from any military base or secret installation. Still, it is inextricably linked with the man who for eleven years was its sole prisoner and most famous citizen.

It was August 18, the night before the anniversary of the coup, when my guide appeared with good news about the miracle he had worked. I asked him why arranging such a seemingly innocuous trip should be so difficult. By his expression he seemed to tell me that if I understood Iran better, I would not have asked such a foolish question.

"For three reasons it is difficult," he explained. "First of all, this is not a routine site. It's not on the tourist program. The ministry of culture has a list of places that tourists can visit, and you're supposed to stick to those places. No tourist ever goes to Ahmad Abad! Second, you did not list Ahmad Abad as a place you wanted to visit when you requested your tourist visa. We made a program for you based on your requests, and that program has been approved by the ministry. You're supposed to stick to the program. And third, you don't have the right visa to visit a place like that. If you had a journalist's visa, you could travel anywhere, but not on a tourist visa. It was all very difficult and very complicated. A whole machinery had to be set in motion."

The guide must have noticed my scowl, because after this litany he hastened to add, "You don't have to feel specially obligated to me. I would have done it for any of my tourists."

Ahmad Abad lies an hour's drive west of Tehran. A highway runs most of the distance, and after leaving it, visitors wind their way past small factories and through barley and sugar beet fields. No sign points the way, nor does any mark the entrance to the village. There is only a small kiosk where sweets are sold. On the day I arrived, two small boys were sitting in the shade in front of it.

"Ask them who Mossadegh was," I said to my guide. He did, and the boys broke into smiles, shaking their heads as if we must be dunces.

"He nationalized the oil industry!" one of them replied. The other one laughed. I was impressed.

The road into Ahmad Abad stops at the gate of a compound surrounded by a high brick wall. There is no name on the gate, but a quick look around made clear that there is no place in town nearly as imposing as this. It had to be Mossadegh's home. I rang the bell and waited.

After a minute or two, a young woman opened the gate. Before us stretched a footpath about eighty yards long, lined on both sides by tall elm trees. Through the trees we could see a handsome two-story brick home with green frames around the doors and the windows.

For more than a decade Mossadegh never left this compound. He could have, because his sentence confined him only to the village, not strictly to the compound. Police agents, however, were under orders to follow and observe him if he stepped beyond the gates. He preferred solitude to their company.

The compound is quite a pleasant place, with paths through gardens and arbors, and the manor house is comfortable though hardly luxurious. Mossadegh was not idle here during his long imprisonment. He supervised the work of about two hundred peasants who worked in nearby fields, training them in the use of modern farm equipment and even winning an agricultural prize for a scheme that increased sugar beet production. His family had traditionally produced lawyers and doctors, and since he had already learned most of what there was to know about law, he devoted himself to studying medicine. He read medical texts and boiled local roots to make antimalaria medicine. When villagers became sick, he treated them. For those who fell seriously ill, he wrote notes that gained them admission to the Najmieh Hospital in Tehran, which his mother had founded. Many brought him their small problems and found him unfailingly attentive and generous.

During his long hours of solitude, Mossadegh spent much time in his upstairs library. He immersed himself in old interests, reading Islamic philosophy and the works of political theorists like Montesquieu and Rousseau, and developed new ones like cooking. He eliminated fried foods from his diet and ate only those that had been steamed or boiled. One of his favorite books, which is still in his study, was the *Larousse Gastronomique.*

Still, for one who lived within the walls of this compound for so long, it must have taken on something of the air of a prison. During his years there, Mossadegh was often unwell, suffering from periodic bouts of bleeding ulcers and other ailments. Relatives who visited him say that he was depressed, discouraged, and demoralized. He mourned not for the loss of his own power but for the collapse of his dreams for Iran. Nothing he did in Ahmad Abad was able to raise his spirits.

"I am effectively in jail," he wrote in his memoir. "I am imprisoned in this village, deprived of all personal freedoms, and wishful that my time would be up soon and I would be relieved of this existence."

The caretaker who escorted my guide and me into Mossadegh's compound said that visitors appear there regularly, especially on weekends. On this day, however, the forty-ninth anniversary of the coup that brought down his government on August 19, 1953, we were the only ones. I had come halfway around the world to be here.

In his will Mossadegh expressed a desire to be buried at the Ebne Babooyeh cemetery in Tehran, alongside the graves of those killed defending his government during the clashes of July 1952. Mohammad Reza Shah, fearing that Mossadegh's grave might become a focus of opposition, would not permit that. Relatives then decided to bury his remains without ceremony in Ahmad Abad. He had instructed them to construct no memorial, not even a gravestone, to mark the place. Those wishes were carried out. He now lies beneath the floor of what was once his dining room.

The carpeted room is small but pleasant, with windows that admit streams of sunlight. Over the years it has taken on the air of a shrine. A low wooden table covered with woven cloth stands over the spot where Mossadegh's body is buried. On it there are two candles and a Koran. Most Iranian visitors follow tradition by laying a hand lightly on the cloth and reciting a verse that acknowledges God's mercy and compassion.

Walls of this room are covered with images of Mossadegh. Some are painted in oil, others sketched in pen or pencil. One is an embroidery that shows him against the background of an Iranian flag. A silk-screen print carries a quote from one of his speeches: "As I am an Iranian and a Muslim, I oppose anything that is against Iran or Islam." There is a photo of him vigorously defending himself at his trial and another, more plaintive one of him sitting alone and lost in thought during his house arrest. The one I liked best shows him at the Liberty Bell in Philadelphia, laying his finger on the famous crack.

This was the room where Mossadegh ate his daily meals and often received visitors. I spent a long time there, allowing my imagination to take me back to those days. Finally I thanked the caretaker and asked if I could walk around the grounds. She had no objection. I wandered among the shade trees and peered into a garage where a pale green 1948 Pontiac that belonged to Mossadegh's wife sits unused.

After a few minutes, another, more intriguing object caught my attention. Leaning against the back wall were the tall double doors of a sturdy iron gate. It was the only object salvaged from the house in Tehran where Mossadegh lived most of his life, including his tumultuous years as prime minister.

What history this gate has seen! Through it, the American and British ambassadors to Iran, along with special emissaries like Averell Harriman, passed countless times as they sought to persuade Mossadegh to give up or modify his plan to nationalize his country's oil industry. Crowds of thugs banged on it as they shouted "Death to Mossadegh!" during the aborted 1952 uprising. During that same uprising, a jeep carrying Shaban the Brainless crashed through the gate as Mossadegh scurried to safety over a back wall. There is still a large dent near the bottom that is probably a result of that crash.

The house before which this gate once stood was wrecked and burned on the night of August 19, 1953, and later the debris was bulldozed to make way for an apartment building. All that remains is the gate. This gives it great historical importance and, for those who knew Mossadegh or have tried to learn about him in the years since his death, an almost spiritual aura. I placed my hand on it and held it there for a long time.

Only a few people in Ahmad Abad could remember Mossadegh.

I found one of them, Abolfathi Takrousta, working on his car in the dusty street outside his home. He is a truck driver and a farmer who worked as a cook in the Mossadegh complex when he was a teenager. When I told him why I had come, he brightened instantly and invited me onto his patio for tea and pistachio nuts. Birds sang as we sat under a grape arbor and talked about bygone days.

Although many accounts describe Mossadegh as having suffered from various ailments, especially in his later years, and although his three years in solitary confinement cannot have been healthy for a man his age, Mr. Takrousta remembered him as strong and vigorous. Once Mr. Takrousta began talking, stories flowed out. Mossadegh had opened a pharmacy where medicine was distributed free to villagers, loaned money to those in need, built an insulated shed to keep ice in summertime, and distributed free bags of grain to each of his laborers at Ramadan and on New Year's Day.

"Mossadegh was not like a normal landlord," Mr. Takrousta told me. "He ran his estate like a charity. Most of what he grew, he gave back to the workers. Everyone here loved him. Any kind of a problem that you had, you would go to him and he would take care of it. From the highest official to the poorest worker, he treated everyone the same."

One day, my new friend told me, a peasant came to Mossadegh to complain that he had been detained by some of the local Savak agents, taken to their headquarters, and beaten while they shouted questions about Mossadegh's habits and conversations.

"It was the only time I ever saw him get angry. He called the police chief and shouted at him to come to the house immediately. When he got to the house, Mossadegh pushed him against a wall, held his cane against the guy's throat and shouted: 'You are here to watch me, and you have no right to abuse anyone else. If you have a problem, you come to me and only me! Don't ever, ever lay a finger on one of my people again!' This was a Savak officer and not a nice man at all, but when this happened he started apologizing and begging forgiveness. After that, the police never went near us. The jailer was afraid of the prisoner!"

I asked if Mr. Takrousta and his neighbors felt different from people in other villages, and he assured me that they did.

"We not only *feel* different, we *are* different," he told me. "We're different because of the effect Mossadegh had on us. Visitors come here from far away. They don't come to any other village. People here are proud that we had the privilege of having such a great man here. We try to behave according to the example he gave us. We have a sense of charity, cooperation, unity, solidarity. We take the hands of people in need. People from other villages know we're like this, and when they have problems, they come to us and we help them. You can't think of Ahmad Abad without thinking of Mossadegh. He's the father of our nation but also the father of this village. It's really a shame that they destroyed his government."

I asked who "they" were. Mr. Takrousta paused, unsure of himself. He stared up at the sky for a long moment and then spoke slowly.

"I'm a simple, uneducated villager," he said. "I don't know who 'they' are. But whoever they are, they don't want our people to be free and raise ourselves up."

We had spent more than an hour talking, and my host followed Iranian tradition by inviting me to stay for lunch. I declined as politely as I could, shook his hand, and thanked him profusely. For a while afterward I wandered aimlessly through the village. Later I checked back at the manse to see whether any other guests had appeared to mark this anniversary. None had. A group of Mossadegh's admirers had considered holding a rally that day, but several were facing prosecution for various political offenses and did not want to provoke the authorities.

Beginning in the 1990s, and especially after the reform-minded Mohammad Khatami was elected president in 1997, Iranians used Mossadegh as a symbol in their political debates. Anyone who paid tribute to him or waved his portrait was implicitly challenging the principles of Islamic rule. Laws forbade calling for a democratic republic to replace the Islamic regime, but praising Mossadegh's legacy was another way of doing the same thing. I found that many Iranians still associated his name with the idea of freedom.

"Oh, he was a good leader," one young man told me. "When he was in power, you could say what you wanted. Not like today. Shah killed him, right?" Not exactly, I replied. But in a sense perhaps yes.

Islamic leaders do not know quite what to make of Mossadegh.

They take his defeat as proof of their view that Iran is the eternal victim of cruel foreigners. Because he was a secular liberal, however, they cannot embrace him as a hero.

The Iranian press reflected this ambivalence in the way it covered the forty-ninth anniversary of the 1953 coup. One television station broadcast a damning documentary about it, but there was hardly a mention that Mossadegh was the victim. A small group of pro-government students rallied outside what was once the American embassy, but they, too, limited themselves to condemning "the crimes of the Great Satan against the Iranian nation" and did not refer to Mossadegh.

Only two of Tehran's fourteen daily newspapers ran stories to mark the anniversary. One of them, *Entekhab,* which is a mouthpiece for hard-liners, described the coup as having been launched "against Mossadegh and also Kashani," a bizarre rewriting of history that portrays Ayatollah Kashani as a victim of foreign intervention rather than as one of its agents. The lesson of the coup, this article said, was that Iranians must support their leaders because dissent only served the interests of "warmongers in the White House."

The other article, in the moderate paper *Fereydoon Shayesteh,* was quite different. It described August 19, 1953, as "the day despotism returned," and although carefully avoiding any praise of Mossadegh, it summarized the episode quite well: "The coup was carried out by professionals from both inside and outside Iran, and it cost millions of dollars. It is not at all true that, as some people have said and written, the coup happened because of internal opposition and mistrust of Mossadegh. It became possible when various well-known politicians, many of whom owed their careers to Mossadegh, broke with him and used all their means to ruin his reputation. These accusations have had no lasting effect, and in the years after the coup, those who made them never managed to win back the people's respect."

During my stay in Tehran, I tried to find some of the buildings associated with the coup, but without much success. Tehran has grown enormously since then, and as in many big cities, growth has meant the destruction of many old neighborhoods. I did drive slowly past the now-empty American embassy compound from which Kermit Roosevelt worked and where American hostages were imprisoned years later. Slogans were painted in large letters on the outside walls, conveniently translated into English. "We Will Make America Face a Severe Defeat," one says. Another proclaims: "The Day the US Praises Us, We Should Mourn."

The only other landmark I could find that Mossadegh would have recognized was the Saad Abad Palace. On the lawn outside, he sat for three days in 1949, demanding that the Shah annul that year's fraudulent election. Inside are rooms where he met often with the Shah, including on the day in 1952 when he had his dramatic fainting fit. The palace is now open to visitors. As I approached, I asked my driver to pull to the side of the long driveway before we reached the entrance. He was mystified, but I had calculated that this must have been where the car carrying Kermit Roosevelt stopped on the nights when he had his clandestine meetings with the Shah. I could easily visualize the Shah walking down the steps ahead, coming through the darkness, and sliding into the car beside him.

Inside, the palace is opulent to the point of excess. Marble, fine woods, old paintings, and richly woven carpets define its décor. I spent much time looking around the Shah's private reception room, which I guessed was where he received Roosevelt on the night they celebrated their victory and bid each other farewell. A large salon upstairs might have been the place where the Shah sat on a table during his meeting with General Schwarzkopf, but of course there was no one who could tell me for sure.

Even though I had been forbidden to interview Iranians about Mossadegh and his regime, the casual conversations I had with ordinary people made it abundantly clear that most held him in high regard. Someday his house in Ahmad Abad will be a museum and will draw streams of pilgrims from across Iran and beyond. I mentioned this to the caretaker while I was there, and she told me that creating such a museum was exactly what the Mossadegh family wished.

"The Mossadegh family?" I asked. During a visit to London, I had met Hedayat Matine-Daftary, the grandson who had fled Iran one step ahead of a vigilante mob. Now I learned that another grandson, Mahmoud Mossadegh, had stayed behind and become a prominent physician in Tehran. It was he who paid to maintain the house at Ahmad Abad, including building the caretaker's cottage and paying her salary. She did not have his telephone number, but with the help of my guide I located him in Tehran. Mahmoud Mossadegh agreed to come to my hotel for dinner that night.

I came down from Room 911 a few minutes before the appointed time. For the better part of an hour I sat waiting near the hotel's main entrance. Just as I began wondering if I had somehow missed my guest, he appeared. I had no idea what he would look like but recognized him immediately. He was tall and fair-skinned, with a strong, self-confident air about him. Most striking of all were his clothes. He wore a business suit and tie, a fashion I had never seen in Iran. As I approached him, I saw that the tie was from Harvard. It turned out that he had just returned from celebrating his forty-fifth class reunion.

"Actually, the whole thing was Averell Harriman's idea," he told me. "I translated for a few of Harriman's meetings with my grandfather. One day he asked me where I wanted to go to college. I told him I assumed I would go somewhere in England, but he said the United States would be better. I asked him where in the United States. He was a Yale man, but for whatever reason he suggested Harvard. So when the time came I applied, and that was that!"

Even before we reached the elevator, Doctor Mossadegh had taken me back to the days when his grandfather was in power. His father was none other than Gholan-Hussein Mossadegh, who had been the prime minister's physician and had accompanied him on his trips to the United Nations in New York and the World Court in The Hague. Gholan-Hussein Mossadegh had passed away years earlier, as had all of the prime minister's five children except one, his daughter Majid, who had spent most of her life at a mental hospital in Switzerland. Grandchildren and great-grandchildren had scattered and, for the most part, avoided politics. Doctor Mossadegh told me that he had never been involved in anything other than medicine. The only public position he ever held was general secretary of the Iranian Society of Fertility and Sterility.

Doctor Mossadegh did not turn up alone that night. With him, dressed in jeans and a white T-shirt, was his son Ali, who was in his mid-twenties. Most of our conversation centered on Prime Minister Mossadegh. The doctor was full of stories and memories. Some were sad, particularly those about how morose Mossadegh became during his decade of enforced isolation. Even the trivial stories were insightful. Mossadegh, for example, used to peel Kleenex tissues apart because he thought that using them at full two-ply strength was a wasteful extravagance.

A few of the doctor's recollections were of true historic interest. He told me that a few weeks before the 1953 coup, he attended a reception at the home of an Iranian diplomat in Washington and overheard the wife of Colonel Abbas Farzanegan, a military attaché who was on the CIA's secret payroll, boast that her husband was involved in a plot that would soon make him a cabinet minister. The next morning Mahmoud Mossadegh cabled this intelligence home to his grandfather.

"Later on, after the coup, I asked him if he had received my cable. He said, 'Of course I did.' When I asked him why he hadn't done something about it, he told me there was nothing he could have done. He said he knew full well that this coup was coming. His choice was to surrender or arm his supporters and call them out to civil war. He hated to think about giving up everything he believed in, but the other alternative was out of the question."

As we spoke, Ali Mossadegh, the late prime minister's great-grandson, listened intently but said little. As dessert was served, I tried to draw him out. In fluent English, he told me that he was studying international relations. Nothing, I thought, could be more appropriate for an intelligent young man with such a pedigree. So did he dream of a career in public life?

The two Mossadeghs, father and son, looked at each other after I asked this question. Obviously they had discussed it between themselves, probably many times. The doctor remained silent as we both waited for the answer.

"No, I won't go into politics," Ali Mossadegh told me. "I'm afraid of the risk. Not the risk to me, but to our family name. We have a very family-oriented society in this country. Wherever you go, even before people ask who you are, they ask whose son you are. Everything you do reflects on your family. If any of us commits even the slightest error, it tarnishes the name of our family and of Prime Minister Mossadegh. I'm just an ordinary human being. I make mistakes like everyone else. That's fine as long as I'm just a private person, but if I become a politician, my mistakes will be held against the family, even against family members who are dead. My life is going to be like my father's life. All we want to do is preserve the heritage of our family. I want to practice honesty, generosity, and the other qualities that people associate with the name Mossadegh. Public life is not for me. I doubt it will be for anyone else in our family. It's too great a responsibility."

NOTES

Chapter 1: Good Evening, Mr. Roosevelt

Firsthand accounts of the events of August 15–19, 1953, appeared in the *New York Times* and in newspapers served by the Associated Press, among them the *Chicago Tribune*. An official account is included in the CIA's clandestine service history, *Overthrow of Premier Mossadeq of Iran, November 1952–August 1953*, written by Donald M. Wilber and referred to here as "Service History." A summary of this history was published in the *New York Times* on April 16, 2000, and the full document is available at www.nytimes.com. Kermit Roosevelt's memoir is *Countercoup: The Struggle for Control of Iran* (New York: McGraw-Hill, 1979). Other accounts of the coup appear in Ambrose, Stephen, with Immerman, Richard H., *Ike's Spies: Eisenhower and the Intelligence Establishment* (Garden City, N.Y.: 1981); Diba, Farhad, *Mohammad Mossadegh: A Political Biography* (London: Croom Helm, 1986); Dorril, Stephen, *MI6: Inside the Covert World of Her Majesty's Secret Intelligence Service* (New York: Free Press, 2000); Elm, Mostafa, *Oil, Power and Principle: Iran's Oil Nationalization and Its Aftermath* (Syracuse, N.Y.: Syracuse University Press, 1992); Gasiorowski, Mark J., *U.S. Foreign Policy and the Shah: Building a Client State in Iran* (Ithaca, N.Y.: Cornell University, 1991); Goode, James F., *The United States and Iran: In the Shadow of Mussadiq* (New York: St. Martin's, 1997); Katouzian, Homa, *Mussadiq and the Struggle for Power in Iran* (London: I. B. Tauris, 1999); Mosley, Leonard, *Power Play* (Baltimore: Penguin, 1974); Prados, John, *Presidents' Secret Wars: CIA and Pentagon Covert Operations Since World War II* (New York: William Morrow, 1986); Woodhouse, C. M., *Something Ventured* (London: Granada, 1982); and Zabih, Sepehr, *The Mossadegh Era: Roots of the Iranian Revolution* (Chicago: Lake View Press, 1982); in articles, including Abrahamian, Ervand, "The 1953 Coup in Iran," in *Science & Society*, vol. 65, no. 2 (Summer 2001); Gasiorowski, Mark J., "The 1953 Coup d'Etat in Iran," in *International Journal of Middle East Studies*, no. 19 (1987); Louis, William Roger, "Britain and the Overthrow of the Mossadeq Government," in Gasiorowski, Mark J., and Byrne, Malcolm (eds.), *Mohammad Mossadeq and the 1953 Coup in Iran* (Syracuse, N.Y.: Syracuse University Press, forthcoming 2003); Gasiorowski, Mark J., "The 1953 Coup d'Etat Against Mossadegh" in that same volume; and Love, Kennett, *The American Role in the Pahlavi Restoration on August 19, 1953* (unpublished), the Allen Dulles Papers, Princeton University (1960); and in two videos, History Channel, *Anatomy of a Coup: The CIA in Iran*, Catalogue No. AAE-43021; and *Mossadegh*, Iranian Movies (www.IranianMovies.com), Tape No. 3313.

Mossadegh fried in Persian oil: *Frankfurter Neue Presse,* October 17, 1952.

Woodhouse emphasizes communist threat: Woodhouse, C. M., op. cit., p. 117.

Philby on Roosevelt: Roosevelt, op. cit., p. 110.

Roosevelt's feeling at border crossing: Roosevelt, ibid., pp. 138–40.

Roosevelt at tennis: Roosevelt, ibid., p. 154.

Zahedi receives over $100,000: Service History, p. B2; and Gasiorowski, Mark J., "The 1953 Coup d'Etat Against Mossadegh," in Gasiorowski and Byrne, op. cit.

Groups CIA wished to influence, Service History, ibid., p. 7.

Cottam on Iranian press: *Anatomy of a Coup* (video), op. cit.

Shah hates taking decisions: Falle, Sam, *My Lucky Life in War, Revolution, Peace and Diplomacy* (Lewes, Sussex: Book Guild, 1996), p. 80.

Shah sent Ashraf away: *Foreign Relations of the United States 1952–1954, Volume X, Iran 1951–1954,* (Washington, D.C.: Government Printing Office, 1989), p. 675.

Ashraf's eyes lit up: Dorril, op. cit., p. 586.

Ashraf's meeting with Shah: Service History, op. cit., p. 24.

Schwarzkopf brings bags of money: Mosley, op. cit., pp. 216–219; and Roosevelt, op. cit., p. 147.

CIA gave Shah cover mission: Service History, op. cit., p. 25; and Katouzian, op. cit., pp. 39–40.

Schwarzkopf meets Shah: Service History, op. cit., p. 29.

Roosevelt presumed meeting Shah would be necessary: Roosevelt, op. cit., p. 149.

Roosevelt authorized to speak: Roosevelt, ibid., p. 154.

Roosevelt's costume: Roosevelt, ibid., p. 155.

Roosevelt's first meeting with Shah: Roosevelt, ibid., pp. 156–157.

Roosevelt tells Shah United States will not accept second Korea: Service History, op. cit., pp. 33–34.

Roosevelt meets agents in cars: Roosevelt, op. cit., p. 162.

Roosevelt's later meetings with Shah: Roosevelt, ibid., pp. 163–166.

Shah feels stubborn irresolution: Service History, op. cit., p. 35.

Shah will fly to Baghdad: Roosevelt, op. cit., p. 161.

Fake message from Eisenhower: Roosevelt, ibid., p. 168.

Firmans arrive: Roosevelt, ibid., pp. 170–171.

Time moved slowly: Roosevelt, ibid., p. 171.

CIA report on coup preparations: Service History, op. cit., pp. 36–38.

Nothing to do but wait: Service History, ibid., p. 38.

"Luck Be a Lady": Roosevelt, op. cit., p. 172.

Roosevelt drives past Riahi's home: Roosevelt, ibid., p. 172.

Shah will look for work: *Foreign Relations of the United States 1952–1954, Volume X,* op. cit., p. 747.

Roosevelt close to despair: Roosevelt, op. cit., p. 173.

Waller telegram: Waller's remarks at conference in Oxford, England, June 10, 2002.

Fatemi speech: *New York Times,* August 17, 1953.

Chapter 2: Curse This Fate

Ferdowsi lament: Mackey, Sandra, *The Iranians: Persia, Islam and the Soul of a Nation* (New York: Plume, 1996), p. 62.

Hidden Imam: Tabatabai, Allamah Sayyid Muhammad Husayn, *Shi'ite Islam* (Albany: State University of New York, 1977), p. 214.

Fischer on Shiites: Fischer, Michael M. J., *Iran: From Religious Dispute to Revolution* (Cambridge, Mass.: Harvard University Press, 1980) pp. 24–27.

Battle cry of Ismail: Mottadeh, Roy, *The Mantle of the Prophet: Religion and Politics in Iran* (New York: Pantheon, 1985), p. 173.

Ismail adopts Shiism: Arjomand, Said Amir, *The Shadow of God and the Hidden Imam* (Chicago: University of Chicago Press, 1984), p. 109.

Modern author on Isfahan: *Nagel Encyclopedia Guide*, quoted in Arab, Gholam Hossein, *Isfahan* (Tehran: Farhangsara, 1996), p. 1.

Curzon on Qajars: Ghods, M. Reza, *Iran in the Twentieth Century: A Political History* (Boulder, Colo.: Lynne Rienner, 1989), p. 2.

Chapter 3: The Last Drop of the Nation's Blood

Curzon on Reuter concession: Curzon, George Nathaniel, *Persia and the Persian Question*, Vol. 1 (London: Longmans, Green and Co., 1892), p. 480.

Tobacco revolt and *fatwa:* Afary, Janet, *The Iranian Constitutional Revolution, 1906–1911: Grassroots Democracy, Social Democracy, and the Origins of Feminism* (New York: Columbia University Press, 1996), pp. 29–33.

Shah borrows half a million pounds: Keddie, Nikki, *Roots of Revolution: An Interpretive History of Modern Iran* (New Haven, Conn.: Yale University Press, 1981), p. 67.

D'Arcy concession: Ferrier, R. W., *The History of the British Petroleum Company, Vol. 1: The Developing Years 1901–1932* (London: Cambridge University Press, 1982), p. 42.

Demand for national assembly: Martin, Vanessa, *Islam and Modernism: The Iranian Revolution of 1906* (Syracuse, N.Y.: Syracuse University Press, 1989), p. 74.

British secretary accepts *bast:* Afary, op. cit., p. 55.

Majlis must decide: Martin, ibid., p. 99.

British diplomat: Martin, ibid., p. 199.

Thrown out law of the Prophet: Martin, ibid., p. 125.

Constitutional government not advisable: Martin, ibid., p. 114.

Overthrow of Islam: Martin, ibid., p. 62.

Two enticing words: Martin, ibid., p. 128.

Openness against insularity: Mackey, op. cit., p. 136.

We want the Koran: Mackey, ibid., p. 152.

Lying between life and death: Bayat, Mangol, *Iran's First Revolution: Shi'ism and the Constitutional Revolution of 1905–6* (New York: Oxford University Press, 1991), p. 244.

Prize from fairyland: Churchill, Winston, *The World Crisis 1911–1914* (New York: Charles Scribner's Sons, 1923), p. 134.

Curzon on Persia's importance: *Documents on British Foreign Policy 1919–1939*, First Series, Vol. IV (London: Government Printing Press), pp. 1119–1121.

Reza Khan in disturbances: Farmanfarmaian, Manucher, and Farmanfarmaian, Roxane, *Blood and Oil: Inside the Shah's Iran* (New York: Modern Library, 1999), p. 115.

Reza's speech: Elwell-Sutton, L. P., "Reza Shah the Great: Founder of the Pahlavi Dynasty," in Lenczowski, George, *Iran Under the Pahlavis* (Stanford, Calif.: Hoover Institute, 1978), p. 18.

Involvement of British officers: Katouzian, Homa, op. cit., pp. 16–17.

Nicholson on Persia: Ferrier, op. cit., p. 589.

Khorasan massacre: Mackey, op. cit., p. 182.

Hamedan baker: Author's interviews in Iran, 2002.

Reza orders mail returned: Mackey, op. cit., p. 178.

Reza largest landowner in Iran: Mackey, ibid., p. 173.

Only one thief in Iran: Ghods, op. cit., p. 93.

Newspaper on common goals in Iran and Germany: Ghods, ibid., p. 166.

Allied leaflet: Goode, James F., *The United States and Iran: In the Shadow of Mussadiq* (New York: St. Martin's, 1997), pp. 9–10.

Chapter 4: A Wave of Oil

Helpless crew: Longhurst, Henry, *Adventure in Oil: The Story of British Petroleum* (London: Sidgwick and Jackson, 1959), p. 21.

Petroliferous territory: Longhurst, ibid., p. 17.

Ahmad Shah as elderly child: Yergin, Daniel, *The Prize: The Epic Quest for Oil, Money and Power* (New York: Simon and Schuster, 1991), p. 136.

Telegram to Reynolds: Longhurst, op. cit., p. 31.

Mastery itself was the prize: Churchill, op. cit., p. 136.

Sunshine, mud, and flies: Longhurst, op. cit., p. 45.

Curzon on wave of oil: *London Times*, November 22, 1918.

Production increases at Abadan: Heiss, Mary Ann, *Empire and Nationhood: The United States, Great Britain, and Iranian Oil, 1950–1954* (New York: Columbia University Press, 1997), p. 6.

Royalty payment in 1920: Heiss, ibid., p. 6.

Reza burns file: Elm, op. cit., p. 31.

Cadman had attended Reza's coronation: Bill, James A., *The Eagle and the Lion: The Tragedy of American-Iranian Relations* (New Haven, Conn.: Yale University Press, 1988), p. 59.

Terms of 1933 oil accord: Heiss, op. cit., p. 13.

Cadman cable: Longhurst, op. cit., p. 78.

Strike at Abadan: Farmanfarmaian, op. cit., p. 186.

Increase in oil production during 1940s: Bamberg, J. H., *The History of the British Petroleum Company: Vol. II: The Anglo-Iranian Years, 1928–1954* (Cambridge, U.K.: Cambridge University Press, 1994), p. 242.

Assessment of young Mossadegh: Katouzian, op. cit., p. 1.

Mossadegh's reaction to Anglo-Persian Agreement: Katouzian, ibid., p. 13.

Cousin's view of Mossadegh: Farmanfarmaian, op. cit., pp. 166–170.

If subjugation were beneficial: Azimi, Fakhreddin, "The Reconciliation of Politics and Ethics, Nationalism and Democracy: An Overview of the Political Career of Dr. Mohammad Musaddiq," in Bill, James A., and Louis, William Roger (eds.), *Mussadiq, Iranian Nationalism, and Oil* (London: I. B. Tauris, 1988), p. 50.

Cut off my head: Katouzian, op. cit., p. 25.

Mossadegh taken prisoner: Katouzian, ibid., p. 33.

Chapter 5: His Master's Orders

(The notation FO refers to numbered documents of the British Foreign Office.)

Shah's affairs: Forbis, William H., *Fall of the Peacock Throne: The Story of Iran* (New York: Harper and Row, 1980), p. 53.

Chauffeur in one-way street: Arfa, Hassan, *Under Five Shahs* (New York: William Morrow, 1965), p. 305.

Succession to Reza Shah: Farmanfarmaian, op. cit., pp. 141–142; and Katouzian, pp. 39–40.

General Schwarzkopf's background: Schwarzkopf, H. Norman, *It Doesn't Take a Hero* (New York: Bantam, 1992), pp. 3–4.

Anglo-Iranian's 1947 profits and Iran's share: Farmanfarmaian, op. cit., p. 212.

Conditions at Abadan: Farmanfarmaian, ibid., pp. 184–185.

Bevin on British standard of living: Yergin, op. cit., p. 427.

Fraser proposes Supplemental Agreement: Heiss, op. cit., p. 7.

British want the whole world: Elm, op. cit., p. 55.

Iskandari threat to nationalize oil: Katouzian, op. cit., pp. 67–68.

Shah's visit to United States: Bill, op. cit., p. 40.

Visit did not go well: McGhee, George, *Envoy to the Middle World: Adventures in Diplomacy* (New York: Harper and Row, 1983), pp. 66–71.

Joint communiqué: Alexander, Yonah, and Nanes, Allen (eds.), *The United States and Iran: A Documentary History* (Frederick, Md.: Alethia Books, 1980), p. 208.

No intention of carrying out orders: FO 371/91448, quoted in Elm, op. cit., p. 63.

British will treat hysterical deputies: FO 371/91512.

Sharogh role: Elm, op. cit., p. 70.

Work of oil committee: Farmanfarmaian, op. cit., pp. 241–242.

Kashani on foreign yoke: Cottam, Richard W., *Nationalism in Iran* (Pittsburgh: University of Pittsburgh Press, 1979), p. 152.

Mossadegh warns Razmara of disgrace: Elm, op. cit., p. 71.

Northcroft says nationalists unimportant: FO 371/91524, quoted in Elm, op. cit., p. 74.

Fateh letter to Elkington: Elm, ibid., pp. 75–76.

Britain's immense service to mankind: Elm, ibid., p. 79.

Shepherd wrote the gist: Elm, op. cit., p. 80.

Statement of Razmara's assassin: Cottam, op. cit., p. 151.

Mossadegh doubts effectiveness of bodyguards: Katouzian, op. cit., p. 83.

Colonel on Colt bullet: Katouzian, ibid., p. 84.

Shepherd messages to Shah and Ala, and Ala's response: Elm, op. cit., pp. 81–82.

Morrison urges troops toward Iran: Elm, op. cit., p. 83.

Qualities of typical Persian: Goode, op. cit., p. 24.

Foreign Office strategy: Elm, op. cit., p. 84.

Emami on British payroll: Dorril, op. cit., p. 573.

Chapter 6: Unseen Enemies Everywhere

CIA mandate: NSC 10/2, "National Security Council Directive on Office of Special Projects," quoted in Etzold, Thomas H., and Gaddis, John Lewis, *Containment: Documents on American Policy and Strategy, 1945–1950* (New York: Columbia University Press, 1978), pp. 125–128.

NSC-68: *Foreign Relations of the United States, 1950, Vol. I*, pp. 237–292.

Truman points to Iran: Truman conversation with George M. Elsey, June 26, 1950, quoted in Byrne, Malcolm, "The Evolution of U.S. Policy Toward Iran After World War II," in Gasiorowski and Byrne, op. cit.

Baskerville as American Lafayette: Bill, James A., op. cit., p. 17.

American contribution: Farman Farmaian, Sattareh, *Daughter of Persia: A Woman's Journey From Her Father's Harem Through the Islamic Revolution* (New York: Anchor, 1992), pp. 56–57.

Unbounded confidence in America: Cottam, Richard W., *Iran and the United States: A Cold War Case Study* (Pittsburgh: University of Pittsburgh Press, 1988), p. 39.

McGhee finds Shah's plans grandiose: McGhee, op. cit., p. 69.

Nothing in the till: McGhee, ibid., p. 320.

Funkhouser report: *Foreign Relations of the United States, 1950, Vol. V,* pp. 76–96.

One penny more: Bill, op. cit., p. 72.

Fergusson report: Louis, William Roger, "Britain and the Overthrow of the Mossadeq Government," in Gasiorowski and Byrne, op. cit.

McGhee meeting in Istanbul: *Foreign Relations of the United States, 1951, Vol. V,* pp. 60–71.

Bevin on nationalization: Bill and Louis, op. cit., p. 6.

McGhee meets Shah: McGhee, ibid., pp. 326–328.

McGhee meets Shepherd: McGhee, op. cit., p. 326.

Meetings in Washington: *Foreign Relations of the United States 1952–1954, Vol. X,* op. cit., pp. 37–42; also McGhee, op. cit., p. 335.

Radio Tehran's broadcast: Goode, op. cit., p. 31.

Morrison cable to Franks: FO 371/91535, quoted in Elm, op. cit., p. 112.

Acheson on Mossadegh: Chase, James, *Acheson: The Secretary of State Who Created the American World* (New York: Simon and Schuster, 1998), p. 353.

New York Times profile of Mossadegh: May 7, 1951.

State Department recognizes sovereign rights of Iran: Alexander and Nanes, op. cit., p. 216.

Morrison annoyed: FO 371/91535, quoted in Elm, op. cit., p. 17.

Morrison message to Acheson: FO 371/91471, quoted in Abrahamian article in *Science and Society,* op. cit.

Truman exchange with Attlee: *Foreign Relations of the United States 1952–1954, Vol. X,* op. cit., pp. 59–63.

Grady on nationalization: *Wall Street Journal,* June 9, 1951.

Jackson proposal: Elm, op. cit., pp. 115–116.

Iranian oil clearly British property: *Security Council Official Records,* 559th Meeting, October 1, 1951, p. 11.

They will come crawling: *New York Herald Tribune,* July 15, 1951.

Drake on staying forever: Interview in *Mossadegh* (video), op. cit.

Morrison in House of Commons: Elm, op. cit., p. 89.

Patrick Hurley testimony: *Baltimore Sun,* June 21, 1951.

British press on Mossadegh: Abrahamian article in *Science and Society,* op. cit.

Washington Post sees stricken state: April 7, 1951.

New York Times on comparisons of Mossadegh to American patriots: November 8, 1951.

Chicago Daily News on McGhee: June 30, 1951.

Leggett on Anglo-Iranian: FO 371/91522, quoted in Elm, op. cit., p. 90.

Younger on Anglo-Iranian: Sampson, Anthony, *The Seven Sisters: The Great Oil Companies and the World They Made* (New York: Viking, 1975), p. 120.

Mountbatten on Morrison: Elm, op. cit., pp. 90–91.

Labor attaché on Abadan: FO 371/91628, quoted in Elm, ibid., p. 103.

Jerusalem Post: FO 371/91628, citing *Post* article of July 6, 1951, quoted in Elm, ibid., pp. 103–104.

Mossadegh appeal to British technicians: Elm, op. cit., p. 118.

Secret British documents: Elm, op. cit., p. 120.

Throw them to the dogs: Elm, ibid., p. 121.

National Security Council report: NSC 107/2, in *Foreign Relations of the United States 1952–1954, Vol. X,* op. cit., pp. 71–76.

Mossadegh letter to Truman: *Foreign Relations of the United States 1952–1954, Vol. X,* ibid., pp. 77–79.

Grady cable: *Foreign Relations of the United States 1952–1954, Vol. X,* ibid., pp. 79–81.

Shepherd wants to get Mossadegh out: FO 371/91582, quoted in Heiss, op. cit., p. 94.

Iranian minister at The Hague: *New York Times,* July 6, 1951.

Truman letter to Mossadegh: Alexander and Nanes, op. cit., pp. 218–219.

Morrison opposes Harriman mission: *Foreign Relations of the United States 1952–1954, Vol. X,* op. cit., pp. 82–84.

Acheson view of Morrison and Shepherd: Abrams, Rudy, *Spanning the Century: The Life of W. Averell Harriman, 1891–1986* (New York: Morrow, 1992), p. 470.

Shepherd opposes Harriman mission: *New York Herald Tribune,* July 13, 1951.

Foreign Office directs Shepherd to apologize: FO 371/91562, cited in Elm, op. cit., pp. 126–127.

Grady should urge Mossadegh to accept Harriman mission: *Foreign Relations of the United States 1952–1954, Vol. X,* op. cit., p. 88.

Chapter 7: You Do Not Know How Evil They Are

Mossadegh tells Harriman he doesn't know British: Walters, Vernon A., *Silent Missions* (New York: Doubleday, 1978), p. 242.

Mossadegh sends grandson to English school: Walters, ibid., p. 253.

Harriman finds Mossadegh rigid and obsessed: *Foreign Relations of the United States 1952–1954, Vol. X,* op. cit., p. 94.

Harriman's impression of Mossadegh: Abramson, Rudy, op. cit., p. 472.

Mossadegh on foreign influence, and "Tant pis pour nous": Walters, op. cit., pp. 251–252.

Walters on Mossadegh's negotiating style: Walters, ibid., p. 250.

Walters compares Mossadegh to Jimmy Durante: Walters, ibid., p. 248.

Walters's translations: Walters, ibid., pp. 253–254.

Mossadegh on crafty and evil British: Walters, ibid., p. 247.

Levy colloquy: *New York Times,* October 7, 1951.

Harriman's failed news conference: Abramson, op. cit., p. 473.

Harriman meets Kashani: Abramson, op. cit., pp. 474–475; and Walters, ibid., p. 255.

Harriman cable on Anglo-Iranian's absentee management: Abramson, op. cit., p. 476.

Mossadegh agrees to negotiate if British accept nationalization: Abramson, op. cit., p. 476.

Instructions to Stokes: FO 371/91575, quoted in Elm, op. cit., p. 134.

Mossadegh and Stokes on divorce: FO 371/91577, quoted in Elm, op. cit., p. 135.

Stokes finds proposals too transparent: FO 371/91578, quoted in Elm, ibid., p. 137.

Stokes visit to Abadan: FO 371/91580, quoted in Elm, ibid., p. 136.

Harriman shocked by conditions at Abadan: Abramson, op. cit., p. 479.

Harriman says lack of British cooperation endangers his mission: *Foreign Relations of the United States 1952–1954, Vol. X,* op. cit., p. 103.

Harriman's trips to cool off: Walters, op. cit., p. 257.

Stokes told to offer no further concessions: FO 371/91579, quoted in Elm, op. cit., p. 141.

The result is nothing: *Newsweek,* September 3, 1951.

Attlee-Truman exchange: Goode, op. cit., p. 43.

Walters recalls a mission unlike any other: Walters, op. cit., p. 263.

Franks says British troops would have a steadying influence: *Foreign Relations of the United States 1950, Vol. V,* op. cit., pp. 233–237.

Bolton suggests direct intervention: FO 371/91525, quoted in Elm, op. cit., p. 156.

Shinwell doesn't want tail twisted: Elm, ibid., p. 157.

British could bring Africans to Abadan: Elm, op. cit., p. 160.

Plans to invade Abadan: Elm, op. cit., pp. 155–168; and Goode, op. cit., p. 33.

Lord Fraser on dumps and doldrums: Elm, op. cit., p. 162.

Gifford tells Acheson of invasion plans: *Foreign Relations of the United States 1952–1954, Vol. X,* op. cit., pp. 54–55.

Acheson warns Franks against invasion: FO 371/91534, quoted in Elm, op. cit., p. 158.

Wall Street Journal laments threats: April 7, 1951.

Philadelphia Inquirer warns of World War III: August 28, 1951.

Howard K. Smith commentary: May 20, 1951, reported in FO 371/91538, quoted in Elm, op. cit., p. 159.

Morrison on Mossadegh's fanaticism: Morrison, Herbert, *An Autobiography* (London: Odhams, 1960), p. 281.

Acheson warns of disastrous consequences: Elm, op. cit., p. 165.

Attlee tells cabinet there will be no invasion: Elm, op. cit., pp. 166–167.

Lambton advises Foreign Office on propaganda lines: Louis article in Gasiorowski and Byrne, op. cit.

Zaehner combines high thought with low living: Louis article, ibid.

Drake on lack of cooperation with Iranians: Interview in *Mossadegh* (video), op. cit.

British prevent foreign oil experts from traveling to Iran: Elm, op. cit., pp. 148–150.

Foreign Office places advertisements: FO 371/91613, with text of ads, quoted in Elm, ibid., p. 146.

Mason intercepts telegrams: Elm, ibid., pp. 146–147.

Acheson on Grady's strong personality: Acheson, Dean, *Present at the Creation: My Years at the State Department* (New York: Norton, 1969), p. 224.

Henderson considers Mossadegh a madman: Heiss, op. cit., p. 180.

Grady warns against giving Iran a forum: *London Daily Standard,* October 15, 1951.

Acheson warns Morrison against U.N. debate: *Foreign Relations of the United States 1952–1954, Vol. X,* op. cit., p. 201.

Gifford on his meeting with Morrison: *Foreign Relations of the United States 1952–1954, Vol. X,* ibid., p. 205.

Chapter 8: An Immensely Shrewd Old Man

Mossadegh is symbol of surging nationalism: *New York Times,* October 9, 1951.

Daily News on Mossy: *Newsweek,* August 15, 1953.

Mossadegh statement upon arriving in New York: *New York Times,* October 9, 1951.

Newsweek on Mossadegh: August 15, 1953.

Jebb opening statement to Security Council: *Security Council Official Records,* 559th Meeting, October 1, 1951.

New York Times on idle Abadan: October 19, 1951.

Jebb urges Mossadegh not to brood: *Security Council Official Records,* 560th Meeting, October 15, 1951.

Mossadegh speech to Security Council: *Security Council Official Records,* ibid.

Mossadegh and Jebb on British-Iranian friendship: Goode, op. cit., p. 57.

McGhee on Liaquat: McGhee, op. cit., p. 93.

Churchill in Liverpool: *London Times,* October 3, 1951.

Second day of Security Council meeting: *Security Council Official Records,* 561st Meeting, October 16, 1951.

Third day: *Security Council Official Records,* 562nd Meeting, October 17, 1951.

Reston column: *New York Times,* October 18, 1951.

Truman received profile of Mossadegh: *White House Declassified Documents* (Washington: Government Printing Office, 1975), Doc. 780.

Adjectives British applied to Mossadegh: Abrahamian article in *Science & Society,* op. cit.

Mossadegh arrival at Union Station: Acheson, op. cit., pp. 503–504.

Mossadegh meets with Truman: Acheson, ibid., p. 504.

New York Times describes compromise proposal: October 25, 1951.

Strang rejects proposal: FO 371/91609, quoted in Elm, op. cit., p. 187.

Butler on Britain's viability: FO 371/91602, quoted in Elm, ibid., p. 188.

Reston says United States intervened too late: *New York Times,* October 18, 1951.

McGhee's efforts with Mossadegh: McGhee, op. cit., pp. 390–391.

McGhee bids farewell to Mossadegh: McGhee, op. cit., p. 403.

Walters pays final visit to Mossadegh: Walters, op. cit., p. 262.

Egyptian newspapers hail Mossadegh: Elm, p. 193.

Mossadegh and Nahas Pasha issue statement: McGhee, op. cit., p. 404.

Churchill says Attlee had scuttled and run: Dorril, p. 560.

Churchill directs Attlee to be stubborn: FO 371/91609, quoted in Elm, op. cit., p. 189.

Churchill describes Mossadegh as elderly lunatic: Goode, op. cit., pp. 34–35.

McGhee sees almost the end of the world: McGhee, op. cit., p. 403.

Mossadegh as man of the year: *Time,* January 7, 1952.

Chapter 9: Block Headed British

Shah will pack his suitcase: Katouzian, op. cit., p. 122.

Mossadegh argues and faints: Katouzian, op. cit., p. 123; and Musaddiq, Mohammad (edited by Homa Katouzian), *Musaddiq's Memoirs: Dr. Mohammad Musaddiq, Champion of the Popular Movement of Iran and Former Prime Minister* (London: Jebhe, 1988), p. 340.

Mossadegh's resignation letter: Zabih, Sepehr, *The Mossadegh Era: Roots of the Iranian Revolution* (Chicago: Lake View Press, 1982), p. 40.

Mossadegh statement on suspending election: Zabih, ibid., p. 38.

Churchill on Italians: FO 371/10465, quoted in Elm, op. cit., p. 268.

Mossadegh at World Court: Elm, ibid., pp. 208–214; and Heiss, op. cit., p. 129.

Voyage of *Rose Mary:* Heiss, ibid., p. 130.

Mossadegh leaves favorable impression: Elm, op. cit., p. 213.

Drop in oil revenue and Mossadegh reaction: Elm, ibid., pp. 271–272.

Zaehner on Qavam: Katouzian, op. cit., pp. 121–122.

Majlis members split between Mossadegh and Qavam: Zabih, op. cit., pp. 41–41.

Qavam statements as prime minister: Zabih, ibid., p. 44; and Katouzian, op. cit., p. 124.

Kashani denounces Qavam: Elm, op. cit., p. 242.

Tudeh protests against Qavam: Zabih, op. cit., p. 63.

Mossadegh presents Koran to Shah: Elm, op. cit., p. 247.

Mossadegh tells Shah he could go down in history: Zabih, op. cit., p. 66.

Middleton cables: Louis article in Gasiorowski and Byrne, op. cit.

New York Times on Zahedi: August 20, 1953.

MacLean on Zahedi's arrest: MacLean, Fitzroy, *Eastern Approaches* (London: Penguin, 1991), pp. 266–274.

Churchill has no regard for timid diplomatists: Woodhouse, op. cit., p. 125.

Churchill concerned about Jones trip, and exchange with Truman: Elm, op. cit., pp. 250–252; and Goode, op. cit., p. 87.

Acheson says British want rule or ruin: Elm, op. cit., p. 257.

Truman says nationalization has become as sacred as the Koran: Heiss, op. cit., p. 140.

Joint letter to Mossadegh: Elm, op. cit., pp. 250–252.

Mossadegh says Britain has plundered poor nations: Elm, ibid., p. 253.

Churchill urges Truman not to go further: Elm, ibid., p. 254.

Eden on Persian language: Eden, Anthony, *Full Circle: The Memoirs of Sir Anthony Eden* (Boston: Houghton Mifflin, 1960), p. 211.

Acheson on Eden's view of Iranians: Chase, op. cit., p. 353.

Truman letter to Grady: Henry Grady Papers, Box 2, 1952, at Harry Truman Library.

Roosevelt didn't talk spook: *New York Times,* June 11, 2000.

Roosevelt is coolness personified: *The Independent* (London), June 15, 2000.

Roosevelt thinks Republicans might be different: Roosevelt, op. cit., p. 107.

Chapter 10: Pull Up Your Socks and Get Going

Rashidians receive £10,000 monthly: Dorril, op. cit., p. 564; and Woodhouse, op. cit., p. 118.

Recipients of foreign bribes: Service History, op. cit., p. 7.

Description of Rashidian brothers: Bill, op. cit., p. 91.

Woodhouse on Anglo-Iranian directors: Dorril, op. cit., p. 580.

Woodhouse on his Washington presentation: Woodhouse, op. cit, pp. 117–118.

Background of John Foster Dulles: Preussen, Ronald W., *John Foster Dulles: The Road to Power* (New York: Free Press, 1982).

Background of Allen Dulles: Grose, Peter, *Gentleman Spy: The Life of Allen Dulles* (Boston: Houghton Mifflin, 1994).

Allen Dulles urges CIA to launch worldwide covert action program: Grose, ibid., p. 292.

Smith tells Roosevelt to get going: Roosevelt, op. cit., pp. 115–116.

Henderson says Mossadegh lacks stability: Goode, op. cit., p. 82.

Henderson on National Front: Ambrose, op. cit., p. 109.

Joint cable from Henderson and Middleton: Brands, op. cit., p. 272.

Henderson in touch with Zahedi: Brands, ibid., pp. 272–279.

United States can no longer approve of Mossadegh government: Service History, op. cit., p. 2.

Eisenhower complains about British efforts: Elm, op. cit., p. 277.

Sinclair visits Washington: Louis article in Gasiorowski and Byrne, ibid.

Shah in hysterical state: *Foreign Relations of the United States 1952–1954, Vol. X*, op. cit., pp. 681–683.

Shaban crashes through gate: Kennett Love article in Allen Dulles papers, op. cit.; and *New York Times*, August 23, 1953.

Mob organized by Kashani: FO 371/10562, quoted in Elm, op. cit., p. 295.

Allen Dulles warns of communist takeover: *Foreign Relations of the United States 1952–1954, Vol. X*, op. cit., p. 689.

March 4 meeting of National Security Council: *Foreign Relations of the United States 1952–1954, Vol. X*, op. cit., p. 693.

Eisenhower considers Mossadegh only hope for West and wants to give him $10 million: FO 371/104614, quoted in Elm, op. cit., pp. 282–283.

Dulles and Eden issue communiqué: Elm, op. cit., pp. 277–283.

Pardon for Tahmasibi: Azimi, Fakhreddin, *Iran: The Crisis of Democracy 1941–53* (London: I. B. Tauris, 1989), p. 298.

Zaehner report on splitting National Front: Abrahamian article in *Science & Society*, op. cit.

Eisenhower has real doubts: *Foreign Relations of the United States 1952–1954, Vol. X*, op. cit., p. 713.

Wisner says CIA ready to discuss plot: Louis article in Gasiorowski and Byrne, op. cit.

Allen Dulles approves $1 million: Service History, op. cit., p. 3.

Afshartus kidnapping: Louis article in Gasiorowski and Byrne, op. cit., note 170; and Dorril, op. cit., p. 585.

Eisenhower letter to Mossadegh: *New York Times*, July 10, 1953.

Eisenhower and Churchill approve plot: Service History, op. cit., p. vi; Prados, John, *Presidents' Secret Wars: CIA and Pentagon Covert Operations Since World War II* (New York: William Morrow, 1986), p. 95; Dorril, op. cit., p. 587; Woodhouse, op. cit., p. 125; and Louis article in Gasiorowski and Byrne, op. cit.

Wilber and Darbyshire begin work in Cyprus: Service History, op. cit., pp. 5–6.

Initial plan for coup: Service History, pp. B1–B10 and 16–18; and Gasiorowski article in Gasiorowski and Byrne, op. cit.

Dulles on getting rid of this madman: Roosevelt, op. cit., p. 8.

Dulles polls advisers and then decides to get going: Roosevelt, ibid., p. 18; Elm, op. cit., p. 299; and Bill and Louis, op. cit., p. 283.

Bohlen opposes coup: FO371/98603.

Goiran opposes coup: Dorril, op. cit., p. 584.

Bedamn budget compared to worldwide covert action budget: Gasiorowski article in Gasiorowski and Byrne, op. cit.

John Foster Dulles asks Allen Dulles if plot is still on: *Foreign Relations of the United States 1952–1954, Vol. X*, op. cit., p. 737.

John Foster Dulles makes public statement: *Foreign Relations of the United States 1952–1954, Vol. X*, op. cit., p. 338.

Wilber on anti-government propaganda: Wilber, Donald N., *Adventures in the Middle East: Excursions and Incursions* (Princeton, N.J.: Darwin, 1986), pp. 188–189.

Chapter 11: I Knew It! They Love Me!

For sources of information about the events of mid-August 1953 in Tehran, see notes for Chapter 1.

Roosevelt meets Zahedi: Roosevelt, op. cit., pp. 166–167; and Service History, p. 45.

Smith on snuggling up to Mossadegh: *Foreign Relations of the United States 1952–1954, Vol. X*, op. cit., p. 748.

Ardeshir Zahedi receives journalists: Kennett Love article, op. cit.; and Dorril, op. cit., p. 592.

Love on copying machine: *Anatomy of a Coup* (video), op. cit.

Roosevelt had sent Rashidians to Washington: Roosevelt, op. cit., p. 80.

Jalili and Keyvani vitally important: *Service History*, op. cit., p. 7.

Fatemi on royal robbery: *London Times*, August 17, 1953.

McClure mission: Elm, op. cit., p. 306; and Service History, op. cit., p. 46.

Jalili and Keyvani prefer money to execution: Dorril, op. cit., p. 595; and Gasiorowski article in Gasiorowski and Byrne, op. cit.

Roosevelt sees slight chance of success: Service History, op. cit., p. 51.

Roosevelt prepares escape plan: Gasiorowski article in *International Journal*, op. cit.

Love on military-looking car: *Mossadegh* (video), op. cit.

Roosevelt on anti-Shah protesters: Roosevelt, op. cit., p. 180.

Roosevelt admits small complications, gives Henderson assignment: Roosevelt, ibid., pp. 183–184.

Roosevelt describes Mossadegh as old bugger: Roosevelt, op. cit., p. 163.

Monday was active and trying time: Service History, op. cit., p. 56.

Riots scare Roosevelt: Roosevelt, op. cit., p. 179.

Henderson meets Mossadegh: Roosevelt, op. cit., p. 185; and *Foreign Relations of the United States 1952–1954, Vol. X*, op. cit., p. 750.

Mossadegh's fatal mistake: *Time*, August 31, 1953.

Daftary leads troops to royalist side: Dorril, op. cit., p. 593; and Katouzian, op. cit., p. 191.

New York Times on policemen swinging into action: August 19, 1953.

Shah arrives in Rome: *London Times*, August 19, 1953.

Shah doesn't expect to return home in immediate future: *New York Times*, August 19, 1953.

Shah likely to join colony of exiled monarchs: *London Daily Telegraph*, August 19, 1953.

Waller on crowds in Iran: *Anatomy of a Coup* (video), op. cit.

Ten thousand dollars sent to Kashani: Dorril, op. cit., p. 593; and Gasiorowski article in *International Journal*, op. cit.

Zirkaneh giants: Ambrose, *Ike's Spies*, op. cit., p. 210.

Mossadegh refuses to arm Tudeh: Author's interview with former Tehran mayor, Nosratollah Amini, June 23, 2002; and Lapping, op. cit., p. 215.

Tribal chiefs paid by Roosevelt's agents: Gasiorowski article in Gasiorowski and Byrne, op. cit.

New York Times on bully-boys: August 23, 1953.

Cottam on mob: *Mossadegh* (video), op. cit.

Smith exchanges cables with Roosevelt: Roosevelt, op. cit., p. 190.

Roosevelt hears radio broadcast: Roosevelt, ibid., pp. 187–191.

Roosevelt fetches Zahedi: Roosevelt, op. cit., pp. 193–194.

Roosevelt toasts impending victory: Roosevelt, ibid., p. 194.

Radio plays "Star-Spangled Banner": Interview with Malcolm Byrne in *Anatomy of a Coup* (video), op. cit.

Shah and Empress react to news of coup: *London Times*, August 20, 1953.

Shah regrets not playing important part: *New York Times*, August 19, 1953.

Mossadegh says he prefers to die: Saheb interview in *Mossadegh* (video), op. cit.

Kissing party: Elm, op. cit., pp. 307–308; and Katouzian, op. cit., p. 192.

Roosevelt and comrades full of jubilation: Roosevelt, op. cit., p. 195.

Meeting of Roosevelt, Henderson, and Ardeshir Zahedi: Roosevelt, ibid., pp. 195–196.

Roosevelt speaks at victory party: Roosevelt, ibid., pp. 195–197.

Some victims had banknotes in their pockets: Elm, op. cit., p. 308.

Three hundred killed: *New York Times*, August 20, 1953; and *Time*, August 31, 1953.

New York Times on sudden reversal: August 23, 1953.

Associated Press on Zahedi's coup: *Chicago Tribune*, August 20, 1953.

A day that should never have ended: Secret History, op. cit., p. 77.

Zahedi sends Batmanqelich to pick up Mossadegh: Diba, op. cit., p. 186.

Mossadegh arrives and greets Zahedi: *Chicago Tribune*, August 21, 1953.

Zahedi orders that Mossadegh be addressed respectfully: *Chicago Tribune*, August 21, 1953.

British airliner unsuitable: London *Times*, August 21, 1953.

Dutch airline charter: *New York Times*, August 23, 1953.

Shah on Mossadegh's crimes: *New York Times*, August 23, 1953.

Shah's airport reception: *New York Times*, August 23, 1953.

Shah's radio speech: London *Times*, August 24, 1953.

Zahedi will send Mossadegh to city jail: London *Times*, August 24, 1953.

Zahedi's government receives millions from CIA: Service History, op. cit., p. xiii.

Zahedi receives $1 million for himself: Gasiorowski, *US Foreign Policy and the Shah*, op. cit., p. 90.

Roosevelt's final meeting with Shah: Roosevelt, pp. 199–202.

Roosevelt leaves with tears in his eyes: Roosevelt, ibid., p. 203.

Chapter 12: Purring Like a Giant Cat

Mossadegh on his only crime: Musaddiq, op. cit., p. 74.

Riot outside Mossadegh's home: Author's interview with Mahmoud Mossadegh, August 19, 2002.

Officers arrested and executed: Diba, op. cit., p. 191.

Tudeh activists executed: Abrahamian, Ervand, *Iran between Two Revolutions* (Princeton, N.J.: Princeton University Press, 1982), p. 280.

Fatemi on traitor Shah, and snake who bites: Goode, op. cit., p. 123.

1962 rally: Diba, op. cit., p. 193.

Mossadegh wants God to take him: Musaddiq, op. cit., p. 80.

Consortium agreement: Elm, op. cit, pp. 310–331; Heiss, op. cit., pp. 187–220; and Goode, op. cit., pp. 138–153.

Shah on Mossadegh's xenophobia: Pahlavi, Mohammad Reza, *Mission for My Country* (New York, McGraw-Hill, 1960), pp. 302, 127.

Shah on Mossadegh's nationalism: Pahlavi, Mohammad Reza, *Answer to History* (New York: Stein and Day, 1980), p. 84.

Shah on worst years of his life: Goode, op. cit., p. 155.

Bakhtiar visits Mossadegh's grave: Goode, ibid., p. xiii.

Khomeini rants at Bakhtiar: Farmanfarmaian, op. cit., p. 452.

Ardeshir Zahedi denies CIA involvement: Zahedi, Ardeshir, "What Really Happened," www.ardeshirzahedi.com.

Shaban receives Cadillac: Diba, op. cit., p. 190.

Ashraf on unsubstantiated allegations: Pahlavi, Ashraf, *Faces in a Mirror* (Englewood Cliffs, N.J.: Prentice-Hall, 1980), p. xiv.

Dulles on Woodhouse's nice little egg: Dorril, op. cit., p. 596.

Woodhouse on first step toward catastrophe: Woodhouse, op. cit., p. 131.

Morrison recalls little about Iran: Morrison, op. cit., pp. 281–282.

Eden defends decision not to wage war: Eden, op. cit., pp. 246–247.

Eden on Morrison: Harris, Kenneth, *Attlee* (London: Weidenfeld and Nicholson, 1982), p. 472.

Churchill considers Ajax finest operation: Service History, op. cit., p. 81.

Roosevelt meets Churchill: Roosevelt, op. cit., p. 207.

Eisenhower awards medal to Roosevelt: Prados, op. cit., pp. 91–92.

Hostage-taker fears another coup: Zahrani, Mostafa T., "The Coup That Changed the Middle East: Mossadeq v. the CIA in Retrospect," in *World Policy Journal* (Summer 2002).

Khamenei says his movement not like Mossadegh's: Abrahamian article, op. cit.

Iranian intellectual on legacy of coup: Zahrani article in *World Policy Journal*, op. cit.

Waller defends coup: Statement to conference in Oxford, England, June 10, 2002.

Falle on legacy: Falle, op. cit., p. 81.

Tudeh strength exaggerated: Gasiorowski article in Gasiorowski and Byrne, op. cit.; Behrooz, "The 1953 Coup in Iran and the Legacy of the Tudeh," in Gasiorowski and Byrne, ibid.; and Abrahamian article in *Science & Society*, op. cit.

Acheson on losing so much so stupidly: Acheson, op. cit., p. 503.

Acheson on Mossadegh's responsibility: Acheson, ibid., p. 504.

Nixon on Acheson's cowardly college: *New York Times*, November 2, 1952.

Dulles purrs: Roosevelt, op. cit., p. 209.

Bakhtiar says Mossadegh should have shot plotters: *Mossadegh* (video), op. cit.

CIA says some facts will never be known: Service History, op. cit., p. 67.

Eisenhower meets Shah: *New York Times*, December 15, 1959.

Eisenhower refers obliquely to coup: Eisenhower, Dwight, *Mandate for Change: The White House Years, 1953–1956* (Garden City, N.Y.: Doubleday, 1963), p. 164;

and Ambrose, Stephen, *Eisenhower: The President* (New York: Simon and Schuster, 1984), p. 129.

Albright acknowledges American responsibility: *New York Times,* March 18, 2000.

Bill on legacy: Bill, op. cit., pp. 288–289.

Cottam on legacy: Cottam, *Iran and the United States,* op. cit., pp. 261–263.

Gasiorowski on legacy: Gasiorowski article in *International Journal,* op. cit.

Goode on legacy: Goode, op. cit., p. 124.

Heiss on legacy: Heiss, op. cit., pp. 234–238.

Keddie on legacy: Keddie, op. cit., pp. 142, 275–276.

Louis on legacy: Bill and Louis, op. cit., pp. 255–256.

BIBLIOGRAPHY

Abrahamian, Ervand. *Iran Between Two Revolutions* (Princeton, N.J.: Princeton University Press, 1982).

——. "The 1953 Coup in Iran" (article), in *Science & Society*, vol. 65, no. 2 (Summer 2001).

Abramson, Rudy. *Spanning the Century: The Life of W. Averell Harriman, 1891–1986* (New York: William Morrow, 1992).

Acheson, Dean. *Present at the Creation: My Years at the State Department* (New York: Norton, 1969).

Afary, Janet. *The Iranian Constitutional Revolution, 1906–1911: Grassroots Democracy, Social Democracy, and the Origins of Feminism* (New York: Columbia University Press, 1996).

Akhavi, Sharough. *Religion and Politics in Contemporary Iran: Clergy State Relations in the Pahlavi Period* (Albany: State University of New York Press, 1980).

Alexander, Yonah, and Nanes, Allen (editors). *The United States and Iran: A Documentary History* (Frederick, Md.: Alethia Books, 1980).

Ambrose, Stephen. *Eisenhower: The President* (New York: Simon and Schuster, 1984).

——, with Immerman, Richard H. *Ike's Spies: Eisenhower and the Intelligence Establishment* (Garden City, N.Y.: Doubleday, 1981).

Amirsadeghi, Hossein (editor). *Twentieth-Century Iran* (London: Heinemann, 1977).

Andrew, Christopher. *Secret Service: The Making of the British Intelligence Community* (London: Heinemann, 1985).

Arab, Gholam Hossein. *Isfahan* (Tehran: Farhangsara, 1996).

Arfa, Hassan. *Under Five Shahs* (New York: William Morrow, 1965).

Arjomand, Said Amir. *The Shadow of God and the Hidden Imam* (Chicago: University of Chicago Press, 1984).

——. *The Turban for the Crown: The Islamic Revolution in Iran* (New York: Oxford, 1988).

Attlee, Clement R. *As It Happened: The Autobiography of Clement R. Attlee* (New York: Viking, 1954).

Avery, Peter. *Modern Iran* (New York: Praeger, 1965).

——, et al. (editors). *The Cambridge History of Iran* (7 vols.) (Cambridge, U.K.: Cambridge University Press, 1968–1991).

Azimi, Fakhreddin. *Iran: The Crisis of Democracy 1941–53* (London: I. B. Tauris, 1989).

244

Bamberg, J. H. *The History of the British Petroleum Company: Volume II: The Anglo-Iranian Years, 1928–1954* (Cambridge, U.K.: Cambridge University Press, 1994).

Banani, Amin. *The Modernization of Iran 1924–41* (Stanford, Calif.: Stanford University Press, 1966).

Bayat, Mangol. *Iran's First Revolution: Shi'ism and the Constitutional Revolution of 1905–6* (New York: Oxford University Press, 1991).

Bill, James A. *The Eagle and the Lion: The Tragedy of American-Iranian Relations* (New Haven, Conn.: Yale University Press, 1988).

—— and Louis, William Roger (editors). *Mussadiq, Iranian Nationalism, and Oil* (London: I. B. Tauris, 1988).

Blair, John M. *The Control of Oil* (New York: Pantheon, 1976).

Brands, H. W. *Inside the Cold War: Loy Henderson and the Rise of the American Empire 1918–1961* (New York: Oxford University Press, 1991).

Brock, Ray. *Blood, Oil and Sand* (Cleveland: World, 1952).

Butler, D. E. *The British General Election of 1951* (London: Macmillan, 1952).

Central Intelligence Agency (written by Donald N. Wilber). *Overthrow of Premier Mossadeq of Iran, November 1952–August 1953* (Clandestine Service History, 1954, unpublished); summary published in *New York Times,* April 16, 2000, text available at www.nytimes.com.

Chace, James. *Acheson: The Secretary of State Who Created the American World* (New York: Simon and Schuster, 1998).

Churchill, Winston S. *The World Crisis, Volume I* (New York: Scribners, 1928).

Cottam, Richard W. *Nationalism in Iran* (Pittsburgh: University of Pittsburgh Press, 1979).

——. *Iran and the United States: A Cold War Case Study* (Pittsburgh: University of Pittsburgh Press, 1988).

Curzon, George Nathaniel. *Persia and the Persian Question* (London: Longmans, Green and Co., 1892).

Department of State. *Foreign Relations of the United States 1952–1954, Volume X: Iran 1952–1954* (Washington, D.C.: Government Printing Office, 1989).

Diba, Farhad. *Mohammad Mossadegh: A Political Biography* (London: Croom Helm, 1986).

Donoughue, Bernard, and Jones, G. W. *Herbert Morrison: Portrait of a Politician* (London: Weidenfeld and Nicholson, 1973).

Donovan, John C. *The Cold Warriors: A Policy-Making Elite* (Lexington, Mass.: Heath, 1974).

Donovan, Robert A. *Conflict and Crisis: The Presidency of Harry S Truman 1948–1953* (New York: Norton, 1982).

Dorril, Stephen. *MI6: Inside the Covert World of Her Majesty's Secret Intelligence Service* (New York: Free Press, 2000).

Dulles, Allen. *The Craft of Intelligence* (New York: Harper and Row, 1963).

Durraj, Manocher. *From Zarathustra to Khomeini: Popular Dissent in Iran* (Boulder, Colo.: Lynne Rienner, 1990).

Eden, Anthony. *Full Circle: The Memoirs of Sir Anthony Eden* (Boston: Houghton Mifflin, 1960).

Eisenhower, Dwight. *Mandate for Change: The White House Years, 1953–1956* (Garden City, N.Y.: Doubleday, 1963).

Elm, Mostafa. *Oil, Power and Principle: Iran's Oil Nationalization and Its Aftermath* (Syracuse, N.Y.: Syracuse University Press, 1992).

Elwell-Sutton, L. P. *Persian Oil: A Study in Power Politics* (London: Lawrence and Wishart, 1955).

Etzold, Thomas H., and Gaddis, John Lewis. *Containment: Documents on American Policy and Strategy, 1945–1950* (New York: Columbia University Press, 1978).

Eveland, Wilbur C. *Ropes of Sand: America's Failure in the Middle East* (New York: Norton, 1980).

Falle, Sam. *My Lucky Life in War, Revolution, Peace and Diplomacy* (Lewes, Sussex: Book Guild, 1996).

Farman Farmaian, Sattareh. *Daughter of Persia: A Woman's Journey From Her Father's Harem Through the Islamic Revolution* (New York: Anchor, 1992).

Farmanfarmaian, Manucher, and Farmanfarmaian, Roxane. *Blood and Oil: Inside the Shah's Iran* (New York: Modern Library, 1999).

Fatemi, Faramarz S. *The U.S.S.R. in Iran: The Background History of Russian and Anglo-American Conflict in Iran and Its Effect on Iranian Nationalism and the Fall of the Shah* (South Brunswick, N.J.: Barnes, 1980).

Fatemi, Nasrollah Saifpour. *Oil Diplomacy: Powderkeg in Iran* (New York: Whittier Books, 1954).

Ferrier, R. W. *The History of the British Petroleum Company: Volume I: The Developing Years, 1901–1932* (London: Cambridge University Press, 1982).

Foran, John (editor). *A Century of Revolution: Social Movements in Iran* (Minneapolis: University of Minnesota Press, 1994).

Forbis, William H. *Fall of the Peacock Throne: The Story of Iran* (New York: Harper and Row, 1980).

Ford, Alan W. *The Anglo-Iranian Oil Dispute of 1951–1952* (Berkeley: University of California Press, 1954).

Gasiorowski, Mark J. *U.S. Foreign Policy and the Shah: Building a Client State in Iran* (Ithaca, N.Y.: Cornell University Press, 1991).

——. "The 1953 Coup d'Etat in Iran" (article), *International Journal of Middle East Studies*, no. 19 (1987).

——, and Byrne, Malcolm (editors). *Mohammad Mossadeq and the 1953 Coup in Iran* (Syracuse, N.Y.: Syracuse University Press, forthcoming 2003).

Ghani, Cyrus. *Iran and the Rise of Reza Shah: From Qajar Collapse to Pahlavi Power* (London: I. B. Tauris, 2000).

Ghods, M. Reza. *Iran in the Twentieth Century: A Political History* (Boulder, Colo.: Lynne Rienner, 1989).

Gilbert, Martin. *Winston S. Churchill: Volume VIII: Never Despair, 1945–1965* (Boston: Houghton Mifflin, 1988).

Goode, James F. *The United States and Iran: In the Shadow of Mussadiq* (New York: St. Martin's, 1997).

Graham, Robert. *Iran: The Illusion of Power* (New York: St. Martin's, 1980).

Grose, Peter. *Gentleman Spy: The Life of Allen Dulles* (Boston: Houghton Mifflin, 1994).

Hairi, Abdul-Hadi. *Shi'ism and Constitutionalism in Iran* (Leiden, The Netherlands: E. J. Brill, 1977).

Halliday, Fred. *Iran: Dictatorship and Development* (London: Penguin, 1980).

Hamilton, Charles W. *Americans and Oil in the Middle East* (Houston: Gulf Publishing, 1962).

Harris, Kenneth. *Attlee* (London: Weidenfeld and Nicholson, 1982).

Heikal, Mohamed. *Iran, the Untold Story: An Insider's Account of America's Iranian Adventure and Its Consequences for the Future* (New York: Pantheon, 1982).

Heiss, Mary Ann. *Empire and Nationhood: The United States, Great Britain, and Iranian Oil, 1950–1954* (New York: Columbia University Press, 1997).

History Channel. *Anatomy of a Coup: The CIA in Iran* (video), Catalogue No. AAE-43021.

Iranian Movies. *Mossadegh and the 1953 Coup by CIA* (video), Tape No. 3313, IranianMovies.com.

Irving, Clyde. *Crossroads of Civilization: 3,000 Years of Persian History* (New York: Barnes & Noble, 1979).

Jeffreys-Jones, Rhodri. *The CIA and American Democracy* (New Haven, Conn.: Yale University Press, 1989).

Katouzian, Homa. *The Political Economy of Modern Iran: Despotism and Pseudo-Modernism 1926–79* (New York: New York University Press, 1981).

——. *Mussadiq and the Struggle for Power in Iran* (London: I. B. Tauris, 1999).

Keddie, Nikki R. *Religion and Rebellion in Iran: The Tobacco Protest of 1891–1892* (London: Frank Cass, 1966).

——. *Roots of Revolution: An Interpretive History of Modern Iran* (New Haven, Conn.: Yale University Press, 1981).

——, and Gasiorowski, Mark J. (editors). *Neither East nor West: Iran, the Soviet Union, and the United States* (New Haven, Conn.: Yale University Press, 1990).

Krause, Walter W. *Soraya, Queen of Persia* (London: Macdonald, 1956).

Lapping, Brian. *End of Empire* (London: Granada, 1985).

Ledeen, Michael, and Lewis, William. *Debacle: American Failure in Iran* (New York: Alfred A. Knopf, 1981).

Lenczowski, George. *Iran Under the Pahlavis* (Stanford: Hoover Institute, 1978).

Levy, Walter J. *Oil Strategy and Politics, 1941–1981* (Boulder, Colo.: Westview, 1982).

Limbert, John W. *Iran: At War with History* (Boulder, Colo.: Westview, 1987).

Longhurst, Henry. *Adventure in Oil: The Story of British Petroleum* (London: Sidgwick and Jackson, 1959).

Longrigg, Stephen H. *Oil in the Middle East: Its Discovery and Development* (Oxford: Oxford University Press, 1968).

Louis, William Roger. *The British Empire in the Middle East 1945–1951* (Oxford: Oxford University Press, 1984).

Love, Kennett. *The American Role in the Pahlavi Restoration on August 19, 1953* (unpublished), the Allen Dulles Papers, Princeton University (1960).

Lytle, Mark Hamilton. *The Origins of the Iranian-American Alliance 1941–1953* (New York: Holmes and Meier, 1987).

Mackey, Sandra. *The Iranians: Persia, Islam and the Soul of a Nation* (New York: Plume, 1998).

MacLean, Fitzroy. *Eastern Approaches* (London: Penguin, 1991).

Martin, Vanessa. *Islam and Modernism: The Iranian Revolution of 1906* (Syracuse, N.Y.: Syracuse University Press, 1989).

McGhee, George. *Envoy to the Middle World: Adventures in Diplomacy* (New York: Harper and Row, 1983).

McLellan, David S. *Dean Acheson: The State Department Years* (New York: Dodd, Mead, 1976).

Milani, Mohsen M. *The Making of Iran's Islamic Revolution: From Monarchy to Islamic Republic* (Boulder, Colo.: Westview, 1994).

Millspaugh, Arthur C. *American in Persia* (Washington, D.C.: Brookings Institution, 1946).

Monroe, Elizabeth. *Britain's Moment in the Middle East, 1914–1971* (Baltimore: Johns Hopkins University Press, 1981).

Morrison, Herbert. *An Autobiography* (London: Odhams, 1960).

Mosley, Leonard. *Power Play: The Tumultuous World of Middle East Oil, 1890–1973* (London: Weidenfeld and Nicholson, 1973).

Mottahedeh, Roy. *The Mantle of the Prophet: Religion and Politics in Iran* (New York: Pantheon, 1985).

Musaddiq, Mohammad (edited by Homa Katouzian). *Musaddiq's Memoirs: Dr. Mohammad Musaddiq, Champion of the Popular Movement of Iran and Former Prime Minister* (London: Jebhe, 1988).

Nicholson, Harold. *Curzon: The Last Phase, 1919–1925* (London: Constable, 1934).

Pahlavi, Ashraf. *Faces in a Mirror* (Englewood Cliffs, N.J.: Prentice-Hall, 1980).

Pahlavi, Mohammad Reza. *Mission for My Country* (New York, McGraw-Hill, 1960).

——. *Answer to History* (New York: Stein and Day, 1980).

Prados, John. *Presidents' Secret Wars: CIA and Pentagon Covert Operations Since World War II* (New York: William Morrow, 1986).

Preussen, Ronald W. *John Foster Dulles: The Road to Power* (New York: Free Press, 1982).

Ramazani, Rouhullah K. *Iran's Foreign Policy 1941–1973* (Charlottesville: University Press of Virginia, 1975).

——. *The United States and Iran: Patterns of Influence* (New York: Praeger, 1982).

Rand, Christopher T. *Making Democracy Safe for Oil: Oilmen and the Islamic East* (Boston: Little Brown, 1975).

Roosevelt, Kermit. *Countercoup: The Struggle for Control of Iran* (New York: McGraw-Hill, 1979).

Rose, Kenneth. *Superior Person: A Portrait of Curzon and His Circle in Late Victorian England* (New York: Weybright and Talley, 1969).

Rubin, Barry. *Paved with Good Intentions: The American Experience and Iran* (New York: Oxford University Press, 1980).

Saikal, Amin. *The Rise and Fall of the Shah* (Princeton, N.J.: Princeton University Press, 1980).

Sampson, Anthony. *The Seven Sisters: The Great Oil Companies and the World They Made* (New York: Viking, 1975).

Schwarzkopf, H. Norman. *It Doesn't Take a Hero* (New York: Bantam, 1992).

Seldon, Anthony. *Churchill's Indian Summer: The Conservative Government 1951–1955* (London: Hodder and Stoughton, 1981).

Shawcross, William. *The Shah's Last Ride: The Fate of an Ally* (New York: Simon and Schuster, 1988).

Shuster, William Morgan. *The Strangling of Persia* (New York: Century, 1912).

Sick, Gary. *All Fall Down: America's Tragic Encounter with Iran* (New York: Random House, 1985).

Stassen, Harold, and Houts, Marshall. *Eisenhower: Turning the World Toward Peace* (St. Paul, Minn.: Merrill Magnus, 1990).

Tabataba'i, Allamah Sayyid Muhammad Husayn. *Shi'ite Islam* (Albany: State University of New York Press, 1977).

Truman, Harry S. *Years of Trial and Hope, 1946–53* (Garden City, N.Y.: Doubleday, 1978).

Vicker, Ray. *Kingdom of Oil: The Middle East, Its People and Its Power* (New York: Charles Scribner's Sons, 1974).

Walters, Vernon A. *Silent Missions* (New York: Doubleday, 1978).

Warne, William E. *Mission for Peace: Point Four in Iran* (New York: Bobbs-Merrill, 1956).

Wilber, Donald N. *Adventures in the Middle East: Excursions and Incursions* (Princeton, N. J.: Darwin, 1986).

——. *Contemporary Iran* (New York: Praeger, 1963).

——. *Iran: Past and Present* (Princeton, N. J.: Princeton University Press, 1976).

Woodhouse, C. M. *Something Ventured* (London: Granada, 1982).

Wright, Denis. *The Persians Amongst the English: Episodes in Anglo-Persian History* (London: I. B. Tauris, 1985).

Yergin, Daniel. *The Prize: The Epic Quest for Oil, Money and Power* (New York: Simon and Schuster, 1991).

Zabih, Sepehr. *The Mossadegh Era: Roots of the Iranian Revolution* (Chicago: Lake View Press, 1982).

INDEX